The Quest for Power in the UNSC

Diplomatic Studies

Series Editor

Jan Melissen
(*Leiden University and University of Antwerp*)

VOLUME 21

The titles published in this series are listed at *brill.com/dist*

The Quest for Power in the UNSC

The Campaigns and Selection of Non-permanent Members

Edited by

Ann-Marie Ekengren and Ulrika Möller

BRILL | NIJHOFF

LEIDEN | BOSTON

Originally published in hardback in 2023.

Cover illustration: "Quest for Power in the UN Security Council", 2023, courtesy of Benjamin Løzninger, www.frenchbk.com

The Library of Congress has cataloged the hardcover edition as follows:

Names: Ekengren, Ann-Marie, editor. | Möller, Ulrika, editor.
Title: The quest for power in the UNSC : the campaigns and selection of
  non-permanent members / edited by Ann-Marie Ekengren and Ulrika Möller.
Description: Leiden ; Boston : Brill/Nijhoff, 2024. | Series: Diplomatic
  studies, 1872-8863 ; volume 21 | Includes index.
Identifiers: LCCN 2023038123 (print) | LCCN 2023038124 (ebook) |
  ISBN 9789004686885 (hardback) | ISBN 9789004687110 (ebook)
Subjects: LCSH: United Nations. Security Council. | United Nations.
  Security Council–Membership. | United Nations. Security
  Council–Decision making. | United Nations. Security Council--Rules and
  practice. | Security, International.
Classification: LCC KZ5037 .Q84 2024 (print) | LCC KZ5037 (ebook) |
  DDC 341.23/23–dc23/eng/20231002
LC record available at https://lccn.loc.gov/2023038123
LC ebook record available at https://lccn.loc.gov/2023038124

Typeface for the Latin, Greek, and Cyrillic scripts: "Brill". See and download: brill.com/brill-typeface.

ISSN 1872-8863
ISBN 978-90-04-71989-7 (paperback, 2024)
ISBN 978-90-04-68688-5 (hardback)
ISBN 978-90-04-68711-0 (e-book)
DOI 10.1163/9789004687110

Contents

Acknowledgments   VII
List of Figures and Tables   IX
Notes on Contributors   XI

1   The Candidates for a Nonpermanent Seat in the Security Council: Who, Why and How?   1
    Ann-Marie Ekengren and Ulrika Möller

2   Competing for an Elected Seat on the Security Council: Who, Why and How?   18
    Ann-Marie Ekengren and Ulrika Möller

3   Candidatures and Terms: Detecting Winners and Losers   49
    Ulrika Möller and Ann-Marie Ekengren

4   Why do States Want a Seat on the UNSC? Expectations between Different Types of States   67
    Ann-Marie Ekengren, Fredrik D. Hjorthen and Ulrika Möller

5   Candidature Decisions: Six In-depth Examinations   96
    Ann-Marie Ekengren, Ulrika Möller, Touko Piiparinen, Tarja Seppä, Anni Tervo, Baldur Thorhallsson, Jóna Sólveig Elínardóttir and Anna M. Eggertsdóttir

6   Competing Small Powers: Austria versus Iceland on the UNSC   117
    Baldur Thorhallsson, Jóna Sólveig Elínardóttir and Anna M. Eggertsdóttir

7   Greater Than Its Size? Comparing Finland's and Luxembourg's Campaigns to the Security Council   147
    Touko Piiparinen, Tarja Seppä and Anni Tervo

8   Election 2016: Sweden and the Kingdom of the Netherlands   179
    Ann-Marie Ekengren and Ulrika Möller

9   Results, Conclusions, and Reflections   212
    Ann-Marie Ekengren and Ulrika Möller

Index   229

Acknowledgments

Writing a book is a collaborative effort that involves the contributions, support, and inspiration of numerous individuals. With deep gratitude, we would like to acknowledge the following people who have played a significant role in the creation of this book, 'The Quest for Power in the UNSC: The Campaigns and Selection of Non-permanent Members'.

First and foremost, we are indebted to the ambassadors, diplomats and senior officials who shared their invaluable insights and experiences with us. Their knowledge and expertise have been instrumental in shedding light on the complexities of the campaign and election processes to the UNSC and we are very grateful for their willingness to provide their firsthand accounts of the election campaigns.

We are also deeply grateful to all members of the research group working on the project The Quest for Power in International Politics: Campaigns by and Selection of Non-Permanent Members to the United Nations Security Council which has been funded by the Swedish Research Council, 2016-01585. A warm thank you to Anna Margrét Eggertsdóttir, Jóna Sólveig Elínardóttir, Fredrik Dybfest Hjorthen, Touko Piiparinen, Tarja Seppä, Anni Tervo and Baldur Thorhallsson. Their dedication to gather and analyze the extensive data and literature on UNSC elections and campaigns has greatly enriched the quality of the research presented in this book. Thank you to Ruben Dieleman for excellent research assistance on the Dutch case. A special thank you goes to Hanna Ojanen who read the entire first draft and gave us invaluable comments on how to improve the coherence of the manuscript.

Over the years, we have been able to present our work at numerous academic occasions; a warm collective thanks to all participants attending our panels and working groups at EISA, ISA, SWEPSA, the Swedish Network for Foreign Policy Analysis, and the research seminars at Lund University and Södertörn University.

We are also very thankful for being part of such an inspirational environment as the Department of Political Science at the University of Gothenburg. A warm thank you to everyone who is supporting us. For recurring support, we say a special thanks to Ulf Bjereld, Marie Demker, Henrik Friberg-Fernros, Marcia Grimes, Marina Nistotskaya, Henrik Oscarsson, and Maria Solevid.

Finally, we would also like to acknowledge our anonymous reviewer, our editor and the publishing team for guidance and expertise. Their meticulous review, insightful suggestions, and unwavering support have been invaluable in refining and polishing this manuscript. Thank you!

Ann-Marie Ekengren and Ulrika Möller
Göteborg
June 8th, 2023

Figures and Tables

Figures

4.1   To what extent would your country be able to influence the agenda of the SC, if you were elected? Comparison of responses between WEOG and non-WEOG countries (N)   72

4.2   What might affect your possibility to influence the agenda when having a nonpermanent seat? Comparison of responses between WEOG and non-WEOG countries (N)   73

4.3   Would an elected seat improve your country's ability to establish stronger relationships with other significant actors in global politics? Comparison of responses between WEOG and non-WEOG countries (N)   74

4.4   What might affect your possibility to establish stronger relationships with other important actors through a nonpermanent seat on the UNSC? Comparison of responses between WEOG and non-WEOG countries (N)   75

4.5   Would an elected seat elevate your country's status in the global community? Comparison of responses between WEOG and non-WEOG countries (N)   76

4.6   What would affect your elevated status from a nonpermanent seat on the UNSC? Comparison of responses between WEOG and non-WEOG countries (N)   76

4.7   What might affect your possibility to influence the agenda when having a nonpermanent seat? Comparison of responses between big, small, and Nordic countries, within the WEOG (N)   78

4.8   Would an elected seat improve your country's ability to establish stronger relationships with other significant actors in global politics? Comparison of responses between big, small, and Nordic countries within the WEOG (N)   79

4.9   Would an elected seat elevate your country's status in the global community? Comparison of responses between big, small, and the Nordic countries within the WEOG (N)   80

4.10   What might affect your possibility to influence the agenda when having a nonpermanent seat? Comparison of responses between big, small, and the Nordic-Baltic countries, within the WEOG and the EEG (N)   81

4.11   Would an elected seat improve your country's ability to establish stronger relationships with other significant actors in global politics? Comparison of responses between big, small, and the Nordic-Baltic countries within the WEOG and the EEG (N)   82

4.12   Would an elected seat elevate your country's status in the global community? Comparison of responses between big, small, and the Nordic-Baltic countries within the WEOG and the EEG (N)   83

4.13   What might affect your possibility to influence the agenda if you held a nonpermanent seat? Comparison of responses between small, big, and the Nordic countries within the WEOG (percent)   92

4.14   Would an elected seat improve your country's ability to establish stronger relationships with other significant actors in global politics? Comparison of responses between small, big, and the Nordic countries within the WEOG (percent)   92

4.15   Would an elected seat elevate your country's status in the global community? Comparison of responses between small, big, and the Nordic countries within the WEOG (percent)   93

4.16   What might affect your possibility to influence the agenda if you held a nonpermanent seat? Comparison of responses between small, big, and the Nordic countries within the WEOG (percent)   93

4.17   Would an elected seat improve your country's ability to establish stronger relationships with other significant actors in global politics? Comparison of responses between small, big, and the Nordic countries within the WEOG (percent)   94

4.18   Would an elected seat elevate your country's status in the global community? Comparison of responses between small, big, and the Nordic countries within the WEOG (percent)   94

Tables

2.1   Reasons for a candidature, and expectations connected to an elected seat on the Security Council   30

2.2   Logics of international campaigning   37

3.1   Times elected to the Security Council 1946–2022   51

3.2   Regional groups: membership and available seats in the Security Council   55

3.3   Candidatures and times elected 1990–2022   58

3.4   Regional groups. competition measure 1990–2022   64

4.1   Responding countries to our telephone survey 2017–2018   70

9.1   Summary of identified factors for seeking a seat in the Security Council among UN member states in general, as well as in Finland, Luxembourg, Austria, Iceland, Sweden, and the Netherlands in particular   219

9.2   Summary of identified factors for success   221

Notes on Contributors

Anna M. Eggertsdóttir
M.A. (2009), currently working in the wind energy industry. She has worked as a project manager and researcher in the Faculty of Political Science at the University of Iceland and has participated in several publications on small states.

Ann-Marie Ekengren
Ph.D. (1999), University of Gothenburg, is a Professor in Political Studies. She has published several monographs and articles on foreign policy decision-making, including *The Mediatization of Foreign Policy, Political Decisionmaking and Humanitarian Intervention* (Palgrave, 2017).

Jóna Sólveig Elínardóttir
M.A. (2011), University of Iceland, is an Icelandic Diplomat currently serving in the role of Political Advisor to the Commander of NATO Joint Force Command Norfolk. Previously, as Member of Parliament, she served as Deputy Speaker and Chair of the Foreign Affairs Committee. Prior to that she held the position of Adjunct Lecturer and Researcher in the Faculty of Political Science at the University of Iceland and co-authored a number of publications on small states.

Fredrik D. Hjorthen
Ph.D. (2017), University of Oslo, is a Researcher at ARENA Centre for European Studies. His research has focused on international and global justice, especially relating to the ethics of humanitarian intervention, burden sharing, and climate justice.

Ulrika Möller
Ph.D. (2007), University of Gothenburg, is an Associate Professor in Political Studies. Her research interests include Security Council candidatures and memberships, Nordic states' foreign- and security policy, and multilateral diplomacy for nuclear non-proliferation and disarmament.

Touko Piiparinen
Ph.D. (2005), University of Wales, Aberystwyth. He has the title of Docent of International Politics at the University of Tampere and Docent of World Politics at the University of Helsinki. His areas of expertise include

conflict management, International Relations theory, critical realism, and Responsibility to Protect principle.

Tarja Seppä

Dr. Soc. Sci. (2019), Tampere University, is a Visiting Scholar at the Politics Unit. Her main areas of research comprise the UN, especially Security Council, the principle of Responsibility to Protect, human rights, politics and law, and the Council of Europe.

Anni Tervo

M. Soc. Sci. (2016), Tampere University, currently works at the United Nations in New York on peacebuilding, crisis management, new technologies and innovation. However, the views presented in this research do not reflect the views of the UN.

Baldur Thorhallsson

Ph.D. (1999), University of Iceland, is a Professor in Political Science and Research Director of the Centre for Small State Studies. His research focuses primarily on small European states - including the Nordic states. He has published extensively on small states, including *Small States and Shelter Theory: Iceland's External Affairs*, Routledge 2019.

CHAPTER 1

The Candidates for a Nonpermanent Seat in the Security Council: Who, Why and How?

Ann-Marie Ekengren and Ulrika Möller

1   Introduction

The annual elections of the nonpermanent (or elected) seats of the Security Council are a major event at the top-level of United Nations diplomacy, but they attract limited public interest and have received modest scholarly attention in the past. Research having eyes firmly focused on the most powerful states – the five states with permanent membership (the P5) – is the main reason for why this specific competition between states has gone under the radar. In contrast, we suggest that the Security Council electoral procedure, which selects the non permanent members of the Security Council (the E10), constitutes a condensed version of the broader power struggle at the core of world politics. By this book, we conduct an extensive scrutiny of the various aspects of this microcosm of power: We explore who is elected, why representation in the Security Council is of great relevance for many states, and how they design their campaigns to reach their goals. Deviations within this microcosm from the power macrocosm is of special interest; sometimes a resourceful favorite 'bites the dust' to the advantage of a less prominent competitor. Why is that? We explore the relevance of how the electoral campaigns are carried out to infer on the outcome.

We address five questions in this book: Who wins a seat? Why do UN member states seek representation in the Security Council? What kind of opportunities do states expect from having a seat? How do they campaign? What accounts for a successful campaign? The results rely on three empirical studies that 1) maps and scrutinizes a three-decades-pattern of candidatures and elected memberships, 2) examines reasons for why states prioritize a candidature, and what they hope to achieve by an elected seat, and 3) detects how states campaign, and compares between competing campaigns to infer on the electoral outcome. Broadly, our attention to the state competition for representation in the Security Council substantiates a positional understanding of power associated with the hierarchical turn in the study of IR and the complex interplay between material and ideational attributes, social skills, and competences for competitive success implied by the study of status.[1] Foremost, by inferring on the relevance on how a campaign is conducted, and on the opportunities for smaller states to gain representation in the Security Council, we are also able to contribute with knowledge about state agency that goes beyond the established patterns of power. The empirical studies rely on a variety of material collected through different data collecting techniques, to be presented in further detail in the empirical chapters. Here it suffices to say that we have collected our main data through; a telephone survey with national diplomatic representatives to the United Nations; personal interviews with diplomats and senior officials involved in designing and executing states' campaigns for being elected to the Security Council; searching the web for written campaign material; compiling data on the outcomes of the elections and memberships over time from the the UN and through Security Council Reports. On basis of the conclusions from our study, we give some advice about the design of campaigns to increase the chances of electoral success and Security Council representation.

States signal their interest for a nonpermanent seat in the Security Council by announcing a candidature. To seek positions in International Organizations (IOs) is one important way for states to increase their participation in world politics. Representation in the Security Council is certainly as high-level as it gets. The responsibility for international peace and security granted by the UN charter accounts for its supreme position in world politics.[2] Through the procedure of rotating the ten nonpermanent seats by election, the opportunity to serve in the Security Council is open to all states. Still, to become a candidate for membership requires careful planning long ahead of the election. It is also contingent on the nomination procedure of the regional groups that dispose the Security Council seats.[3] Belonging to a regional group who endorses only one candidate per available seat is especially frustrating to the member states eager for the opportunity to try its luck in the election. To run a candidature all the way to the election is also a major commitment, which finalizes in a phase of active campaigning. As the competition over an elected seat has become tougher, states often announce candidatures more than a decade ahead of the election and the campaigns goes on for years. These campaigns promote the strengths and suitability of the candidate on basis of past and current contributions to the United Nations and other relevant foreign policy characteristics. They are an interesting hybrid between features that resemble national

---

1   Bially Mattern and Zarakol 2016; Götz 2021.
2   Luck 2006; Sievers and Daws 2014.
3   Malone 2000; Schrijver and Blokker 2020.

election campaigns and tools adopted from the diplomatic field. To run an active campaign is becoming more decisive for governments who have made a Security Council candidature into a foreign policy priority. We suggest that several different objectives are associated with the prioritization of a Security Council candidature and that the design of the campaign has explanatory value to the electoral results. Our study is, to the best of our knowledge, the very first theoretically structured comparative study of these campaigns.

As already indicated, we suggest that the appointment of nonpermanent members of the Security Council requires attention as this procedure both discerns a prevailing pattern of power among states in world politics *and* offers a rare opportunity to operate at the very center of global authority. Even single states with an otherwise low international profile can take advantage of a seat in the Security Council. On the one hand, only a handful of resourceful states have proven capacity to frequent representation in the Security Council. On the other hand, occasionally even small developing states manage to reach all the way to the Council. Often, a term in the Council is an opportunity brought to the smaller and less resourceful states by the turn-taking order some regional groups apply to select candidates for the elected seats at their disposal. At times, however, a less resourceful candidate matches and even defeats some stronger competitors in a 'contested slate', which is an election-round with more candidates than available seats. Luxembourg and Estonia are examples of smaller states who have experienced this victory, while India, Canada and Australia are among the populous and resourceful states who share the experience of electoral defeat. Thus, our approach rests upon the presumption that the candidatures for nonpermanent seats in the Security Council is an important feature of the struggle for power and influence among states. We propose that active campaigning for support, as part of states' candidatures for a seat, inherits potential to counter electoral outcomes expected solely on basis of traditional measures of state power. In addition to learning more about how and why these campaigns for a nonpermanent seat are important to states, we suggest that our close inquiry of candidatures and election results also contributes to the broader study of the relationship between states in world politics, and of the legitimacy of the Security Council.

For the further introduction of our line of inquiry, we proceed in the subsequent two sections by discussing 1) the implications of our focus on elections and campaigns within the broader study of power and legitimacy of the Security Council, 2) candidatures as a foreign policy priority, and 3) campaigns as a political and diplomatic activity. Thereafter, we outline the content of the book on basis of our research-questions.

2   The Broader Relevance of Our Approach: on Power and Legitimacy

The common scholarly departure on the Security Council is the legal subordination of all states that gives this international body unparalleled power in world politics. Less frequently noted are the legal entitlement of all UN member states to seek office in this powerful institution. To clarify, the UN charter dictates the universal subjugation of states to the authority of the Council *and* grants them with the right to seek representation within the Council on equal terms. The widely recognized exception is the privilege of permanent representation granted to five UN member states: China, France, Russia, United Kingdom, and United States (the P5). The Council is infamous for this eternal right to representation to a privileged few. Commonly, experts and scholars characterize the Security Council as controlled by these five permanent members. The literature describes it as a 'vetocracy' and as 'a creature of the world's strongest states'.[4] The institutional design of a few permanent seats reflects the distribution of capabilities at the inception of the Security Council. It accounts for a binary categorization of states – those with and without permanent membership – and remains one of the most obvious differences for their opportunity to exercise power and influence in world politics.

The effects of the permanent membership with associated advantages are also a main source of concern in the political and scholarly debates on the legitimacy of the Security Council. On matters of international peace and security, the Security Council is entitled to make binding decisions, as well as to enforce them through various sanctions, ultimately by military means (article 41, 42). In spite if this political authority, the Security Council is still an international body that suffers from a lack of perceived legitimacy.[5] The frequently targeted criticism from members of the UN, as well as from other international actors, concerns severe shortcomings in addressing the threats to international peace and security that the Council is set up to handle. The analysis relies on the theoretical insight that input legitimacy i.e., quality of terms for participation, affects output legitimacy i.e., quality of decisions.[6] Scholars identify the inability to appropriately exercising authority because of institutional design, foremost caused by the abovementioned favorable conditions that come with permanent membership. If advocacy of the UN embodies the vision of a rule-based order that is equal to all states, the executive inability of the Security Council rather accentuates the opposite, by and through the

---

4   Barnett and Finnemore, 2018, 4; von Einsiedel and Malone, 2018, 19.
5   Hurd 2002; 2008a; 2008b.
6   Corbett et al. 2018.

power asymmetries among its members. In addition to the formal veto right in decisions, the P5 benefit from institutional memory, accumulated political and diplomatic abilities, and opportunities to expand their influence by establishing beneficial working methods and taking control of important practices, such as pen-holding.[7] This is quite a smorgasbord of power-tools that enables the permanent members to impose their will on occasions when they have identified common interests and makes it possible for each permanent member to work against and ultimately block political initiatives perceived in conflict with their own national interest. Thus, when addressing main issues of power and legitimacy there are certainly good reasons for the emphasis on the institutional order, established through five permanent seats. Still, from this one-sided focus on the P5 maneuvers, the role of the E10 will always be marginal and the procedures surrounding their appointment seem less interesting as well. In this book, we speak to the contrary. We see the relevance in exploring the efforts taken by many states for the purpose of political representation. By our choice of approach, we set the five permanent members aside for the purpose of examining the intense political activity among the remaining majority to exercise their right to representation. We suggest that this does not only improve our knowledge on the relevance of the campaigns but contribute to the analysis of the relationship between states in world politics, and of the legitimacy of the Security Council.

First, the procedure with appointing nonpermanent members by election is relevant in the sense that proving capable to frequent representation in the Security Council is an obvious expression of state power, while zero times in the Council may be read as a sign of political weakness. The equal right of each member state of the United Nations to seek representation on the Security Council has not resulted in an equal distribution of times each member state has served. Instead, the electoral procedure accounts for a further stratification of states, which is more fine-grained than the binary categorization constituted by permanent membership to a selected few. We map out the variation in access to the Council established over time and discuss how this pattern mirrors a broader international hierarchy of states. We also address the relevance of the regional groups for this pattern; differences in nomination procedure and in composition of members affect the opportunity to an elected term in the Council. The variation of terms in the Council between states, depending on their regional group belonging, sheds light also on rather profound differences in regional power relations. The gap is particularly wide

---

7   Keating in Von Einsiedel et al 2016: 139; Schia 2017.

among members in the Asia-Pacific group in which the strong interest of several regional powers to frequent representation seems to be at the expense of the many small states who have not even served once. Over time, this gap may also widen if many states calculate in terms of maximizing the possible impact from each elected member in the power struggle between the P5 and the E10. In such calculus the experienced regional power is likely to defeat a small first-time candidate in the regional nomination procedure as well as in the election.

Second, the procedure with appointing nonpermanent members by election is relevant for the legitimacy of the Security Council, both in spite of and because of the legitimacy deficit caused by the dominance of the permanent five. To specify, the pattern of uneven opportunity to representation in the Security Council between UN member states may raise concerns about input legitimacy and the quality of participation. On the other hand, it is also possible to argue that a small number of frequently elected members is the best way to counter some of the P5 influence, as these states gather capacities and skills from their experience of frequent representation, and thereby have a better chance to affect the quality of the decisions.

In the context of the uneven representation in the Security Council mapped out, our problem approach reveals that the electoral outcomes do not merely reflect a systemic pattern where traditional attributes of power always dominate, because seemingly stronger candidates are sometimes defeated. This point to the relevance of examining the types of power at stake. By addressing the hierarchical ordering of states, through the pattern of elected memberships, our study contributes to the analysis that goes beyond international politics as dictated by a distribution of capabilities in anarchy. By our explanatory approach, with focus on the campaigns, we also reveal the more complex set of power tools that states have and use in their quest for climbing in the social hierarchical order. Further described below, we examine the power enhancing benefits associated with an elected seat in the Security Council. Before we proceed, next section puts the growing interest in serving in the Security Council in a historical and broader IO context.

3   The Growing Interest in an Elected Seat: Historical Change and IO Reform

The most enduring paralysis of the Security Council occurred during the Cold War, when the hostility between the US and the Soviet Union resulted in their frequent use of veto to circumvent each other's influence. The breakdown of the bipolar order paved the way for an initial increase in UN activity, including

peace operations initiated by the Security Council. It is in this historical setting that we see an increasing interest among UN member states to serve in
the Security Council. The past decade of deteriorating relations between
permanent members, in particular the US, Russia, and China, has yet again
crippled the agency of the Security Council and cast doubts on its relevance.
During periods when the elected members have been more influential than
usual, they have also concluded that the power of the P5 is difficult to circumvent, preventing the SC to act.[8] Despite this, the interest in serving in the UN
Security Council remains high among the members of the UN. We suggest that
this reflects a broader pattern by which states excluded from great power competition seek to increase their share of participation in international organizations.[9] Not even the Security Council stands unaffected by a broader process
through which an increasing number of states are becoming more involved in
IOs.

The gradual increase of opportunities for participation for a larger share of
IO members reflects how IOs are seeking to improve their legitimacy, which
attests to effectively raised demands by groupings of smaller states.[10] While the
Security Council might not qualify as a reform eager IO for legitimacy enhancing purposes, there are signs such as a protruding position for smaller states in
the procedure of appointing nonpermanent members. As one expression, no
candidate involved in a 'contested slate' (more candidates than available seats)
can afford to ignore the members of Small Island Developing States (SIDS) in
their efforts to gather sufficient support. This group of small islands with similar challenges on sustainable development includes close to a fifth of all UN
member states. The members of SIDS do not formally coordinate their votes,
but their 'competent performance of vulnerability' relies on a shared agenda.[11]
This agenda requires attention to secure enough votes in the Security Council
elections.

As an additional expression, small states are not only an important constituency, but manage with some regularity to get a two-year access to the Security
Council chamber in New York. While this, as mentioned, often reflects a turn-
taking order and the praxis of 'clean slates' adopted by the regional group to
whom the candidatures belong, at occasions small state candidatures in 'contested slates' manage to match, and even defeat, their larger state contestants.
One illustration of this is when Luxembourg, inhabiting 0.6 million, in 2012,

8   Keating in Einsiedel et al 2016: 149.
9   Malone 2000; Corbett et al. 2018; Corbett et al. 2019; Vahid and Postolski 2022.
10   Corbett et al. 2018; 2019.
11   Corbett et al. 2019, 647.

could rejoice with Australia, residence of 25 million, over a forthcoming term in the Council, and to the great disappointment of its competitor Finland, a country with 5 million people. To get a sense of Luxembourg's achievement in defeating Finland, a country with close to ten as many inhabitants, it is also worth to consider that Luxembourg has less than half the diplomatic missions of Finland, as these missions become important campaign sites during a candidature.[12] The Finnish loss was an unpleasant surprise to its government, and a wake-up call for all the Nordic states, who thereby had faced two failed candidatures in a row. We consider the Nordic states as an interesting group in the Security Council elections. They are a group of small but wealthy states, who shares a sense of community and have aimed for a high profile in UN-politics. This has rewarded them with a positive reputation in UN circles, but they also faced a period of decline in the post-Cold War period, with several failed candidatures for office, including the Security Council. In our study, we pay special attention to the Nordic states as a sub-group within the Western European and Others Group (WEOG) to conduct comparisons between successful and unsuccessful campaigns in contested slates.

4   The Security Council Candidature: Reasons and Expressions

Regardless of the institutional disadvantages associated with elected membership, there is considerable interest among the 188 UN members who lacks the permanent equivalent for a two-year term in the Security Council. Also, in the light of the many restraints to actual achievements as an elected member, there are several conceivable reasons for why UN member states without a permanent seat in the Council quest the elected seats. These reasons may stem from the Security Council as the established platform of power, from its adaptation to become a more accurate platform of power, as well as from the voices for its more profound reform to remain a legitimate platform of power. From all these angles, an elected term in the Security Council brings power enhancing benefits to the holder of this office. As an established platform, it provides the temporary office holder opportunity to participate in the decision-making on international peace and security, simultaneously with unique access to the small group of privileged powers. As an adapted platform, it provides the temporary office holder improved opportunities to maneuver. Indeed, the Security Council has proven some ability to adapt to new circumstances, by adjusting

---

12   Lowy index 2016–19.

procedures and by inventing new ways of acting, which in turn contribute to staying topical.[13] As a result, the E10 seek to exercise normative influence through the choice of thematic debate, by requesting improved transparency, and by getting access to pen holding on country-specific issues.[14] Finally, in the context of voices of a reformed platform, frequent elected membership has significant political value for states with prospects for a future permanent seat. This clarifies that successful candidatures and reputation for regular and competent membership of the Council are attributes to status. To elaborate further on this link with status; as a token of their success, terms in the Council is beneficial also to small states with ambitions of a high-profile foreign policy. Accepting the idea of recurrent terms in the Security Council as an attribute of status in world politics also underlines the relevance of considering the stratified pattern constituted by the electoral procedure for nonpermanent seats in the Security Council.

Turning from the possible reasons to states' interest in the elected seats, which we will discuss in further detail below, to its different expressions; making a candidature into a foreign policy priority will keep the Ministry of Foreign Affairs busy for years. As mentioned, the combined activities to gather support includes tools adopted from the diplomatic field, such as confirming a promise of support by a written agreement, and features from national rallies, such as a campaign message with an associated slogan, to promote achievements and issue priorities. The growing importance of an active campaign implies that the candidature turns diplomats and public servants into campaign workers, a role that deviates from the typical tasks associated with their positions. If the concept of *parliamentary diplomacy* captures how national parliaments – and Members of Parliament – are becoming international actors, the concept of *candidature diplomacy* captures how states – and state officials – are becoming involved in election activities to secure a sufficient number of votes.[15] While there is a growing literature on parliaments as agents in international politics, there is no comparative study on how governments launch candidatures for international offices on behalf of their states. As part of candidature diplomacy, state agents target especially important groups of voters; they send individuals with authority and reputation to launch the message, and they seek to keep close track of the support they gather.[16] We know that there is a

---

13   von Einsiedel et al. 2016, 1–2.
14   Keating in Einsiedel et al. 2016: 149–152; Security Council Report; Gifkins 2021; Farrall et al. 2020.
15   Stavridis and Jančić 2016; van Wyk 2020.
16   Byrne 2011; Ekengren and Möller 2021; Langmore and Farrall 2016; Thorhallsson and Eggertsdóttir 2021.

diplomatic practice of learning from recently successful candidatures among friends and neighbors, but the scholarly knowledge of the campaigns for international office is underdeveloped.

We proceed to specify our contribution with departure in our research-questions: Who wins a seat? Why do UN member states seek representation in the Security Council? What kind of opportunities do states expect to get from having a seat? How do they campaign? What accounts for a successful campaign?

5   Who Wins a Seat? The Procedure for Election to the Security Council

In the appointment of representatives to the nonpermanent seats, the UN Charter instructs member states to pay special attention to contributions 'to the maintenance of international peace and security and to the other purposes of the Organization'.[17] Winning an elected seat on the Security Council requires two thirds of the votes from the present member states. Each term lasts for two years, and there is a rotation of five seats on each occasion. Since 2015, the elections take place in June each year.

The nomination of candidatures occurs within five regional groups. The distribution of seats between regional groups are as follows: three for the African Group (AG), two for the Asia and the Pacific Group, one from the Eastern European Group (EEG), two from the Latin American and the Caribbean (GRU-LAC), and two from the Western Europe and Others group (WEOG) (including Canada, Australia, and New Zealand).[18] On even calendar years, there are elections for one seat from the African group, one from the Asia-Pacific group, one from the Latin America and Caribbean group, and two from the WEOG. On odd calendar years, there are elections for two seats from the African group, one from the Asia-Pacific group, one from the Latin America and Caribbean group, and one from the Eastern European group.[19]

The distribution of nonpermanent seats for the purpose of regional representation is the result of a reform from 1963, which expanded the number

---

17   Article 23, 1.
18   UN Doc. A/RES/1991 (XVIII) (1991); Malone 2000; Hurd 2002.
19   Security Council Report 2017.

from six to ten. The reform was in response to a changing international community, with an increasing number of newly independent states. A further increase in the number of states since then, from 104 in 1963 to 193 in 2021, attests to the current competition among states to serve as nonpermanent members. Broadly speaking, this means that states seeking an elected seat are now up against even more competitors and need to win the support of even more countries in order to secure the required number of votes.[20] Another consequence is that they might have to wait longer for a renewed opportunity after a failed candidature. In accordance with such a development, experts and scholars suggest that the competition over the elected seats has intensified over the past decades.

We are interested in a closer examination of the results from the Security Council elections over time as we suggest that the electoral pattern is relevant to the broader power relations on the global as well as the regional level. Our first empirical step, in Chapter 3, is to map out the distribution of terms in the Security Council between the UN member states since the inception of the Council, and to examine competitiveness in the post-Cold War period further. We use data from both the UN and the non-profit organization Security Council Reports. We examine competitiveness by looking at the relationship between candidatures and times elected, and by scrutinizing the opportunity to an elected seat for states depending on their regional group belonging. As a result, we detect the winners and losers in the post-Cold War competition for representation in the Security Council. A majority of the UN member states have tried to get a seat in the Security Council on at least one occasion in the post-Cold War period. More than half of them have also been successful in this endeavor on at least one occasion. Still, close to one third of the world's states awaits the opportunity to serve their first term in the Council, while a small group of states visits the Council on frequent intervals. We reveal the shrinking chances in the opportunity to serve in the Council for a majority of members as the consequence of the successful few. However, there is significant variation in the share of time that the successful few seizes between the regional groups.

---

20   Two-thirds (10 of 15) of the seats on the SC are appointed via an election in the General Assembly. Each year, member states choose between the candidates for five available seats to the next biennial term (Article 23). A two-thirds majority in the General Assembly (UNGA) is required for election.

6   Why Do UN Member States Seek Representation? What Do They
         Expect from a Term?

Great many UN member states have launched a Security Council candidature
in the post-Cold War era. Why is that? We explore the many possible reasons
why a short two year-term on the SC is so attractive to states. Why do member
states contend for a spot, and what do they hope to achieve? In our second
empirical study, we rely on a phone interview survey to the permanent representations in New York. We do comparisons both between UN member states
within different regional groups, and comparisons between states within the
Western European and Others Group (WEOG).

    By exploring why states find a term on the Security Council attractive, and
what they hope to achieve if elected, we are able to offer some insight on the
perceived relevance of the Security Council. The analysis will give us evidence
on how and why states participate in international organizations, especially
by winning positions in international bodies and committees. In our comparison on why states seek representation on the Security Council and what they
expect from it, we pay special attention to regional group membership and
state size. We find state size especially relevant since wealth and population
are among the most recently detected determinants to a successful candidature regardless of the overall increase of opportunities for smaller states to participate in international organizations.[21] Because of their size, smaller states
have a more limited ability to maneuver in global politics, since their smaller
population and economy affect their diplomatic and military capacities.[22] Yet
smaller states still aim for a term on the Security Council and, although not
as frequently as their bigger counterparts, sometimes they manage to achieve
their goal. We contribute with insight that size can also matter to differences
when it comes to motivational drives for a candidature and expectations on
what a nonpermanent seat can entail. Regardless of size, member states are,
of course, aware of the expert view on the relationship between the P5 and
the E10, which tempers their expectations of the extent to which they will be
able to exercise influence. Yet the increasing interest to serve suggests that
states certainly see benefits from having the opportunity. The commitment
of smaller states to the United Nations for the purpose to enhancing their
national security through a rule-based order might explain their keen interest
to serve on the Security Council. On the other hand, we might expect states

---

21   Dreher et al. 2014; Corbett et al. 2018.
22   Thorhallsson and Bailes 2016.

with even stronger sets of positional attributes to have an equally strong interest. States might view serving on the Security Council at regular intervals to sustain a middle power identity. It is even more important for regional powers with hope for a permanent seat to demonstrate their capacity for frequent representation, as electoral defeats might weaken their political claims.

In Chapter 2 we delve deeper into this issue and suggest that states see a nonpermanent seat offering at least three power enhancing benefits: to influence, to network and to gain status. The empirical analysis for the reasons behind candidatures and expected benefits with a seat take place in Chapter 4 and 5. Our empirical study isolates the differences in the expected benefits among states in different regional groups and of different types. Our study can also contribute with insights into the beliefs and strategies when it comes to the strong position of the P5.

7   How Do They Campaign? What Accounts for a Successful Campaign?

As the competition for a seat on the Security Council has intensified, states announce their candidatures earlier and they campaign more actively. As the competition for a seat has become tougher, campaigning has become increasingly important.

In our third main empirical step, we do a comparison between successful and unsuccessful campaigns. The electorate of UN member states does not reward all campaigns equally; they elect some countries more often. Yet, prior success does not necessarily lead to future success. Further, the circumstance that smaller states indeed are capable to contest their larger competitors speaks to the relevance of examining the campaigns. States tend to follow the routine of learning from best practice, in the sense that they seek campaign advice from those most recently elected. In terms of research, however, we lack systematic inquiry on these campaigns, i.e., how they are carried out and what leads to success. Such inquiry is obviously relevant considering the electoral record of surprising defeats by a more prosperous candidate with size-related advantages in the competition for a term on the Security Council to the advantage of a less resourceful competitor. The absence of systematic inquiry on campaigning means that we lack extensive descriptions as well as theoretical insights on campaign performance.

We carry out the empirical study for how campaigns are conducted and what accounts for success in Chapter 6, 7 and 8. The Charter instructs members to pay special attention to contributions 'to the maintenance of international peace and security and to the other purposes of the Organization'.[23] When it comes to the selection of nonpermanent members, we can expect candidates to try to communicate that they possess qualities that relate to these specifications. In addition, we use a theoretical framework (set up in Chapter 2) based on insights rendered from literature on national campaigns and on Olympic Games site decisions to structure our comparisons. We identify three logical elements of campaigning: contribution, competence, and commitment. We conduct our study of campaigns as three pairwise comparisons. We have limited the scope to the Nordic states, and one of their WEOG competitors in each of the three elections. Our attention on the Nordic states enables us to infer with some additional accuracy regarding the conditions and prospects for smaller states to gain access to the highest international office. The Nordic states coordinate their candidatures, which reflects a long tradition of deep collaboration in United Nations politics. The selection of nonpermanent members to the Security Council relies on dividing the ten available seats between regional groups of member states. Each regional group decides whether they want to nominate only one candidate per available seat, so-called clean slates, or hold a competition among several candidates ahead of the election, so-called contested slates. The frequent use of contested slates is characteristic of the WEOG. All Nordic states are members of WEOG, but they constitute a sub-group that coordinates and supports each other's candidatures. As mentioned, the election for the two available WEOG seats takes place every other year. The Nordic states contribute with a candidate every fourth year. Since we are interested in mapping out campaigns in order to determine how states are successful, we have used the Nordic states because they are a sub-group within the WEOG. To establish three comparisons between one successful and one unsuccessful candidature, we have paired each of the three Nordic candidatures in the 2000s with one of their competitors: Iceland with Austria for the 2008 election, Finland with Luxembourg for the 2012 election, and Sweden with the Kingdom of the Netherlands for the 2016 election.

8   The Structure of the Book

In Chapter 2, we will further elaborate on our theoretical departure, design and method. Once this is in place, we conduct a three-stage empirical investigation. In Chapter 3, we focus on who is elected, how many times different

---

23   Article 23, 1.

states are elected or if they are not elected at all. We also study which states candidate and fail and to which regional group they belong. In Chapter 4 and 5, we investigate why states seek representation in the Security Council and what they expect from receiving a seat. Here, we rely on results from a telephone interview survey conducted with various states' permanent representations in New York, as well as in-depth interviews with diplomatic representatives from six different countries in three comparative case studies. In Chapters 6, 7 and 8, the same countries reappear in three comparative case studies. This time we analyze how states campaign for a seat and what leads to a successful candidature. We study campaign material, official records, as well as interviews with leading diplomats. Chapter 9 concludes the book.

Bibliography

Barnett, Michael and Marta Finnemore. 'Political Approaches'. In *The Handbook on United Nations,* eds. Thomas G. Weiss and Sam Dawns, (New York: Oxford University Press, 2018).

Bially Mattern, Janice and Ayse Zarakol. 'Hierarchies in World Politics'. *International Organization,* 70 (2016), 623–654.

Byrne, Caitlin. 'Campaigning for a Seat on the Security Council: a Middle Power Reflection on the Role of Public Diplomacy'. *CDP Perspectives on Public Diplomacy,* paper 10, 2011.

Corbett, Jack, Xu Yi-Chong and Patrick Weller. 'Small States and the 'Throughput' Legitimacy of International Organizations'. *Cambridge Review of International Affairs.* 31(2) (2018), 183–202.

Corbett, Jack, Xu Yi-Chong and Patrick Weller. 'Norm Entrepreneurship and Diffusion 'from below' in International Organisations: How the Competent Performance of Vulnerability Generates benefits for Small States'. *Review of International Studies,* 45(4) (2019), 647–668.

Dreher, Axel, Matthew Gould, Matthew D. Rablen and James Raymond Vreeland. 'The Determinants of Election to the United Nations Security Council'. *Public Choice,* 158 (2014), 51–83.

Ekengren, Ann-Marie, Fredrik D. Hjorthen and Ulrika Möller. 'A Nonpermanent Seat in the United Nations Security Council: Why Bother?'. *Global Governance: a Review of Multilateralism and International Organizations,* (26) (2020), 21–45.

Ekengren, Ann-Marie and Ulrika Möller. 'Campaigning for an Elected Seat in the UN Security Council'. In *Elected Members of the Security Council: Lame Ducks or Key Players?, eds.* Schrijver, Nico J. and Niels M. Blokker (Leiden: Brill Nijhoff, 2020).

Ekengren, Ann-Marie and Ulrika Möller. 'Campaigning for the prize: the quests by Sweden and the Kingdom of the Netherlands for Security Council Membership, 2017–2018'. *The Hague Journal of Diplomacy*, 16 (2021), 1–26.

Farrall, Jeremy, et al. 'Elected member influence in the United Nations Security Council'. *Leiden Journal of International Law* 33.1 (2020): 101–115.

Gifkins, Jess. 'Beyond the veto: Roles in UN Security Council Decision-Making'. *Global Governance* 27(1) (2021), 1–24.

Götz, Elias. 'Status Matters in World Politics'. *Review of International Studies,* 23(1) (2021), 228–247.

Hurd, Ian. 'Legitimacy, Power and the Symbolic Life of the UN Security Council'. *Global Governance,* 8 (2002), 35–51.

Hurd, Ian. *After Anarchy: Legitimacy and Power in the United Nations Security Council* (Princeton: Princeton University Press, 2008a).

Hurd, Ian. 'Myths of Membership: the Politics of Legitimation in UN Security Council Reform'. *Global Governance,* 14 (2) (2008b), 199–217.

Keating, Colin. 'Power Dynamics between Permanent and Elected Members'. In *The UN Security Council in the 21st Century,* eds. Sebastian von Einsiedel, David M. Malone, and Bruno Stagno Ugarte (Boulder: Lynne Rienner, 2016).

Langmore, John and Jeremy Farrall. 'Can Elected Members Make a Difference in the Security Council? Australia's Experience in 2013–2014'. *Global Governance,* 22 (1) (2016), 59–77.

Lowy Diplomacy Index.

Luck, Edward C. *UN Security Council: Practice and Promise* (New York: Routledge, 2006).

Malone, David. 'Eyes on the Prize: the Quest for Nonpermanent Seats on the UN Security Council'. *Global Governance,* 6 (1) (2000), 3–23.

Melissen, Jan. 'Diplomatic Studies in the Right Season'. *International Studies Review,* 1 (2011), 723–725.

Schia, Niels Nagelhus. "Horseshoe and Catwalk': Power, Complexity and Consensus-Making in the United Nations Security Council'. In *Palaces of Hope – the Anthropology of Global Organizations,* eds. Niezen, Ronald and Maria Sapignoli (Cambridge: Cambridge University Press, 2017).

Security Council Report.

Schrijver, Nico J. and Niels M. Blokker (eds.). *Elected Members of the Security Council: Lame Ducks or Key Players?* (Leiden: Brill Nijhoff, 2020).

Sievers, Loraine, and Sam Daws. *The Procedure of the UN Security Council.* 4th ed. (Oxford: Oxford University Press, 2014).

Stavridis, Stelios and Davor Jančić. 'The Rise of Parliamentary Diplomacy in International Politics'. *The Hague Journal of Diplomacy,* 11(2016), 105–120.

Thorhallsson, Baldur and Alyson J.K. Bailes. 'Small State Diplomacy'. In Constantinou, Costas M., Pauline Kerr, and Paul Sharp eds. *The Sage Handbook of Diplomacy* (London: Sage, 2016).

Thorhallsson, Baldur and Anna Margrét Eggertsdóttir. 'Small States in the UN Security Council: Austria's Quest to Maintain Status'. *The Hague Journal of Diplomacy*, 16 (2021), 53–81.

UN Doc. A7RES/1991 (XVIII) (1991).

Vahid Nick Pay and Przemysław Postolski. 'Power and Diplomacy in the United Nations Security Council: the Influence of Elected Members'. *The International Spectator*, 57(2) (2022), 1–17.

van Wyk, Jo-Ansie. 'Candidature diplomacy: South Africa and Nkosazana Dlamini-Zuma's candidature to chair the AU Commission, 2011–2012'. *South African Journal of International Affairs*, 27 (3) (2020) 317–338.

Veenendaal, Wouter P. and Jack Corbett. 'Why Small States Offer Important Answers to Large Questions'. *Comparative Political Studies*, 48 (4) (2015), 527–549.

Von Einsiedel, Sebastian, David M. Malone, and Bruno Stagno Ugarte. *The UN Security Council in the 21st Century*, (Boulder: Lynne Rienner, 2016).

Von Einsiedel, Sebastian and David M. Malone. 'Security Council'. In *The Oxford Handbook on the United Nations*, eds. Weiss, Thomas G. and Sam Daws (Oxford: Oxford University Press, 2018).

Vreeland, J.R., and A. Dreher. *The Political Economy of the United Nations Security Council: Money and Influence* (New York: Cambridge University Press, 2014).

CHAPTER 2

Competing for an Elected Seat on the Security Council: Who, Why and How?

Ann-Marie Ekengren and Ulrika Möller

1 Introduction

For UN member states willing to take on the challenge, a candidature for a seat on the Security Council has become an increasingly work intensive and high-profiled activity. The announcement to run for election takes place earlier and the campaigns have extended in scope and been prolonged in time. Stakes are particularly high if the slate is contested, that is when the number of candidates exceeds the available seats. Long before the active campaigning begins, there are diplomatic interactions to ponder support and pave the way for vote exchange agreements. Efforts to secure votes continue up until the final minutes ahead of the election. On the day of the election, all the Permanent Representatives (PRS) are gathered in the General Assembly, some with an Election Officer (EO) by their side, to cast the votes on behalf of their countries. The candidate countries have member(s) of government present, along with senior officials, PRS and other diplomats. The high-level political and diplomatic representatives of the candidature countries socialize in what might seem like a casual manner, but more likely, these chats are carefully planned to maximize the chances of sufficient support. Members of the campaign teams hand out the final bags with branded gifts. All candidates have made efforts to estimate how many supporters they have, based on agreements made and promises pledged, as part of their campaigning efforts.

This intense political and diplomatic competition for nonpermanent seats in the Security Council may appear puzzling in the perspective of the elected members' marginal influence given the more powerful instruments available to the permanent members.[1] In some contrast, our approach illuminates how the competition for a nonpermanent seat reflects a relationship of power between states, as representation in the Security Council is beneficial to them in several different ways. We argue that the design and execution of the campaigns plays

---

1   Engelbrekt 2015; Barnett and Finnemore 2018; von Einsiedel and Malone 2018.

a role for the outcome of the election. The voting result displayed at the board on the election day reveals the quality of the conducted campaign and of the method utilized to estimate support. It provides a reality-check about the current political and diplomatic relations. For some, the result will confirm a self-perception about the role they want to play in the world. Others might realize that they have, at best, misinterpreted their political and diplomatic colleagues and, at worst, been deceived. Electoral loss is not only a missed opportunity for participation in the exercise of international authority, but has implications for possibilities to collaboration, and for reputational standing.

In this chapter, we lay out the theoretical foundation for our approach. We establish the analytical departures for our inquiry, conducted in three main empirical steps: 1) to map out and examine the electoral pattern of the nonpermanent seats over time, 2) to explore expectations with the candidatures, and 3) to conduct pairwise comparisons of campaigns to identify factors of success. We draw on previous research on the determinants to electoral success as to why states prioritize a candidature and what they hope to achieve by a term in the Security Council.[2] We substantiate the relevance of campaigning as an explanation of election outcomes, by clarifying how available explanations fail to account for the cases included in our study. As further guidance, for the first empirical step, we utilize the analytical lens of international hierarchy to reveal how the electoral pattern reflects a stratification of states. For the second empirical step, we specify an analytical framework to study the power-enhancing benefits that may push states towards a candidature decision.[3] For the third empirical step, we specify an explanatory framework that identifies logics of campaigning, which may account for variation in the electoral result.[4]

---

2   A growing body of literature addresses various topics related to Security Council elections, including the why and how of state candidatures. Important themes include determinants for electoral success Dreher et al. 2014, campaigns and electoral outcomes Malone 2000; Ekengren and Möller 2021, power enhancing benefits from a seat Ekengren et al. 2020, single case studies on countries' experiences Langmore and Farrall 2016; Chapnick 2019; Vahid and Postolski 2022, and vote buying, aid-for-policy or other political advantages Kuziemko and Werker 2006; Bueno de Mesquita and Smith 2010; Vreland and Dreher 2014; Dreher, Eichenauer and Gering 2016; Reinsberg 2020; Balci 2022. The more extensive literature on legitimacy, reform, and functionality of the Security Council addresses possibly enhanced roles for elected members Hurd 2002, 2008a; 2008b; Engelbrekt 2015, 2016; Eisendel et al. 2016; Schrijver and Blokker 2020.
3   Ekengren et al. 2020.
4   Ekengren and Möller 2021.

2   Previous Research on UN Elections and Determinants for Electoral Success

The earliest statistical studies on the selection of candidates for international office within the United Nations date back to the Cold War.[5] Subsequent studies of the Security Council candidatures and elections rarely mention these studies, but we suggest that their theoretical and empirical focus are still valid. Singer and Sensenig have explicit focus on the results of Security Council elections over time and inquire the relevance of national power (measured through GNP), political alignment with the US, and economic ties with the US.[6] Weigert et al. study the appointment of UN offices among UN members in Africa and examine qualities of the candidates in terms of 1) contributions to the UN, 2) the image as a 'good' member of the UN, and 3) the personality and reputation of individual delegates.[7] A main difference between these studies, apart from the variation in empirical scope, is that Singer and Sensenig focus on the broader power capital of states, while Weigert et al. focus on the qualities and performance of the candidatures. Certainly, there are overlaps, for instance in the sense that a rich country can make more substantial contributions to the UN, which may also translate into a more positive image of its UN membership. Our inquiry is a contribution in the sense that we both map out the electoral pattern over time to reveal the relationship of power between states and scrutinize the qualities that may possibly overtrump the material attributes if utilized in a campaign.

Indeed, the results from more recent studies suggest that material attributes remain important, but other qualities are at play also. To specify, the most recent statistical analysis on the election to the nonpermanent seats in the Security Council highlights two commonly shared characteristics of successful candidatures: population and wealth.[8] The repeatedly elected states include populous and/or wealthy states, such as Argentina, Brazil, Canada, Germany, India, and Japan. In addition, their results indicate the relevance of two normative standards, referred to as 'the peace norm' and 'the turn-taking norm'. The presence of a peace norm concerns the UN's main mission to prevent conflict and to promote peace; member states are therefore encouraged to take the peace credentials of Security Council candidates into consideration when voting. Hence, members engaged in civil war are less likely to become members

---

5   Singer and Sensenig 1963; Weigert et al. 1969.
6   Singer and Sensenig 1963.
7   Weigert et al. 1969.
8   Dreher et al. 2014.

of the Council. The turn-taking norm addresses the nomination procedure of having a set order for candidatures that regional groups may apply. The study also suggests that for candidates in competitive races, this norm work to the favor of first-time candidates and of those with longer spells away from the Council. In conclusion, Dreher et al. (2014) highlight the presence of a 'compromise between the demands of populous countries to win elections more frequently and a norm of giving each country its turn'.[9]

We suggest that wealth and population as 'determinants' for electoral success both reflect a strong interest among regional powers to serve in the Council, and their advantages in the regional nomination procedure. Because of their relative wealth and population-size, they can argue that they are the best suited to represent the region, and thus to contribute to counter the stronghold of the P5. This poses a dilemma to all the other members of a regional group. They must trade between on the one hand the goal to maximize the possible impact of each elected seat disposed by their regional group, and, on the other hand, their own ambition to gather the possible advantages from this international office. We also suggest that a main reason for why populous and wealthy countries are more successful is because they have more resources to spend on the campaign and a stronger diplomatic presence, both in terms of having more embassies and a larger UN representation.[10] The presence of more embassies and a larger UN mission lay the groundwork for more robust contact with other missions and governments, which is an obvious strength during a candidature. Despite such advantages, surprising defeats of, for example, Australia (for the 1997–98 term) and Canada (for the 2011–12 term, and the 2020–21 term) underscore that the outcome of contested elections is indeed uncertain.[11] To proceed, the two normative aspects examined by Dreher et al. (2014) are interesting in the sense that they point to the relevance of cultivating certain qualities as part of a campaign for a term in the Council. Hence, not being involved in conflict appears close to a necessity for the chances of election and being a first-time candidate might be beneficial in a contested slate. None of the explanations presented above can account for the variation in outcome for the cases we have included in our study. Austria defeated first time candidate Iceland, as a more populous state, with more embassies, and a larger economy than Iceland. First time candidate Luxembourg defeated Finland, despite having fewer embassies and spending less on the campaign. The same pattern applies to the case of Sweden, which defeated the Kingdom

---

9   Dreher et al. 2014, 51; Copeland 2010; Chapnick 2019.
10   Thorhallsson and Bailes 2016; Prantl 2005, 37, on the size of permanent missions.
11   Thakur 1996.

of the Netherlands; Sweden is a less populous country with fewer embassies and a smaller budget for the campaign.[12] We see a room for complementing currently available statistical analysis by descriptive statistics on the electoral pattern over time, and by case comparisons through strategic selection, to examine both the reasoning behind candidatures and the relevance of campaigns for the electoral result.

3   Hierarchies in Formal Anarchy: Stratification through Security Council Representation

We will delineate the electoral pattern to the nonpermanent seats in the Security Council to further illuminate the relationship between states in world politics and to learn more about the relationship between members within regional groups. We suggest that the analytical lens of international hierarchy is a fruitful departure to the study of Security Council elections, as the election pattern over time results in a stratification between states on basis of their proven capacity to win these elections. Reinvigorated scholarly attention on the notion of hierarchy has resulted in a relatively widespread agreement on the presence and importance of various forms of vertical stratification in world politics.[13]

Vertical stratification provides a minimalist definition of hierarchy. Stratification with regards to what, as well as the degree, varies between approaches. Stratification can be restricted to binary categories of supra- and subordination as well as to results in detailed rankings on basis of multiple criteria. As frequently pointed out, one decisive binary categorisation of states is the one constituted through the institutionalisation of a few permanent members of the Security Council, contrary to the nonpermanent members of the Security Council. Here, we are interested in the less noticed but more fine-grained ranking that is constituted through the electoral procedure of appointing the Council's nonpermanent members.[14] Unlike permanent membership, the procedure with elected membership does not establish a fixed binary categorization. Instead, a stratification evolves over time on basis of variation in electoral success between states. Just like the binary categorization established by permanent membership, however, this more fine-grained stratification too reflects access to international authority. To specify further, hierarchy-centred

---

12   Engelbrekt 2020.

13   Bially Mattern and Zarakol 2016; Schulz 2019, 89.

14   See Dunton 2020, 529.

approaches may be divided into a 'thinner' and a 'thicker' view. In essence, the 'thinner' view restricts hierarchy to stratification on basis of the distribution of authority, while the 'thicker' view of hierarchy reveals patterned inequality on basis of various types of normative standards.[15] The thinner view resembles the Weberian understanding of (office) hierarchy as a 'system of super- and subordination in which there is a supervision of the lower offices by the higher ones'.[16] The thicker view reveals the social ranking of superiority and inferiority through norms spread by transnational advocacy.[17]

More evident than most forms, we suggest that the Security Council elections address the authority-related dimension of hierarchy. An important theoretical point of departure to hierarchy-centred approaches has been to reveal the limitations of anarchy-centred approaches. Still, Bially Mattern and Zarakol (2016) argue that 'Hierarchy-centrism does not necessitate abandoning the concept of anarchy altogether, any more than trying to understand the dynamics of our vast universe requires astronomers to deny the importance of the sun altogether'.[18] Similarly, McConnaughey, Musgrave and Nexon argue that the presence of hierarchy as stratifications on basis of normative standards poses no challenge to the states-under-anarchy-framework. Instead, the foremost challenge is hierarchy equivalent to the 'thinner view', focusing on the distribution of command-relations.[19] We suggest that this argument provides additional reason for analytical attention on the Security Council elections, as it is a procedure with effect on the distribution of authority for many states. However, we also acknowledge that there is a status dimension to stratification established by access to international authority; demonstrating capacity to access international authority by elected membership at frequent and periodic intervals is certainly associated with elevated status. Duque (2018) argues that status is not achieved from any fixed set of attributes but the result of 'systematic social processes' that involves recognition on basis of a combination of values and resources. While diplomatic networks have become a frequent measurement of the stratification of status between states, we suggest that Security Council elections is highly relevant as one of the 'systematic social processes' with status implications. We will map out the electoral results over time to reveal and examine the entailed pattern of stratification. Through our empirical investigation of the electoral results, we are also able to detect

15   Lake 2007; Towns and Rumelili, 2017; Bially Mattern and Zarakol 2016; Schulz 2019.
16   Weber in Roth and Wittich 2013, 957.
17   Towns and Rumelili 2017.
18   Bially Mattern and Zarakol 2016, 649.
19   McConnaughey, Musgrave and Nexon 2018, 186.

deviations from expectations that rest on established measures of power. This gives further substance to the relevance of our focus on campaigns; states may possess some agency to improve their chances of an elected seat. The coming sections elaborate on this further, as we address why states become candidates in the first place, and how they carry out their campaigns.

4   Why Do States Become Candidates for an Elected Seat on the Security Council?

Previous research on the actual candidatures for seats on the Security Council is very limited. Most recent studies are either single case studies, some mainly focusing on the term rather than the candidature, or address differences between campaigns mainly by illustration.[20] Malone (2000) focuses on Canada's candidature for the 1999–2000 term and includes some comparison with competitors. Malone has not explicitly focused on why states might want a nonpermanent seat in the first place, but the reasons identified include 'to underscore international prestige', 'to advance a national position in a dispute', and to pursue 'broader objectives'.[21] In another single-case study, Langmore and Farrall examine Australia's experience in the UNSC during 2013–2014. Within the context of studying how successful a nonpermanent member can be in achieving their goals, given the presence of the P5, they touch upon the question of why states choose to campaign. According to Langmore and Farrall, Australia's reasons for pursuing the campaign were that 1) the UNSC had become a more important institution, 2) Australia had certain security interests in Afghanistan, 3) Australia had important assets, 4) it was Australia's turn, and 5) Australia needed to pursue certain ideas and values. They further conclude that the campaign could be seen as a way of 'strengthening Australia's and, therefore [foreign minister Kevin Rudd's] own international influence'.[22]

As single-case studies, the results of Malone and Langmore and Farrall are sensitive to any particularities of the cases being examined. They are, nevertheless, instructive of our aim to present a more systematic empirical examination of why states seek nonpermanent seats on the UNSC. For one thing, the objectives they identify center on different aspects of influence and power. In the context of P5 dominance, they might have an ambition of shaping decisions. They might also have a chance to express their views in dialogue, such

---

20   Malone 2000; Gillissen 2006; Langmore 2013; Langmore and Farrall 2016.

21   Malone 2000, 6–7.

22   Langmore and Farrall 2016, 60–1.

as by influencing UNSC decision making or using their seat to gain prestige. Furthermore, while candidates might have a narrower – more self-interested – security agenda, the studies indicate that we should not rule out the possibility of a broader, value-laden agenda. The success of the Canadian initiative during the 1999–2000 term, to bring the concept of human security, then recently launched by UNDP, to the agenda of the UNSC, has inspired other elected members to follow suit.[23] As Ekengren et al (2020) have asserted, we also believe that a seat on the UNSC is relevant to states, at the very least, as an opportunity to 1) shape decisions, 2) improve network, and 3) work on their prominence. We further introduce these three types of benefits, which form our first analytical framework, below.

5   Shape Decisions

Membership in international organizations may appear strange in the sense that it involves a voluntary restriction of the highly valued sovereignty of states; we expect that states enter IOs only if it helps them to reach goals, which they are unable to attain singlehandedly. The realist analysis emphasizes the great power calculus of relative gains as well as the designs of IOs as a reflection of great power interests.[24] Indeed, the veto of the P5 is a frequently used example. Neoliberal and constructivist analysis, on the other hand, illuminate how IOs may, in fact, evolve towards serving the interest of a larger share of its members.[25] Broadly, membership in IOs is a means for states to solve coordination problems, to enforce bargains, and to shape policies.[26] While all these types of opportunities apply to membership in the United Nations, we believe that the shaping of policies might be especially relevant to states' aspirations to serve on the Security Council. Most states are excluded from the great power competition, which means that they share an interest of improving the multilateral order to restrain the reach and room for maneuver of the powerful few. Indeed, the calls for reform, including restrictions of the veto, illustrate how this ambition certainly applies to the Security Council.[27]

Over the past decades, IOs have also increased the number of opportunities for participation to suit the larger number of members.[28] This trend is

---

23   Malone 2000, 7.
24   Waltz 1979; Mearsheimer 1994.
25   Martin 1992; Keohane and Martin 1995; Keohane and Nye 1998.
26   Abbot and Snidal 1998, 29; i.e., Martin 1992.
27   Drieskens 2015.
28   Corbett 2018.

not as visible in the Security Council, as the most evident example of institutionalized great power interest, but there are changes in its proceedings that attest to the opportunities elected members have in shaping processes and outcomes. One such opportunity comes with the significant expansion of the thematic focus, which has made the UNSC highly relevant to the process of shaping international norms, as well. This development originates from the strategic use of elected members taking the opportunity to address a thematic issue during their month of presidency. Another ongoing process of change concerns the task of acting as penholder, which entails important leadership functions.[29] Elected members are becoming increasingly successful by taking on this task, which members of the P5 have long dominated especially in relation to country-specific issues. Several positive examples, set by a few elected members, relate to this, in the sense that they assert a broader type of leadership during their term on the UNSC as well.[30] These developments occur on the margins, in terms of moving the stronghold of the P5. Still, they suggest that elected members have increased their room to maneuver, and candidates might therefore entertain some expectations on shaping decisions during a term on the UNSC. Since states are aware that decision making in this international body is in the control of the P5, states might also seek office for other reasons than to influence decisions.

6   Extended Network

A nonpermanent seat on the Security Council offers access to the supreme body of the world's main multilateral organization, the United Nations. This can be of value even despite the restraint set by the veto for elected members to exercise influence on decision-making. To specify one such value, the temporary location from within a power center improves the opportunities a country has, to cultivate and expand a current diplomatic or political network, which is important for the maintenance and enhancement of social power. In the language of Social Network Analysis, the UNSC is a central 'hub' in the wider web of social and political interactions. We can regard candidatures to an elected seat as attempts to work on centrality within that web. Despite the term being short, the two years a state spends on the UNSC may provide an opportunity to integrate further in the broader socio-political network. The pattern we see in which certain states are constantly engaged in seeking representation and positions of responsibility at various multilateral

29   Gifkins 2021.
30   Keating 2016, 149–53.

platforms speaks to the accuracy of this view. The relevance of achieving such centrality, and making it as dense as possible, lies in the interchangeability of this network power and other forms of power.[31] Specific elements of the interchangeability process go beyond the scope of our study. Still, we can say that a strong political and diplomatic network is relevant to several forms of social power as presented by differing perspectives, such as liberalism, constructivism, and practice theory. The liberal notion of 'soft power', or 'the ability to get what you want through attraction rather than coercion or payments', is geared towards symbolic and ideational components.[32] The degree to which states have opportunity to exercise this ability 'through attraction' depends on the density of their political and diplomatic networks. Similarly, to exercise influence through norm entrepreneurship, as suggested by constructivism, a sufficient social location is necessary.[33] Finally, power as emergent to social interaction is equally important within practice theory. The tactic of establishing skillfulness, as suggested by practice theory, may both depend on, and lead to, improved political and diplomatic networks.[34] Translated into the candidature for an elected seat, we might expect states to consider a term on the UNSC as an opportunity to shape decisions, as well as to establish stronger networks. Regular access to representatives of the P5 might seem like an opportunity in itself; this regular access might also make a state more interesting to other states, which could open additional doors for dialogue and networking.

7   Work on Prominence

Status refers to the recognized position of an actor within a hierarchy.[35] Commonly assumed, to reach this position requires a set of *valued attributes*, or status markers. Even if the broader IR-debate on material vs. ideational properties applies to the specification of these attributes, the literature shows an awareness of the complexities regarding these status markers at play.[36] For one thing, they are collective beliefs, or intersubjective understandings, on the requirements for achieving a higher rank.[37] These attributes may also range

---

31   Hafner-Burton, Kahler and Montgomery, 2009.
32   Nye 2004.
33   Finnemore and Sikkink 1998.
34   Adler-Nissen and Pouliot 2014; Ralph and Gifkins 2017.
35   Freedman 2016, 83; de Carvahlo and Neumann 2015, 4; Renshon 2016, 513; Ward 2019, 213.
36   See Duque 2018.
37   Larson, Paul, and Wohlforth, 2014, 7–8; Ward, 2019, 213.

from properties that are geopolitical in character, such as weapon systems, to properties, such as political dedication or diplomatic skills within issues that are of normative importance. Furthermore, as indicated above (see section on hierarchy), there is no such thing as an immediate cause and effect-flow between improvement on the set of status markers and an elevated position in the ranking of states. Instead, the acquisition of a valued attribute to substantiate a status claim requires a state agent to acknowledge that the attribute is necessary for achieving a higher social rank.[38] Moreover, as pointed out by Duque (2018), the maintenance of status relies on systematic social processes by which recognition is granted on basis of the combination of values and resources. We have suggested that the Security Council elections establish a systematic social process of this sort, and we also propose that state representatives may be very considerate about the status dimension of the elected seats. From this view, campaigns may even be seen as an instrument to display the combination of values and resources that substantiates the status-claim behind the quest for an elected seat.

The reinvigorated literature on status in world politics focused initially on the exploration of rising powers' experiences of *disrespect* and *status deficit* but is now also considering small states as status seekers.[39] The typical empirical case in the exploration of status deficit was a rising power experiencing inappropriately low social rank, given substantive material assets taken into consideration. These states seek further recognition of their status, and they are prepared to fight for it. Indeed, empirical analysis has confirmed the association between status dissatisfaction and propensity toward conflict.[40] The incorporation of small states as status seekers shifted focus from status seeking via conflictual means towards peaceful ones. As small states, per definition, are disqualified from great power competition, it is argued that they might be more interested in status as the only type of power available to them, and as a way of standing out from the myriad of other small states.[41]

The research on status in world politics also highlights the rights and privileges associated with elite club-membership.[42] This suggests that small states

38   Ward, 2019, 824.
39   Wolf 2011; Larson, Paul, and Wohlforth, 2014; Renshon 2016, 2017; Neumann and de Carvahlo 2015.
40   Wallace 1971; Larson and Shevchenko 2010; Paul, Larson and Wohlforth 2014; Freedman 2016; Renshon 2016; 2017.
41   Neumann and de Carvahlo 2015, 16; Wohlforth et al. 2017.
42   Ward 2019.

may seek status to get 'a seat at the table' and the opportunity to stand in 'the limelight' with the great powers.[43] Although somewhat vaguely put, these reasons for why also small states might invest in status are all applicable to an elected seat in the Security Council as a term certainly brings a state as close to international authority as possible and thereby also a brief period at the center of attention.

To sum up, translated into the candidature for an elected seat, states might consider a term on the UNSC with the expectation to shape decisions, and to establish stronger networks, but also as an opportunity to maintain or elevate their status.

These three theoretically deduced reasons for a candidature guide our empirical investigation, carried out as a phone interview with diplomats at the permanent missions of the United Nations. As reported by Ekengren et al. (2020), these reasons are all valid to diplomats for why one's own state, as well as other states, decide to seek candidatures. Additional reasons include a sense of obligation and country-specific issues, such as seeking the office on a regular basis. Further, there is a discrepancy in estimating one's own reasons and other states' reasons for wanting a seat, especially because a sense of obligation is more important to individual countries and portraying status level is more important to others. We have also detected a discrepancy between the reasons to campaign and the estimated outcome, if elected. While the opportunity to influence is a main reason to seek a candidature, the ratings on actual impact are modest. Conversely, states were optimistic in their assessment of the opportunity to establish networks, but this was not among the most important reasons countries specified for wanting a seat. A similar pattern applies to status; it is not the most important reason for seeking a candidature, but a term on the Council may very well have a positive effect.

While previous studies have addressed the beliefs and expectations connected to campaigns, they have rarely considered *who* is representing the state. We depart from the view that the state is a corporate agent, which implies regularities among those who are representing and acting on its behalf.[44] Typical state agents in the field of international relations are prime ministers, and diplomats. While politicians are the final decision makers, diplomats provide political advice based on their experiences acting as representatives of the state. While politicians enter and exit offices of power on a

---

43   Wohlfort et al., 2017, 534.
44   Pettit 2001; Wendt 2004.

TABLE 2.1   Reasons for a candidature, and expectations connected to an elected seat on the security council

To shape decisions	To expand network	To work on status
– Guard one's national security – Promote specific principles and values – Do the principles/ values/reform remain once the term has ended?	– Access the P5 – Establish other types of contacts – Does access to new networks remain once the term has ended?	– Elevate status – Maintain status – Does status achieved from elected seat remain once the term has ended?

regular basis, diplomats often 'personify' the state for longer periods, albeit through different missions and assignments. For this reason, we have chosen to focus on the diplomatic category; specifically, the permanent missions in New York, since the UN headquarters is the most important site for campaign-related activities. The Permanent Representative of a candidate for a seat on the UNSC needs to meet with as many other PRs as possible, hoping that this will translate into votes. Arguably, diplomats at the permanent missions are experts on what states – especially their own, but also others – hope to gain from a seat. In the table above, we offer illustrations for each theoretical reason. Our research strategy is to assess the extent to which these theoretical reasons are represented in the views and beliefs expressed by diplomats at the permanent missions to the UN in New York. Further, we also compare the stated reasons for a seat, with the estimated outcome from an actual term on the Security Council.

States have different relationships with the UN depending on their size and position in the global system. State size matters for what can be expected from a UN membership in general, but also for more specific positions, including a nonpermanent seat on the UNSC. From this departure, as well as the results from Ekengren et al. (2020), we proceed with a more nuanced analysis as to why states seek a candidature. We examine the 1) differences related to state size, and 2) patterns among members within the WEOG. Through focus on members of one specific group, we control for regional differences regarding the nomination process.

8   Conceptualizing State Size and its Relevance for Expectations on an Elected Seat

In world politics, the distinction of state size is dependent on context, to a certain degree. Within UN politics, states defined as small are also likely to be economically vulnerable, whereas in the field of security, states defined as small are also likely to be militarily non-aligned but may very well be wealthy. Likewise, the small state literature focuses empirically on three groups that differ extensively from one another: small island states, relatively small states in Africa and South America, and small wealthy states in Europe. The conceptualization of state size is also a controversial issue among scholars, with the literature on small states and medium-sized powers facing similar challenges. There are three approaches, which rely mainly on 1) positional attributes, 2) perception and 3) behavior. Typical positional attributes, commonly combined, include territory, population, economic – and military capabilities.[45] In the absence of a conclusive definition through scholarly agreement on the appropriate combination of these factors, we could depart from self-identification, or from a detected behavioral pattern.[46] For example, medium-sized powers are often associated with normative ambitions of playing the role of a good power, enhancing good citizenship throughout the world. Often, they try to build bridges in a regional context and to use international organizations in their effort to influence world politics. Thus, if states identify as small or medium-sized powers, and/or act in what we regard as a typical pattern for any of these categories, we should address them as small states or medium-sized powers.[47] Therefore, if the Nordic states identify as small states, then we should treat them as small states. On the other hand, if the foreign policies of the Nordic states involve bridge building, the active use of IOs, and the promotion of norms, then we should treat them as medium-sized powers.[48] If the problem with the positional approach is an arbitrary line for delineating different categories, the main problem with the alternatives is that they are nearly tautological.

A possible and more appealing alternative is to acknowledge that the identity as small state is tied to 'a specific spatio-temporal context' and involves size-related disadvantages in world politics.[49] A main objective of the study of

45   Thorhallsson and Wivel 2006, Veenendaal, Wouter and Corbett 2015; Thorhallsson and Bailes 2016; Baldacchino and Wivel 2020.
46   Thies and Sari 2018; Robertson 2017.
47   See Thorhallsson and Wivel 2006, 654–5; Corbett et al. 2019.
48   See Ingebritsen 2002.
49   Thorhallsson and Wivel 2006, 654; Baldacchino and Wivel 2020, 7.

small state foreign policy is to examine how small states compensate for size-related disadvantages.[50] For our research purpose to address the relevance that smallness has on expectations of a term in the Security Council, we find it appropriate to address small European states, despite they are not economically vulnerable and have a population size that far exceeds the population of any member of Small Island Developing States. In the context of the Security Council, and the disadvantage of being an elected member rather than a permanent member, we may indeed regard small European states as small, even if they are larger than any member of SIDS. Our focus on small states mainly within the WEOG (and in some analysis including the EEG), allows us to control for the possible influence from the regional procedure of nomination. An additional advantage is that small European states have more experience of a term in the Security Council than small states in general, which means that our large-N comparisons will be between expectations from small and large states, rather than between never elected and frequently elected states. Using a combination of spatio-temporal considered identity and several measures of positional attributes might be the most comprehensive way to define the size of states. As one of the detected determinants of success for UNSC elections, we will rely on population size to differentiate between larger and smaller European states.[51] We consider population as a proxy for the variation in economic and diplomatic capacities ie., size related advantages/disadvantages, between larger and smaller states.

9 States' Candidatures for an Elected Seat on the Security Council: How Do They Campaign?

Candidatures for an elected seat in the UNSC have some resemblances to party rallies in national elections. A campaign is conducted that launches a message – summarized by a slogan – to promote achievements and issue priorities and especially important groups of voters are targeted. The candidature countries send individuals with authority and reputation to launch the message, and they keep close track and make estimates of their number of supporters.[52] Of course, each of these features may spark controversy during a campaign, as could features distinct to the Security Council elections. For example, vote exchange agreements are one of the main instruments for

---

50   Baldacchino and Wivel 2020.
51   See Dreher et al 2014.
52   Ekengren and Möller 2020.

diplomatic representatives at the UN in New York to secure support of a candidature. Their frequent use reflects the diplomatic practice of putting weight to
bilateral promises by a written agreement, but this does not seem as evidently
appropriate to an outside audience. For one thing, the secrecy that surrounds
these agreements makes auditing on whether each agreement is coherent with
important foreign policy principles impossible. However, diplomats and public
servants involved in candidatures consider the use of these agreements of support as an established and legitimate instrument, and qualitatively different
from making policy promises of rewards in return of support. To specify, if vote
exchange agreements are examples of a campaign oddity, previous studies also
reveal the presence of dubious means and practices, including the increase of
aid to developing countries during a UNSC membership, and the possible use
of aid in exchange for votes by donor countries during candidatures. Kuziemko
and Werker (2006) strikingly conclude: 'On average, the typical developing
country serving on the council can anticipate an additional $16 million from
the United States and $1 million from the United Nations. During important
years, these numbers rise to $45 million from the United States and $8 million
from the United Nations'.[53] Another study covering the Cold War has revealed
that if the US intervened in the election of a nonpermanent member in the
Council, the elected country moved closer to the US position in upcoming
Security Council voting.[54]

In a related vein, Dreher, Eichenauer and Gehring (2016) study the effect
from aid in economic growth, on the aid given to nonpermanent members
in the Security Council. Indeed, the results confirm that this aid, given for
political-instrumental reasons, has less effect on economic growth. If research
has confirmed there are economic benefits from a nonpermanent seat for
(elites in) developing countries via an increase of aid, whether donor countries
use foreign aid to gather support for their UNSC candidature is a less explored
venue.[55] Results by Reinsberg (2019) indicate that this might be the case.[56] The
design of our study will allow us to reveal debates and domestic controversies
that a candidature decision and/or features of a campaign my result in, but
not to push knowledge further when it comes to the frequency of illegitimate
means and practices as part of a Security Council candidature. However, we
have noticed that several public officials and diplomats with campaign experience have confirmed either exposure to inappropriate proposals about a

---

53   Kuziemko and Werker 2006, 924.
54   Balci 2022.
55   Dreher, Eichenauer and Gehring 2016.
56   Reinsberg 2019.

vote in return for economic contributions or rumors on the use of illegitimate means surrounding other campaigns in previous elections.[57]

Existing research on the candidatures for a nonpermanent seat confirm the relevance of the UN Charter instructions and that states with extensive contributions to the maintenance of international peace and security are displayed during the campaign. These states also manage better in the elections, than states with lesser contributions. However, the research also points to the fact that other factors than adherence to the Charter are important.

Reflecting on earlier results for campaign success, we need to consider that campaigns have become more competitive in the past decade. Still, in this tougher climate for candidates, actual contributions as well as the image of a good member should be equally relevant today. The opportunity for substantial contributions probably also is one reason for why wealth is such a relevant factor in the more recent research. Further, our work suggests that wealth produces additional advantages for a candidate in terms of a larger budget for each campaign and for a stronger diplomatic network through embassies in more countries as well as Permanent Representations in the UN headquarters. By 'peace norm', Dreher et al. refer to the UN's main mission to prevent conflict and to promote peace, and the above-mentioned instructions for member states to consider peace credentials when voting in the UNSC election. One effect is that members engaged in civil war are less likely to be elected members of the Council. By a 'turn-taking norm', Dreher et al. refer to the practice of a set order for candidatures in some of the regional groups and, in competitive races, the advantage for first-time candidates and candidates with longer spells outside the Council.[58]

Recent single case studies give us valuable help in identifying important campaign categories for further study. These studies also give us reason to assume that quality and attractiveness of campaigns *can* matter for the election outcome. Earlier studies describe how campaigns are organised in the capital and carried out through different *activities* around the world, but with UN headquarters in New York as an especially important site.[59] International campaigning includes activities which otherwise are far from traditional diplomacy.[60] Byrne argues that these activities are important to attract public attention within the targeted diplomatic and political community.[61]

---

57   Interviews 14, 15, 16.
58   Dreher et al. 2014.
59   Malone 2000; Langmore 2013.
60   Byrne 2011; Wiseman 2011; Melissen 2011.
61   Byrne 2011, 14.

These earlier studies also point to the relevance of values made visible through the campaign as well as a communication on what to achieve during the term in the Council. David Malone and Caitlin Byrne underline the importance of a *campaign message*.[62] To specify, Byrne argues that the 'right' message can raise awareness of, and improve, a country's reputation, but the lack of political commitment to a message can also do harm in a campaign.[63] This means that a candidature needs back-up of the message by consistent action and support. Malone (2000) warns against focusing solely on national reputation; he suggests that candidatures that mainly rely on an 'excessively complacent view of their own standing' might very well be heading towards a defeat (Malone 2000, 8). Rather, he argues that candidates 'need to develop one or two themes which they can hammer away [at] consistently'.[64]

Moreover, Adam Chapnick, Mary Whelan and Caitlin Byrne all describe the importance of having *skilful people* running the campaign; they can design a more coherent campaign and enjoy more respect from others. David Chapnick, in his study on Canadian candidatures over time, highlights the relevance of a well-respected Permanent Representative as well as the contributions by individual politicians for the outcome of a campaign.[65] Both Whelan (2002) and Byrne (2011) explain that referred skills are to know when to listen to others and when to pursue their own message.[66] More skilful people can probably adapt their campaign more easily to changes in the context.

We have also incorporated insights from the literature on national campaigns, since these show some interesting resemblances with the international campaigns and the most relevant campaign features. The election of nonpermanent members to the UNSC is indeed different from democratic national elections, targeting a limited number of diplomats and politicians as representatives of a state rather than a majority of a country's citizens. Still, these campaigns must also communicate to be persuasive over a sustained period. The national campaigning literature points to the relevance of very similar categories 1) the campaign organization, 2) individual politicians, such as the party-leader, through their skills to promote the message, and 3) the message being consistent and ideologically coherent.[67] The literature on Olympic

---

62   Malone 2000, 8; Byrne 2011, 8, 19–21.
63   Byrne 2011, 8, 21.
64   Malone 2000, 8.
65   Chapnick 2019, 11, 115, 151, 176–177.
66   Whelan 2002, 19–20; Byrne 2011, 23–25.
67   Panebianco 1988; Hernson 2009; van der Brug and Mughan 2007; Benoit et al. 2011; O'Shaughnessy 2002; Sussman 2005.

Games site decisions also underscores the relevance that a coherent message has for the success of a candidature.[68]

To summarize our main categories for analysing campaign success for a non-permanent seat in the Security Council: With respect to *organisation,* previous studies on UNSC candidatures suggest that the campaigns are set up and run from the state's capital, with the Permanent Mission in New York as the other important unit. We need to learn more about the size of these units and their relationship to each other. With respect to *key participants,* the campaigns seem to engage a mix of politicians, public officials, and diplomats.[69] We need to learn more about the relevance of political versus diplomatic participation, as well as whether there are additional important actors and what role they play. Regarding *activities,* the campaigns are global in scope in the sense that events occur in the capitals and in New York, as well as in embassies around the world. The participants in the campaigns also visit targeted countries for the sake of gathering support.[70] We need to learn more about the relevance and purpose of these different activities. With respect to a *coherent message,* it is relevant to consider candidates' contributions to the UN and their image as 'good' members of the UN. It makes sense that candidates seek to communicate past and current commitments since the UN Charter specifically instructs Member States to pay special regard to contributions to international peace and security. We will also study the domestic context in which the message is launched.

As reported by Ekengren and Möller (2021), and presented below, our theoretical framework addresses 'the three C's for successful campaigning': contributions, commitment, and competence. According to the *first* logic, candidates focus on communicating their *previous and current contributions to the UN.* They seek to disseminate their multilateral merits, or UN CV, to prove the strength of their candidature. This is of immediate relevance to the recommendation in the UN charter that member states consider contributions to international peace and security in these elections. According to the *second* logic, candidates focus on communicating their *commitment,* through a message that specifies certain values, themes, and challenges. Typically, the values, themes, and challenges coincide with some of the strongest merits. According to the *third* logic, candidates focus on communication, the relevant *competences, and skills.* Typically, relevant skills resonate with the values, themes and

---

68   Persson 2000.
69   Langmore 2013.
70   Malone 2000; Langmore 2013.

TABLE 2.2   Logics of international campaigning

Demonstrating contributions	Proving ideational commitment	Claiming competence
– Focus on previous and current contributions to the UN and the multilateral order – Communicating multilateral merits	– Focus on a clear and consistent message, by promoting specific themes, values and defining certain global challenges – Displaying dedication to the message	– Focus on skills and expertise among politicians and diplomats – Displaying competence regarding the themes, values, and challenges identified through the message

challenges identified by the message, which helps to shed light on contributions. Thus, while each of these logics may be followed individually, combined they contribute to reinforcing the attractiveness of the campaign. There is a relevant difference between the first logic and the two remaining ones. The task of communicating past and present contributions may be left to public officials and diplomats mainly but making convincing arguments about current commitment and competence requires politicians, who can demonstrate that they are dedicated to the values, themes, and challenges, and that they know what they are talking about. In contrast, a campaign carried out solely by dedicated and competent diplomats and senior officials runs the risk of facing doubts as to why the government does not invest its time and effort. It risks raising the suspicion that such thin engagement might also characterize the term, if elected. We summarize these three logics in the table above.

Guided by this framework, we will seek to single out the main features of a successful candidature. In the empirical chapters, Chapters 6, 7 and 8, we conduct a qualitative structured case comparison between successful cases of campaigns to the UNSC and less successful ones by two members from the WEOG.[71]

In addition, there has been no detailed exploration of the relevance of the domestic arena to the success of a state's candidature. However, the choice to

---

71   On this method see George and Bennett 2005; Collier 2011.

campaign for a seat takes effort and resources away from other foreign policy issues, which may lead to criticism from the opposition. The opposition and the government may also have different opinions on the role the UN should play in the overall foreign policy. Our study will look deeper into the relationship between the government and the opposition in relation to a candidature. A victorious candidature may be domestically important for some, while mattering little to others. However, a defeat might entail different costs depending on the relationship between government and opposition. A defeat could also be less politically costly if the government has recently changed and could thus be seen as an opportunity to put blame on the predecessors for not carrying out an efficient campaign.[72]

10   Campaign Comparison Design: a Subgroup of Small States in the WEOG

We carry out our study of campaigns as a pairwise comparison between successful and unsuccessful candidatures. All three pairs include a Nordic state, put in comparison with one of its WEOG competitors. By design, this study has a focus on members of the WEOG, and especially on a subgroup of small states within this regional group. Intriguingly, while the WEOG frequently adopt contested slates this will never involve two Nordic countries as they have agreed to avoid intra-Nordic competition by a turn taking order. The Nordic states form an interesting group in the sense that they are small states with a reputation of engagement and capacity to contribute within UN politics. Nevertheless, they have experiences from a period of decline, including a row of failed Security Council candidatures, which they also seem to have overcome. To illustrate, the Nordic state candidatures for the elections in 2008 and 2012 failed, but the Nordic state candidatures for the elections in 2016 and 2020 succeeded. Our empirical study includes the three first of these candidatures. As the final step of this chapter, we do, first, an introduction of the Nordic states in UN politics, second, an introduction of the three elections that are singled out for our pairwise campaign comparisons.

---

[72]   Langmore and Farrall 2016; Malone 2000.

11   The Nordic 'Ticket' and the Fluctuations of 'Nordicness'

The Nordic states have agreed on a turn taking order to ensure a regular Nordic Security Council candidature and to avoid intra-Nordic competition. They always support each other's candidatures, and even contribute to the campaign by, for instance, promoting it with other countries whenever the opportunity presents itself. To illustrate this advantage, when a Nordic country campaigns for a nonpermanent seat, the campaigning Permanent Representative in New York get support from his four close Nordic colleagues to create a positive image for the candidature. A potential disadvantage occurs when the Nordic countries cooperate in relation to several UN elections. So, if a Nordic country is aiming for another of the elected positions at the UN, then the two campaigns are coordinated together, to prevent unintentional additional competition. Consequently, a Nordic country aiming for a Security Council seat might have to postpone its campaign until another Nordic campaign has been completed. This notion of Nordic coordination is beneficial for displaying a united front and gaining additional support, but the available time slot for a campaign may disappear. The practice used by the Nordic countries regarding UN elections demonstrates their sense of shared identity, as well as the strategic belief that their chances of promoting common interests improve if they coordinate and support each other's efforts.

The collaboration between the Nordic states in UN politics dates to the Cold War, when they successfully formed a group broadly distinguished by their dedication to multilateralism. The history of the Nordic group in UN politics illustrates how smaller states seek to exercise influence despite their size, by coordinating their efforts of endorsing a rule-based order for the sake of diminishing unexpected results. Moreover, having a distinct Nordic role through a foreign policy with common features is not only the consequence of a shared Nordic experiences based on a common location, cultural heritage, and domestic politics, but is something that other states and actors in world politics have recognized, as well.[73] However, in the post-Cold War era, the unity as well as the relevance of the Nordic group in the United Nations has diminished somewhat for various reasons, including how the countries have taken separate paths regarding European integration. More recently, the relevance and interest in a Nordic role for world politics seems to be on the rise, yet again.[74] Seemingly symptomatic of the declining relevance of the Nordic group

---

73   Ingebritsen 2002.
74   Laatikainen 2003; Björkdahl 2007; Brommesson 2018. According to Brommesson 2018, 'Nordicness refers to the perception and recognition of a Nordic role in the foreign policy

within the UN, two Nordic candidatures in a row faced electoral defeat, Iceland in 2008, and Finland in 2012. This trend was broken on the third attempt, with Sweden winning a seat in 2016, seemingly confirming the renewed relevance of 'Nordicness', within the United Nations, as well. Whether the Swedish candidature signified a shift in foreign policy orientation, and whether this prioritized the UN at the expense of the EU, became an important topic in the heated domestic debate during the phase of active campaigning.

One distinct development that the Nordic group in the UN has undergone is the establishing of closer contact with the Baltic States, which has occurred despite some remaining diplomatic concerns over Russian disapproval. The Baltic States take part in Nordic consultative discussions, and the Nordic countries endorsed the two recent candidatures from the Baltic States; Lithuania won a seat in 2013, as did Estonia in 2019. The Baltic States are members of the Eastern European Group (EEG), with elections held in odd numbered years, as opposed to the WEOG, which holds its elections in even numbered years. Consequently, when the Nordic and Baltic states have a shared agenda on the exercising of influence on the Security Council, they both improve their chances of a maintained presence by endorsing one candidate every other year instead of every fourth year. The Nordic community certainly relies on a sense of shared characteristics, experiences, and interests. Still, candidatures are country-specific, which reinforces that there are also important differences between the members of the Nordic group. The following sections introduce the Nordic candidates in the 2008, 2012, and 2016 elections, along with each of the contenders that we have included in our study.

12   The 2008 Election: Iceland and Austria

In the 2008 election for a nonpermanent seat on the Security Council, Iceland competed against Austria (included in this study) and Turkey (or Türkiye). Among the three, Iceland lost out.

The Nordic countries are small, but Iceland is the smallest by far, in terms of geographical size as well as population. It is also the youngest; it was part of a union with Denmark and received its independence in 1918. It became an independent republic in 1944. In 1949, Iceland was among the founding

---

of the various Nordic countries', p.356. The recent trend of reinvigorated Nordicness is intriguing considering some main differences in their choices of foreign and security policy paths, including NATO membership/non-membership and EU membership/non-membership.

members of NATO, and established close ties to the United States during the Cold War. Iceland is not a member of the European Union but is involved in other European collaborations for the sake of trade as well as security, including Schengen and OSCE. Iceland became a member of the United Nations in 1946 but did not establish a permanent mission in New York until 1965. Iceland has a significantly smaller foreign service than the other Nordic states, though it has grown since the 1990s. Compared to the other Nordic states, Iceland has a weaker tradition of foreign policy with internationalist features. Since the end of the Cold War, Iceland has however moved towards taking on more responsibilities, even with its identity as a small state. The candidature for a term on the Security Council in 2009–10 was Iceland's first.

In contrast to Iceland, Austria is a populous country and has been a member of the European Union since 1995. Austria is a neutral country, not only by policy, but regulated through law. Austria has been a member of the United Nations since 1955, and has collaborated with NATO, through Partnership for Peace, since 1995. In the post-Cold War era, Austria, a middle-sized power, has actively sought a more prominent international role, taking on responsibilities and engagements within the EU as well as the UN. Vienna is also one of the headquarters of the UN. It hosts several international organizations, including the IAEA and CTBTO, and is frequently the venue of important diplomatic meetings and conferences. The candidature for a term on the Security Council in 2009–10 was Austria's third.

13   The 2012 Election: Finland and Luxembourg

In the 2012 election for a nonpermanent seat on the Security Council, Finland competed with Luxembourg (included in this study) and Australia. Among the three, Finland lost out.

Like Sweden, Finland adopted a policy of neutrality during the Cold War, although it had a special friendship agreement with the Soviet Union. When becoming a member of the United Nations, Finland's neutrality was a concern. After joining the organization in 1955, Finland has been an active member. Like its neighbor Sweden, Finland joined the European Union in 1995. Among the Nordic members of the EU, Finland is the only country that is also part of the euro. Like Sweden, Finland remained military non-aligned in the post-Cold War era but collaborated with NATO through Partnership for Peace from 1995 and became a NATO member in 2023. The candidature for a term on the Security Council in 2013–14 was Finland's third.

Luxembourg is a founding member of the United Nations, NATO, and the European Union. Like the Nordic countries, Luxembourg is a small state, with a population that is only double the size of Iceland's, and one-tenth the size of Finland. Since it identifies as a small state, Luxembourg's foreign policy has consistently aimed at contributions to the multilateral order and is dedicated to European integration as well as to transatlantic collaboration. The candidature for a term on the Security Council in 2013–14 was Luxembourg's first.

14   The 2016 Election: Sweden and the Kingdom of the Netherlands

In the 2016 election for a nonpermanent seat on the Security Council, Sweden competed with the Kingdom of the Netherlands (included in this study) and Italy. Among the three, Sweden ended up winning the seat.

Sweden joined the United Nations in 1946, immediately aiming for an active membership profile. During the Cold War, Swedish foreign policy relied on neutrality and sought to maintain a Nordic balance between the West and the East, at times using an active internationalist approach. Like Finland, Sweden has been a member of the European Union since 1995. Finland and Sweden remained military non-aligned in the post-Cold War era but collaborated with NATO through Partnership for Peace from 1995 and handed in their NATO membership application in tandem in 2022. The candidature for a term on the Security Council in 2017–18 was Sweden's fifth.[75]

The Kingdom of the Netherlands joined the United Nations in 1945, immediately aiming for an active membership profile. Hosting the International Court of Justice, The Hague is one of the main European centers of UN activity. The Netherlands is a founding member of NATO and of the European Union. The Netherlands' foreign policy has consistently aimed at contributing to the multilateral order as well as to European integration. Although the main part of its territory is in Western Europe, three of the constituent countries are in the Caribbean Sea: Aruba, Curacao, and Sint Marten. As a sovereign state constituted by four countries, the Kingdom of the Netherlands has the identity of a middle-sized power, but with the experiences of a small state as well. The candidature for a term on the Security Council in 2017–18 was the Kingdom's sixth.

Bibliography

Abbot, Kenneth W. and Duncan Snidal. 'Why States Act through International Organizations'. *Journal of Conflict Resolution,* 4(1) (1998), 3–32.

---

75   Engelbrekt 2020.

Adler-Nissen, Rebecca and Vincent Pouliot. 'Power in Practice: Negotiating the International Intervention in Libya'. *European Journal of International Relations*, 20 (4) (2014), 889–911.

Balci, Ali. 'Do Gladiators Fight for Their Masters? Voting Behavior of the US-Promoted United Nations Security Council Members in the Early Cold War'. *PS: Political Science and Politics*, (2022) (1–6).

Baldacchino, Godfrey and Anders Wivel. 'Small States: Concepts and Theories'. In *Handbook on the Politics of Small States* Baldacchino. Godfrey and Anders Wivel eds. (Edgar Elgar Publishing, 2020).

Barnett, Michael and Marta Finnemore. 'Political Approaches'. In *The Handbook on United Nations,* eds. Thomas G. Weiss and Sam Dawns (New York: Oxford University Press, 2018).

Benoit, William L., Mark J. Glantz, Anji L. Phillips, Leslie A. Rill, Corey B. Davis, Jayne R. Henson, and Leigh Anne Sudbrock. 'Staying "on Message": Consistency in Content of Presidential Primary Campaign Messages Across Media'. *American Behavioral Scientist*, 55, no. 4 (2011), 457–468.

Bially Mattern, Janice and Ayse Zarakol. 'Hierarchies in World Politics'. *International Organization*, 70 (2016), 623–654.

Björkdahl, Annika. 'Swedish Norm Entrepreneurship in the UN'. *International Peacekeeping*, 14(4) (2007), 538–552.

Brommesson, Douglas. 'Introduction to Special Section: from Nordic Exceptionalism to a Third Order Priority – Variations of "Nordicness" in Foreign and Security Policy'. *Global Affairs,* 4 (4–5) (2018), 355–362.

Bueno de Mesquita, Bruce, and Alastair Smith. 'The pernicious Consequences of UN Security Council Membership'. *Journal of Conflict Resolution,* 54 (5) (2010), 667–686.

Byrne, Caitlin. 'Campaigning for a Seat on the Security Council: a Middle Power Reflection on the Role of Public Diplomacy'. *CDP Perspectives on Public Diplomacy,* paper 10, 2011.

CARICOM. Austria sign co-operation MOU, 2008.

Chapnick, Adam. *Canada on the United Nations Security Council: a Small Power on a Large Stage* (Vancouver, Toronto: UBC Press, 2019).

Collier, David. 'Understanding Process Tracing'. *PS: Political Science and Politics*, 44 (4) (2011), 823–830.

Copeland, Daryl. 'What Canada's Security Council Loss Says About Us'. *The Mark*, 16 October 2010.

Corbett, Jack, Xu Yi-Chong and Patrick Weller. 'Small States and the 'Throughput' Legitimacy of International Organizations'. *Cambridge Review of International Affairs*, 31 (2) (2018), 183–202.

Corbett, Jack, Xu Yi-Chong and Patrick Weller. 'Norm Entrepreneurship and Diffusion 'from below' in International Organisations: How the Competent Performance of

Vulnerability Generates benefits for Small States'. *Review of International Studies*, 45 (4) (2019), 647–668.

De Carvalho, Benjamin, and Iver B. Neumann. *Small State Status Seeking: Norway's Quest for International Standing* (London and New York: Routledge, 2015).

Dreher, Axel, Matthew Gould, Matthew D. Rablen and James Raymond Vreeland. 'The Determinants of Election to the United Nations Security Council'. *Public Choice*, 158 (2014), 51–83.

Dreher, Axel, Vera Z Eichenauer and Kai Gehring. 'Geopolitics, Aid, and Growth: the Impact of UN Security Council Membership on the Effectiveness of Aid'. *The World Bank Economic Review*, 32 (2) (2016), 268–286.

Drieskens, Edith. 'Curb Your Enthusiasm: Why an EU Perspective on UN Security Council Reform Does Not Imply an EU Seat'. *Global Affairs*, 1 (1) (2015), 59–66.

Dunton, Caroline. 'Willing to Serve: Empire, Status, and Canadian Campaigns for the United Nations Security Council (1946–1947)'. *International Journal,* 75 (4), (2020). 529–547.

Duque, Marina G. 'Recognizing International Status: a Relational Approach'. *International Studies Quarterly*, 62 (2018), 577–592.

Ekengren, Ann-Marie, Fredrik D. Hjorthen and Ulrika Möller. 'A Nonpermanent Seat in the United Nations Security Council: Why Bother?'. *Global Governance: a Review of Multilateralism and International Organizations*, (26) (2020), 21–45.

Ekengren, Ann-Marie and Ulrika Möller. 'Campaigning for an Elected Seat in the UN Security Council'. In *Elected Members of the Security Council: Lame Ducks or Key Players?, eds.* Shrijver, Nico J. and Niels M. Blokker (Leiden: Brill Nijhoff, 2020).

Ekengren, Ann-Marie and Ulrika Möller. 'Campaigning for the prize: the Quests by Sweden and the Kingdom of the Netherlands for Security Council Membership, 2017–2018'. *Hague Journal of Diplomacy*, 16 (2021), 1–26.

Engelbrekt, Kjell. 'Responsibility Shirking at the United Nations Security Council: Constraints, Frustrations, Remedies'. *Global Policy*, 6 (4) (2015), 369–378.

Engelbrekt, Kjell. *High-Table Diplomacy: the Reshaping of International Security Institutions* (Washington DC: Georgetown University Press, 2016).

Engelbrekt, Kjell. *Sveriges medlemskap i FN:s säkerhetsråd 2017–18* (Stockholm: Försvarshögskolan, 2020).

Farrall, Jeremy, et al. 'Elected Member Influence in the United Nations Security Council'. *Leiden Journal of International Law,* 33 1 (2020), 101–115.

Finnemore, Martha, and Kathryn Sikkink. 'International Norm Dynamics and Political Change'. *International Organization,* 52 (4) (1998), 887–917.

Freedman, Joshua. 'Status Insecurity and Temporality in World Politics'. *European Journal of International Relations*, 22 (4) (2016), 797–822.

George, Alexander L. and Andrew Bennett. *Case Studies and Theory Development in the Social Sciences* (Cambridge, London: MIT Press, 2005).

Gifkins, Jess. 'Beyond the veto: Roles in UN Security Council Decision-Making'. *Global Governance,* 27 (1) (2021), 1–24.

Gillissen, Christophe. 'The Back to the Future? Ireland at the UN Security Council, 2001–2002' *Nordic Irish Studies,* (5) (2006), 23–24.

Hafner-Burton, Emelie, Miles Kahler and Alexander H. Montgomery. 'Network Analysis for International Relations'. *International Organization,* 63 (2009), 559–92.

Hernson, Paul S. 'The Roles of Party Organizations, Party-Connected Committees, and Party Allies in Elections'. *The Journal of Politics,* 71 (4) (2009), 1207–1224.

Hurd, Ian. 'Legitimacy, Power and the Symbolic Life of the UN Security Council'. *Global Governance,* 8 (2002), 35–51.

Hurd, Ian. *After Anarchy: Legitimacy and Power in the United Nations Security Council* (Princeton: Princeton University Press, 2008a).

Hurd, Ian. 'Myths of Membership: the Politics of Legitimation in UN Security Council Reform'. *Global Governance,* 14 (2) (2008b), 199–217.

Ingebritsen, Christine. 'Norm Entrepreneurs: Scandinavia's Role in World Politics'. *Cooperation and Conflict,* 37 (1) (2002), 11–23.

Keating, Colin. 'Power Dynamics between Permanent and Elected Members'. In *The UN Security Council in the 21st Century,* eds. Sebastian von Einsiedel, David M. Malone, and Bruno Stagno Ugarte (Boulder: Lynne Rienner, 2016).

Keohane, Robert O. and Lisa Martin. 'The Promise of Institutionalist Theory'. *International Security* 20 (1) (1995), 39–51.

Keohane, Robert O., and Joseph S. Nye Jr. 'Power and Interdependence in the Information Age'. *Foreign Affairs,* 77 (5) (1998), 81–94.

Kuziemko, Ilyana, and Eric Werker. 'How Much Is a Seat on the Security Council Worth? Foreign Aid and Bribery at the United Nations'. *Journal of Political Economy,* 114 (5) (2006), 905–930.

Laatikainen, Katie Verlin. 'Norden's Eclipse the Impact of the European Union's Common Foreign and Security Policy on the Nordic Group in the United Nations'. *Cooperation and Conflict,* 38 (4) (2003), 409–441.

Lake, David. 'Escape from the State of Nature: Authority and Hierarchy in World Politics'. *International Security,* 32 (1) (2007), 47–79.

Langmore, John. 'Australia's Campaign for Security Council Membership'. *Australian Journal of Political Science,* 48 (1) (2013), 101–111.

Langmore, John and Jeremy Farrall. 'Can Elected Members Make a Difference in the Security Council? Australia's Experience in 2013–2014'. *Global Governance,* 22 (1) (2016), 59–77.

Larson, Deborah Welch and Alexei Shevchenko. 'Status Seekers: Chinese and Russian Responses to US Primacy', *International Security,* 34 (4) (2010), 63–95.

Larson, Deborah Welch, T.V. Paul and William Wohlforth. 'Status in World Order'. In *Status in World Politics* eds. Paul, T.V., Deborah Welch Larson and William Wohlforth (New York: Cambridge University Press, 2014).

Luck, Edward C. *UN Security Council: Practice and Promise* (New York: Routledge, 2006).

Malone, David. 'Eyes on the Prize: the Quest for Nonpermanent Seats on the UN Security Council'. *Global Governance,* 6 (1) (2000), 3–23.

Martin, Lisa. 'Interests, Power and Multilaterlism'. *International Security* 46 (4) (1992), 765–792.

McConnaughey, Megan, Paul Musgrave and Daniel H. Nexon. 'Beyond anarchy: Logics of Political Organization, Hierarchy, and International Structure'. *International Theory,* 10 (2) (2018), 181–218.

Mearsheimer, John J. 'The False Promise of International Institutions'. *International Security,* 19 (1) (1994), 5–49.

Mearsheimer, John J. *The Tragedy of Great Power Politics* (New York: Norton, 2001).

Melissen, Jan. 'Diplomatic Studies in the Right Season'. *International Studies Review,* 1 (2011), 723–725.

Neumann, Iver B., and Benjamin de Carvalho. Small States and Status. In *Small State Status Seeking: Norway's Quest for International Standing,* eds. Benjamin de Carvalho and Iver B. Neumann, 1–22 (New York: Routledge, 2015).

Nye, Joseph S., Jr. *Power in the Global Information Age: From Realism to Globalization* (London: Routledge, 2004).

O'Shaughnessy, Nicholas J. *The Idea of Political Marketing* (Westport: Praeger Publishers, 2002).

Panebianco, Angelo. *A Political Parties: Organization and Power* (New York: Cambridge University Press, 1988).

Pettit, Philip. *A Theory of Freedom: From the Psychology to the Politics of Agency* (New York: Oxford University Press, 2001).

Persson, Christer. 'The Olympic Games Site Decision'. *Tourism Management,* 23 (1) (2000), 27–36.

Prantl, Jochen. 'Informal groups of states and the UN Security Council'. *International Organization,* 59 (3) (2005), 559–92.

Ralph, Jason, and Jess Gifkins. 'The Purpose of United Nations Security Council Practice: Contesting Competence Claims in the Normative Context Created by the Responsibility to Protect'. *European Journal of International Relations,* 23 (3) (2017), 630–653.

Reinsberg, Bernhard. *Do countries use foreign aid to buy geopolitical influence? Evidence from donor campaigns for temporary UN Security Council seats'.* WIDER Working Paper, No. 2019/4.

Renshon, Jonathan. 'Status Deficits and War'. *International Organization,* 70 (2016), 513–550.

Renshon, Jonathan. *Fighting or Status: Hierarchy and Conflict in World Politics* (Princeton: Princeton University Press, 2017).

Robertson, Jeffrey. 'Middle-power Definitions: Confusion Reign Supreme'. *Australian Journal of International Affairs*, 71 (4), (2017), 355–370.

Schia, Niels Nagelhus. "Horseshoe and Catwalk': Power, Complexity and Consensus-Making in the United Nations Security Council'. In *Palaces of Hope – the Anthropology of Global Organizations*, eds. Niezen, Ronald and Maria Sapignoli (Cambridge: Cambridge University Press, 2017).

Schrijver, Nico J. and Niels M. Blokker eds. *Elected Members of the Security Council: Lame Ducks or Key Players?* (Leiden: Brill Nijhoff, 2020).

Schulz, Carsten-Andreas. 'Hierarchy Salience and Social Action: Disentangling Class, Status, and Authority in World Politics'. *International Relations*, 33 (1) (2019), 88–108.

Sievers, Loraine and Sam Daws. *The Procedure of the UN Security Council.* 4th ed. (Oxford: Oxford University Press, 2014).

Singer, Marshall R. and Barton Sensenig. 'Elections within the United Nations: an Experimental Study Utilizing Statistical Analysis'. *International Organization*, 17 (4) (1963), 901–925.

Stavridis, Stelios and Davor Jančić. 'The Rise of Parliamentary Diplomacy in International Politics'. *The Hague Journal of Diplomacy,* 11 (2016), 105–120.

Sussman, Gerald. *Global Electioneering: Campaign Consulting, Communications, and Corporate Financing* (Oxford: Rowman and Littlefield, 2005).

Thakur, Ramesh. 'Australia's Unsuccessful Bid for the UN Security Council'. *Pacific Research*, 9 (4) (1996), 48–49.

Thies, Cameron G. and Angguntari C. Sari. 'A Role Theory Approach to Middle Powers: Making Sense of Indonesia's Place in the International System'. *Contemporary Southeast Asia*, 40 (3) (2018), 397–421.

Thorhallsson, Baldur and Anders Wivel. 'Small States in the European Union: What Do We Know and What Would We Like to Know?' *Cambridge Review of International Affairs*, 19(4) (2006), 651–668.

Thorhallsson, Baldur and Alyson J.K. Bailes 'Small State Diplomacy'. In *The Sage Handbook of Diplomacy* eds. Constantinou, Costas M., Pauline Kerr, and Paul Sharp (London: Sage, 2016).

Thorhallsson, Baldur and Anna Margrét Eggertsdóttir. 'Small States in the UN Security Council: Austria's Quest to Maintain Status'. *The Hague Journal of Diplomacy*, 16 (2021) 53–81.

Towns, Ann E. and Bahar Rumelili. 'Taking the Pressure: Unpacking the Relation between Norms, Social Hierarchies, and Social Pressures on States'. *European Journal of International Relations*, 23 (4) (2017), 756–779.

Vahid, Nick Pay and Przemysław Postolski. 'Power and Diplomacy in the United Nations Security Council: the Influence of Elected Members'. *The International Spectator*, 57(2) (2022), 1–17.

Van der Brug, Wouter and Anthony Mughan. 'Charisma, Leader Effects and Support for Right-Wing Populist Parties', *Party Politics*, 13 (1) (2007), 29–51.

Veenendaal, Wouter P. and Jack Corbett. 'Why Small States Offer Important Answers to Large Questions'. *Comparative Political Studies*, 48 (4) (2015), 527–549.

Von Einsiedel, Sebastian, David M. Malone, and Bruno Stagno Ugarte. *The UN Security Council in the 21st Century* (Boulder: Lynne Rienner, 2016).

Von Einsiedel, Sebastian and David M. Malone. 'Security Council'. In *The Oxford Handbook on the United Nations* eds. Weiss, Thomas G. and Sam Daws (Oxford: Oxford University Press, 2018).

Vreeland, J.R. and A. Dreher. *The Political Economy of the United Nations Security Council: Money and Influence* (New York: Cambridge University Press, 2014).

Wallace, Michael D. 'Power, Status and International War'. *Journal of Peace Research*, 8 (1) (1971) 23–35.

Waltz, Kenneth N. *Theory of International Politics* (Mass: Addison-Wesley, 1979).

Ward, Steven. 'Logics of Stratified Identity Management in World Politics'. *International Theory*, 11 (2019), 211–238.

Weber, Max. Roth, Guenther and Claus Wittich (eds.) *Economy and Society* (Berkely: University of California Press, 2013, first published 1920).

Wendt, Alexander. 'The State as Person in International Theory'. *Review of International Studies*, 30 (2) (2004), 289–316.

Weigert, Kathleen Maas, and Robert E. Riggs. 'Africa and United Nations Elections: an Aggregate Data Analysis'. *International Organization*, 23 (1) (1969), 1–19.

Whelan, Mary. 'Ireland's Campaign for Election in 2000 to the United Nations Security Council'. *Administration*, 50 (1) (2002), 3–40.

Wiseman, Geoffrey. 'Bringing Diplomacy Back In: time for Theory to Catch Up with Practice'. *International Studies*, 13 (2011), 710–713.

Wohlforth, William C., Benjamin de Carvalho, Halvard Leira and Ivar B. Neumann. 'Moral Authority and Status in International Relations: Good States and the Social Dimension of Status Seeking'. *Review of International Studies*, 44 (3) (2017), 526–546.

Wolf, Reinhard. 'Respect and Disrespect in International Politics: the Significance of Status Recognition'. *International Theory*, 3 (1) (2011), 105–142.

Interviews with Dutch Diplomats

Interview 14 2019, 19 March, Interviewer Ulrika Möller.
Interview 15 2019, 2 April, Interviewer Ulrika Möller.
Interview 16 2019, 3 June, Interviewer Ulrika Möller.

CHAPTER 3

Candidatures and Terms: Detecting Winners and Losers

Ulrika Möller and Ann-Marie Ekengren

1 Introduction

The equal right of each member state of the United Nations to seek representation on the Security Council has not resulted in an equal distribution of times each state has served. After more than 70 years of elections, close to one third of the eligible states have not yet served while a selected few have been elected eight terms or more. This uneven variation in access to political authority through the elected seat constitutes a more fine-grained stratification than the binary categorization through the permanent seat in the Council. Thus, the Security Council election is a procedure that contributes to a relationship between states and to the constitution of international hierarchy. In this chapter, as we begin our empirical examination of Security Council candidatures and elections, the outcome of and conditions for this ranking is at the center of attention. We start with a comprehensive approach through the entire time span of elections and proceed through stepwise specifications by exploring, 1) the relationship between number of candidatures and times elected in the post-Cold War period, and 2) how regional membership corresponds with different opportunities to become a candidate. The pattern that emerges through the chapter confirms the main conclusion in previous research about the relevance of size and wealth to a success play in this political game, but with important analytical additions found in our descriptive data. First, 'the size-and-wealth' effect detected in previous research may be read as a reflection of regional power-dominance.[1] The degree to which regional powers' regular access to the Council is at the expense of the smaller states within the same regional group varies between these groups. A small state in the Asia and the Pacific group (Asia-Pacific) is the most disadvantaged due to competition between several regional powers, including India and Japan, for frequent Council representation. Currently, Japan is at the top of this game with

---

1 Dreher et al. 2014.

12 successful elections. Second, we single out important deviations from 'the size-and-wealth' effect by identifying wealthy states with the experience of electoral loss and smaller states with success. To specify, a small state in the West European and Others Group (WEOG) has the more frequent opportunity to compete for an elected seat.

As a result, this chapter brings further justification of our subsequent choices of research-design, set to 1) map out and compare the varying expectations between groups of states (Chapters 4 and 5), and 2) map out and compare campaigns between successful and unsuccessful campaigns by members in the WEOG (Chapters 6, 7 and 8).

2   Who Wins a Seat? The Pattern Over Time

A categorization of the total number of nonpermanent memberships for each state from 1946 to 2022 reveals an uneven distribution (see Table 3.1 below).

The group with zero times in the Council is the largest, with 60 states. The top-team of four states who have served at least eight times consists of India, Argentina, Brazil, and Japan. It is worth noting that these four states are all mentioned in the discussions on enlarging the Security Council with more permanent members.[2] These four states belong to two different regional groups: Asia-Pacific and the Group of the Latin America and Caribbean Countries (GRULAC). The top-player within this team is Japan, with a record of twelve successful elections, followed by Brazil with eleven, Argentina with nine, and India with eight terms in the time span we examine.

The subsequent groups of states, who have served six to seven times, include at least one member from all regional groups except from the African Group. The WEOG stands out as a regional group, since five states in this category are members: Belgium, Canada, Germany, Italy, and the Netherlands. A similar but less flagrant pattern of overrepresentation for the WEOG apply for the next groups of states, with four to five times in the Council. All regional groups have members in these categories, but eight of the 22 states are members of the WEOG: Australia, Denmark, Ireland, New Zealand, Norway, Spain, Sweden, and Türkiye. The second strongest regional group here is GRULAC with five members that have served in the Council four to five times: Chile, Mexico, Panama, Peru, and Venezuela. Egypt is the country with the strongest representation in the African Group, but still only with five terms in the Council. Poland, a

---

2   Hassler 2013.

TABLE 3.1   Times elected to the Security Council 1946–2022

12	Japan
11	Brazil
9	Argentina
8	India
7	Colombia, Italy, Pakistan. Total: 3
6	Belgium, Canada, Germany, Netherlands, Poland. Total: 5
5	Australia, Chile, Egypt, Mexico, Norway, Panama, Peru, Spain, Venezuela. Total: 9
4	Denmark, Ecuador, Gabon, Ghana, Indonesia, Ireland, Malaysia, New Zealand, Philippines, Romania, Sweden, Tunisia, Türkiye. Total: 13
3	Algeria, Austria, Bolivia, Bulgaria, Costa Rica, Cote D'Ivoire, Cuba, Ethiopia, Jordan, Morocco, Portugal, Senegal, South Africa, Syrian Arab Republic, Uganda, Ukraine, Zambia. Total: 17
2	Angola, Bangladesh, Benin, Burkina Faso, Cameroon, Congo, Democratic Republic of the Congo, Finland, Greece, Guinea, Guyana, Hungary, Iraq, Jamaica, Kenya, Lebanon, Libya, Mali, Mauritius, Nepal, Nicaragua, Republic of Korea, Rwanda, Togo, United Arab Emirates, United republic of Tanzania, Uruguay, Viet Nam, Zimbabwe. Total 29
1	Albanien, Azerbadijan, Bahrain, Belarus, Bosnia and Herzegovina, Botswana, Burundi, Chad, Croatia, Czech Republic, Djibouti, Dominican republic, Equatorial Guinea, Estonia, Gambia, Guatemala, Guinea Bissau, Honduras, Iran, Kazaksthan, Kuwait, Liberia, Lithuania, Luxembourg, Madagascar, Malta, Mauritania, Mozambique, Namibia, Niger, Nigeria, Oman, Paraguay, Qatar, Saint Vincent and the Grenades, Sierra Leone, Singapore, Slovakia, Slovenia, Somalia, Sri Lanka, Sudan, Switzerland, Thailand, Trinidad and Tobago, Yemen. Total: 46
0	Afghanistan, Andorra, Antigua and Barbuda, Armenia, Bahamas, Barbados, Belize, Bhutan, Brunei Darussalam, Cape Verde, Cambodia, Central African Republic, Comoros, Cyprus, Democratic People's Republic of Korea, Dominica, El Salvador, Eritrea, Fiji, Georgia, Grenada, Haiti, Iceland, Israel, Kiribati, Kyrgystan, Lao People's Democratic Republic, Latvia, Lesotho, Lichtenstein, Malawi, Maldives, Marshall Islands, Micronesia, Monaco, Mongolia, Montenegro, Myanmar, Nauru, Palau, Papua New Guinea, Republic of Moldovia, Saint Kitts and Nevis, Saint Lucia, Samoa, San Marino, San Tome and Principe, Serbia, Seychelles, Solmon Islands, South Sudan, Suriname, Swaziland, Taijikstan, Timor-Leste, Tonga, Turkmenistan, Tuvalu, Uzbekistan, Vanuatu. Total 60 (Saudi Arabia has been elected but declined the seat).

Note: The categorization relies on data from the United Nations Security Council (un.org/securitycouncil/)

member of the Eastern European Group (EEG), has the strongest representation in this group by six terms in the Council.

As with the categories one, two, and three, we see that half of the eligible
members have served between one and three times in the Security Council
between 1946 and 2022. As mentioned earlier, we also find that 60 states,
approximately one third of the eligible members, have never served in the
Council. As a reflection of the detected relevance of state size (wealth and
population) in previous research, the listing through Table 3.1 reveals that
small states are indeed overrepresented among those who have never served
in the Council. At least half of the never elected states qualify as small states
on basis of population and/or territory. More than one third (27 of 60) of these
small states also belong to the group of Small Island Developing States (SIDS),
which suggests that economic and political vulnerability are at stake as well.
The circumstance that SIDS includes so many UN member states make their
shared agenda with emphasis on sustainable development, including climate
and security, important to consider for candidates in contested slates to secure
votes. However, while they are an important constituency, they clearly suffer
from underrepresentation as elected members.

One example of a candidature by a small island state is the 2018 election,
when there was a contested slate in the Asia-Pacific Group between the
Maldives and Indonesia. While Indonesia secured the required two-thirds
majority through 144 votes already in the first election round, the Maldives
got 46 votes. To be sure, it is difficult to imagine a greater difference between
two competing candidatures than the Maldives, inhabiting 0.5 million people,
and Indonesia, with a population of 270 million people. This major difference
in size translates into very uneven conditions for running the candidature,
due to differences in available economic resources as well as the diplomatic
and administrative capacities between the two contestants. As Indonesia is
among the frequently elected states, this candidature also entertained the
advantage of previous experience campaigning for an elected seat. Although
this poses an advantage, we also know from other examples that this is not a
sufficient condition for electoral success. The Maldives, we suggest, got support from many members in SIDS for the opportunity to a representative in
the Council to promote its perspective on the link between sustainable development, climate, and security. However, other UN member states might have
had concerns about whether it held sufficient state capacity to face the challenges a term in the Council poses, as this tend to be a tough journey also for
the experienced elected members. Despite the detected advantage of being a
first time candidate, when the difference in state capacity is too large between

contestants, we suggest that this counters the advantage of being a first-time candidate.

Also worth noting is that all regional groups have small states members who have never served in the Council. To illustrate, Papua New Guinea and Tonga are members of the Asia-Pacific Group, Comoros and Swaziland are members of the African Group, San Marino and Moldova are members of the EEG, Grenada and Haiti are members of the GRULAC, and Andorra and Lichtenstein are members of the WEOG. A possible explanation for small state overrepresentation in the zero times category, which we will address later, is that these states do not have a similar strong interest for Security Council membership as the average UN member state, and therefore have abstained from launching a candidature. It is also possible that small states deem their chances of success as low, which might affect their preparedness to turn a candidature into a foreign-policy priority to begin with.

Leaving focus on small state overrepresentation in the category with zero times in the Security Council, we also find that there is an uneven distribution between the regional groups regarding their share of states in the zero times category. More than 40 percent of states who have never served in the Council are members in the Asia-Pacific Group, whereas the other regional groups hold shares in the category of never elected that ranges from 10 to 20 percent. From this view, membership in the Asia-Pacific Group seems highly disadvantageous for a state with ambitions for Security Council representation. As we shall see, variations in the total number of members between regional groups cannot account for this difference. In the next section, we examine the possible effects of regional group membership.

3   Who Wins a Seat? Impact of Regional Group Membership

There are several ways in which regional group belonging can influence the chances for membership of the Security Council. For one thing, the opportunity to a candidature depends on the nomination process applied by the regional group. The most notable difference in the nomination process is, as already indicated, between adopting the principle of a 'clean slate', which is the endorsement of one candidate per seat, and a 'contested slate', which is the endorsement of several candidates competing for each available seat. The contested slate increases the opportunity for more states to get involved in the competition for an elected seat but increases the uncertainty on whether a candidature will lead to a term in the Council. The clean slate shrinks the opportunity but brings a high degree of certainty of an elected seat for those who are endorsed as candidates. The members of the WEOG group are the ones most often involved in contested elections, while the African Group, as well as GRU-LAC, most often have clean slates. Just to illustrate the different approaches among different regional groups; between 2010 and 2022 the GRULAC has had twelve clean slates in the annual elections, Africa has had four contested and eight clean slates, and the Asia-Pacific Group has had six contested and six clean slates. The EEG and the WEOG take part in the elections every other year. First one candidate from Eastern Europe and then two candidates from the WEOG. The EEG has had two contested elections and four clean slates, and the WEOG has had four contested elections and two clean slates.

We have described the differences in candidature nomination procedure between the regional groups. The clear advantage with a clean slate for the member states is the certainty that a candidature will result in an elected seat. The major disadvantage is that it imposes restraints on the opportunities to try. We will also examine other possible effects from differences in conditions between regional groups. A frequently noted difference between the regional groups are whether they have access to permanent seat(s). Here we are more interested in differences when it comes to each individual members' opportunity to get elected to the Security Council. We seek to detect the variation between groups by dividing the elected seats for each regional group into the individual 'share' each regional member has in these seats. We can also understand this as their chances of getting elected if the results were decided by lottery. In Table 3.2 below, we describe the total number of members in each regional group, their number of permanent and elected seats, and these individual shares.

The distribution of permanent seats twists representation to the advantage of the WEOG. Three of the permanent seats belong to members of the WEOG, while the African Group and GRULAC has none. The EEG and the Asia-Pacific Group have one each.

There is a similar bias to the advantage of the WEOG when it comes to the chances of each member (without a permanent seat) to an elected seat, because of differences in the total number of members. In Table 3.2, we illustrate the differences between member states without a permanent seat by their individual share of, or chances to, the elected seats. If lottery decided nonpermanent seats, the chances are as follows: for a state from the WEOG 0,077, for a state from GRULAC 0,061, for a state from the African Group 0,056, for a state from the EEG 0,045, and for a state from the Asia-Pacific Group 0,038. As illustrated, all other things equal, states with prospects for an elected seat have the highest chance if member of the WEOG and lowest if member of the Asia-Pacific Group.

In the previous section, we suggested that membership in the Asia-Pacific Group is the most disadvantageous for a state with ambitions for Security Council representation, on basis of the large number of states in the never elected category from this regional group. The differences in individual chances of an elected seat between regional groups, as presented above, is in the same direction and supports this conclusion. The difference in individual chances reflects the difference in the total number of members between regional groups. Both the WEOG and the Asia-Pacific Group have two elected seats at their disposal, so the difference is a consequence of the difference, and, to some degree, of the number of permanent seats, and, to a higher degree, the total number of members. The WEOG has three permanent seats, and 28 + 1 members, while the Asia-Pacific Group has one permanent seat, and 53 members. Reflecting this difference, WEOG holds the lowest share (nine percent) of the category of states never elected to a term in the Security Council, while Asia-Pacific has the largest share of states in this category (40 percent). However, we suggest that the difference in size between groups cannot fully account for their different shares of the never elected category, since, in theory, there has been enough elected terms for each member states, regardless of group belonging, to serve at least once. To illustrate, the elections to the Security Council in its current form has been conducted since 1965, which means that the number of elected terms exceeds the total number of members also of the two largest regional groups, the African and Asia-Pacific Group, given that they have three and two elected seats at their disposal respectively.

TABLE 3.2   Regional groups: membership and available seats in the Security Council

Regional Group	Members	Members with permanent seat	Elected seats	Individual 'share' of elected seats (permanent members excluded)
African Group	54	0	3	0,0556
Asia-Pacific Group	53	1	2	0,0385
EEG	23	1	1	0,0455
GRULAC	33	0	2	0,0601
WEOG	28 + 1[a]	3	2	0,0769
	192[b]	5	10	-

a   USA belong to the WEOG as observer state (+ 1).
b   The number of UN member states is 193. The number of member states in regional groups adds up to 192, because Kiribati is not a member of any regional group.

Thus, to account for the uneven share between regional groups of the never elected category, we also need to consider the competition for seats within each regional group. As described above, the Asia-Pacific Group has 27 states who have never served in the Council, while the WEOG has six states. This means that 52 percent of the members in the Asia-Pacific Group, who are competing for the elected seats (27/52), have never served in the Council. The equivalent for the WEOG is 23 percent (6/26). As we proceed, we will address the competition between states, including the intra-group competition, through two additional steps. First, we will examine the number of candidatures and their success rate. Second, we will examine intra-group competition by detecting the implications of a successful few on the other members' opportunities for an elected seat.

4   Who Wins a Seat? Candidatures and Times Elected

To launch a candidature for an elected seat in the Security Council reflects a foreign policy priority. A plausible reason for why some member states have not yet served on the Security Council is that their governments have made other priorities. Still, the reasons for different priorities might differ and we will discuss them in relation to states different success rates. In Table 3.3 below we have listed all states who have launched candidatures, including failed ones. We have also noted which states launched successful campaigns and because of this served in the Security Council between 1990 and 2022. As an indicator of overall success, we have specified the relationship between number of terms in the Council and number of failed candidatures. We suggest that this indicator measures the degree to which a state entertain political support in accordance with its political ambitions within UN politics. Japan exemplifies a fulfilled political ambition (+ 6) since they have been elected six times and failed zero times in this period. Canada on the other hand represents a case of unfulfilled political ambitions (-1) since they have been elected once and failed twice in this period.

As seen in Table 3.3, a majority of the UN member states (118 states) have tried to get a seat in the Security Council on at least one occasion in the post-Cold War period 1990–2022. More than half of them have also been successful in this endeavor on at least one occasion. At the same time, 42 states have been unsuccessful in their candidatures on at least one occasion and three states share the experience of two failed candidatures. Noteworthy, 18 of the 60 states who have never served in the Security Council (listed in Table 3.1 above) have been candidates. Countries who have never served in the Council but launched a candidature in the post-Cold War period include for example Eritrea, Georgia, Iceland, Maldives, and Kyrgyzstan. The list becomes longer if we also include states who have sought to launch a candidature but failed on the regional level or have withdrawn their candidatures by an announcement ahead of the election. States not yet elected who have made these efforts include the two small island states Fiji and the Seychelles. Bangladesh, Kazakhstan, and Kenya have also made such candidature attempts. We therefore suggest that lack of political interest is an insufficient explanation for why close to one third of states have not yet served in the Council.

Belarus has not served in the Security Council in these past thirty years, despite having tried on two occasions. Further examples of a second candidature failure (in terms of an electoral loss or withdrawal) are Dominican Republic and Canada, but both these countries have also served on one occasion in this period. Canada is the outlier among the four states with two failed candidatures for an elected seat, in the sense that the detected determinants for success, most notably population, wealth (and the so called 'peace norm') have not been sufficient to repeatedly take Canada to the Council in accordance with its political ambitions. Noteworthy, previous research on Canadian candidatures have detected a broken domestic consensus on the relevance of elected membership of the Security Council, which indicate that domestic politics might affect the prospects for a successful candidature. We suggest that the repeated Canadian candidature failures illuminate the relevance of examining campaigns to explain the electoral outcomes.[3]

If we proceed from candidatures with the lower to the higher success-rates, there are a few countries within each regional group that have served three times or more in this period. Most states have succeeded on all their candidatures. On some, but not every, occasions this success may be the consequence of a clean slate. The single strongest performer is Japan, with six candidatures and as many successful elections in the Security Council in this period. Other states who have succeeded with all their candidatures include Argentina (4), Belgium (3), Brazil (5), Chile (3), Germany (4), Indonesia (3), Pakistan (3), Nigeria (3), South Africa (3) and Spain (3). Similar for all these countries, with Belgium as an exception, is a large population. India and Italy have also served on three occasions but share the experience of a failed candidature.

During the period 1990–2022, frequently elected members of the Security Council are evenly distributed between the regional groups, with exception of the EEG. Nigeria and South Africa are members of the African Group. Japan,

---

3 Chapnick 2019; Ekengren and Möller 2021.

TABLE 3.3   Candidatures and times elected 1990–2022

Country	Candidatures	Times elected	Failed candidature (withdrawal, electoral loss)	Success rate/ Fulfillment of political ambitions
Albania	2	1	1	-1
Algeria	1	1	0	1
Angola	2	2	0	2
Argentina	4	4	0	4
Australia	2	1	1	0
Austria	2	2	0	2
Azerbaijan	1	1	0	1
Bahrain	1	1	0	1
Bangladesh	1	1	0	1
Belarus	2	0	2	-2
Belgium	3	3	0	3
Benin	2	1	1	0
Bhutan	1	0	1	-1
Bolivia	2	1	1	0
Bosnia and Herzegovina	1	1	0	1
Botswana	1	1	0	1
Brazil	5	5	0	5
Bulgaria	2	1	1	0
Burkina Faso	1	1	0	1
Cabo Verde	1	1	0	1
Cambodia	1	0	1	-1
Cameroon	1	1	0	1
Canada	3	1	2	-1
Chad	1	1	0	1
Chile	3	3	0	3
Colombia	2	2	0	2
Congo	1	1	0	1
Costa Rica	2	2	0	2
Cote D'Ivoire	1	1	0	1
Croatia	1	1	0	1
Czech Republic	2	1	1	0
Denmark	1	1	0	1

TABLE 3.3 Candidatures and times elected 1990–2022 (*cont.*)

Country	Candidatures	Times elected	Failed candidature (withdrawal, electoral loss)	Success rate/ Fulfillment of political ambitions
Democratic Republic of the Congo	1	0	1	0
Djibouti	2	1	1	0
Dominican Republic	3	1	2	-1
Ecuador	2	2	0	2
Egypt	2	2	0	2
Equatorial Guinea	1	1	0	1
Eritrea	1	0	1	-1
Estonia	1	1	0	1
Ethiopia	2	2	0	2
Finland	1	0	1	-1
Gabon	3	3	0	3
Gambia	2	1	1	0
Georgia	1	0	1	-1
Germany	4	4	0	4
Ghana	2	2	1	1
Greece	2	1	1	0
Guatemala	2	1	1	0
Guinea	1	1	0	1
Guinea Bissau	2	1	1	0
Honduras	1	1	0	1
Hungary	2	1	1	0
Iceland	1	0	1	-1
India	4	3	1	2
Indonesia	3	3	0	3
Iran	1	0	1	-1
Ireland	2	2	0	2
Israel	1	0	1	-1
Italy	4	3	1	2
Jamaica	1	1	0	1
Japan	6	6	0	6
Jordan	1	1	0	1

TABLE 3.3   Candidatures and times elected 1990–2022 *(cont.)*

Country	Candidatures	Times elected	Failed candidature (withdrawal, electoral loss)	Success rate/ Fulfillment of political ambitions
Kazakhstan	1	1	0	1
Kenya	2	2	0	2
Kuwait	1	1	0	1
Kyrgyzstan	1	0	1	-1
Lebanon	1	1	0	1
Libya	1	1	0	1
Lithuania	1	1	0	1
Luxembourg	1	1	0	1
Malaysia	2	2	0	2
Maldives	1	0	1	-1
Mali	1	1	0	1
Mauritania	1	0	1	-1
Mauritius	1	1	0	1
Mexico	3	3	0	3
Mongolia	0	0	1	-1
Mozambique	1	1	0	1
Morocco	2	2	0	2
Namibia	1	1	0	1
Nepal	1	0	1	-1
Netherlands	2	2	0	2
New Zealand	2	2	0	2
Nicaragua	1	0	1	-1
Niger	1	1	0	1
Nigeria	3	3	0	3
Norway	2	2	0	2
Oman	1	1	0	1
Pakistan	3	3	0	3
Panama[a]	0	1	0	1
Peru	2	2	0	2
Philippines	1	1	0	1
Poland	2	2	0	2
Portugal	2	2	0	2
Qatar	1	1	0	1
Republic of Korea	2	2	0	2

TABLE 3.3   Candidatures and times elected 1990–2022 (*cont.*)

Country	Candidatures	Times elected	Failed candidature (withdrawal, electoral loss)	Success rate/ Fulfillment of political ambitions
Rwanda	2	2	0	2
San Marino	1	0	1	-1
Saudi Arabia[b]	1	D	0	X
Senegal	1	1	0	1
Singapore	1	1	0	1
Slovakia	2	1	1	0
Slovenia	2	1	1	0
South Africa	3	3	0	3
Spain	3	3	0	3
Sudan	1	0	1	-1
Sweden	3	2	1	1
Switzerland	1	1	0	1
Thailand	1	0	1	-1
FYR of Macedonia	1	0	1	-1
Togo	1	1	0	1
Tunisia	2	2	0	2
Turkey	2	1	1	0
Uganda	1	1	0	1
Ukraine	2	2	0	2
United Arab Emirates	1	1	0	1
Tanzania	1	1	0	1
Uruguay	1	1	0	1
Venezuela	3	2	1	1
Vietnam	2	2	0	2
Zimbabwe	1	1	0	1
Total: 119			Total: 45	

Note: Main sources are 1) United Nations General Assembly meeting record (1990–94, 1996–97, 1999–2019), 2) Resolutions and decisions adopted by the General Assembly (1995, 1998), and 3) Security Council Report (2020; 2021; 2022).

a   Panama became a member for 2006–07 without a candidature, as a compromise nomination after 47 rounds of deadlock voting between the two candidatures Guatemala and Venezuela in the 2005 election.

b   Saudi Arabia was elected in 2013 but declined the nonpermanent seat.

Indonesia, India, and Pakistan are members of the Asia-Pacific Group. Chile, Mexico, Argentina, and Brazil are members of the GRULAC. Belgium, Germany, Italy, and Spain are members of the WEOG. As indicated, no state within the EEG has established a pattern of frequently elected membership. Moreover, the pattern of regular membership is not as distinct in the African Group with only two states elected three times in this period. We suggest that this is an effect of the clean slate procedure, with many potential candidates to choose from, and a more considerate policy on giving all members an opportunity to serve in the Council. Further, the two regional groups with the four top-performers in terms of total number of times in the Council (see Table 3.1) are the same groups who have the most regular members in the post-Cold War period: GRULAC and the Asia-Pacific Group. Shared characteristics among these regular members are the position as regional power and/or an elevated international profile, and/or – for Brazil, Germany, Japan, and India – prospects for a future permanent membership. Taking the ambition of a future permanent membership into consideration, we also understand the relevance for these states to prove a political and diplomatic capacity for regular terms in the Security Council in the competition for elected seats. The group also inherits states with successful experiences as distinctive to the period: the unified Germany and the post-apartheid South Africa. Finally, the group of regular members in the post-Cold War era also holds a few states who are well integrated in the international community but not necessarily qualifying as regional powers. Belgium, Italy, and Spain have managed to outperform several equally strong and qualified states among their WEOG colleagues; not only Canada, but also Australia and New Zealand have the experience of a failed candidature in this period.

Of course, being a frequently elected member of the Security Council may count as an opportunity to yield influence as well as an important marker of international prominence for the individual state who manages to do so.[4] There is also a potential upside on behalf of all the other members of the regional group as well, in the sense that they send an experienced and qualified representative as their elected member to counter the dominance of the permanent members. That is in case the elected consider regional issues. The downside, however, is that these states occupy the larger share of elected seat opportunity available to the regional group. In the next section, we examine how the opportunity for all other members shrinks through this dominance of a successful few.

---

4   Ekengren, Hjorthen and Möller (2020).

5 Who Wins a Seat: Shrinking Opportunities due to the Successful Few

As revealed in the previous section, all regional groups have between two and four members who distinct themselves through a more frequent representation in the Security Council. In several cases, this reflects the political ambition of a permanent membership. We are interested in the implication this has on the opportunity for all the other members to serve on the Council. For that purpose, we have portioned the total amount of available years per member in each regional group and measured how this share of years shrinks when the 'high performers' have gotten their larger share of years. We summarize the results in the table below (Table 3.4). The members of the Asia-Pacific have the fewest year at their disposal (1.15) to begin with, and the members of the WEOG have the most (2.31). This, again, reflects the results from our previous examinations that point to the Asia-Pacific Group as the least advantageous group to belong to if a state wants to serve in the Security Council as a nonpermanent member. When the high performers have gotten their share of years, the remaining members of this group have the fewest years left at their disposal, and they have lost the highest share to the high performers. To illustrate, members of the Asia-Pacific Group have 51 percent of the years left, members of GRULAC have 64 percent, members of the WEOG have 70 percent, and members of the African Group have 88 percent left, after the group of high performers have gotten their share of years. The members of the EEG stand unaffected, since no state in this group have managed to become frequently elected in a similar manner as in the other groups. As mentioned, there might be a collective advantage to all members in a regional group with sending a strong and experienced elected member on frequent intervals. The downside of having a strong voice representative for the region, however, is that it shrinks the chances for representation for the average and, especially, the weaker members in the group. This pattern is the most striking in the Asia-Pacific Group. As the previous example of the Maldives against Indonesia in the 2018 election illustrates, there is a limitation in how much a state can benefit from being a first-time candidate, when facing a competitor with way stronger capacities. This does not mean that smaller states, when given the opportunity to candidate, cannot perform a competitive campaign. We suggest that the design of the campaigns has explanatory value to the outcomes that deviates from detected determinants of success. We also suggest that campaigns between competing candidates within the WEOG is the most futile ground to learn about this. Relative to the other groups, the WEOG has the best initial conditions and best chances for each single member to reach the Security Council. This creates conditions

TABLE 3.4   Regional groups. competition measure 1990–2022

Regional Group	Representation years, total	Years per member, P5 excluded	'High performers': elected three times or more	Remaining years per member, after 'high performers' share
African	96 (3 seats, 32 yrs)	1.78 (96/54)	Egypt (5) South Africa (3) Nigeria (3)	1.57, 88%
Asia and the Pacific	64 (2 seats, 32 yrs)	1.23 (64/52)	Japan (6) India (3) Indonesia (3) Pakistan (3)	0.63, 51%
Eastern European	32 (1 seat, 32 yrs)	1.45 (32/22)	-	1.45, 100 %
GRULAG	64 (2 seats, 32 yrs)	1.93 (64/33)	Argentina (4) Brazil (4) Chile (3) Mexico (3)	1.24, 64%
Western European and Others	64 (2 seats, 32 yrs)	2.46 (64/26)	Belgium (3) Germany (4) Spain (3) Italy (3)	1.72, 70%

for close races between candidatures in contested slates, and accounts for a potentially high impact from the campaigns on the electoral outcome.

6   Results and Conclusions

The equal right of UN member states to seek representation in the Security Council unfolds into an uneven pattern of actual terms each state has served. The few states who serve in the Security Council on a more frequent basis are regional powers, while small states, and especially the economically vulnerable small island developing states, are overrepresented in the large group of states who have never served. As such, Security Council elections contributes to a social stratification of states on basis of the provided opportunities to representation that reflects a broader international hierarchy, more fine-grained than the one captured by the acknowledged division between the P5 and the rest. In line with results from previous studies of the elections to the Security Council, the mapping we have presented attests to the importance of size and wealth for this overall stratification.

A few states have even launched more than one unsuccessful candidature during this time. Further, 18 of the states who have never served in the Council have launched a candidature in this time but failed. We conclude that the lack of political interest for a term in the Council is an insufficient explanation for why almost one third of states have still not served. The extensive number of unsuccessful candidatures, which also includes wealthy and populous countries, speaks to the relevance both of examining why states embark on this journey and the relevance of how the campaign is executed.

It should also be considered that the chances to become a candidate in the first place depends on the nomination procedure of the regional groups, as well as the intensity of competition within regional groups, depending on the total number of members and available seats. As an important addition to differences of the competition within the different regional groups, this chapter has revealed a significant variation regarding the effect of the successful few on the opportunities for the remaining members. The procedure with regional representation is to account for equality between regions but at times criticized for not doing so, especially with the lack of a permanent seat in the African Group. The results in this chapter rather reveal how the within-group dynamics can further reinforce the unequal opportunities between members. The conditions in the Asia-Pacific Group are tough in the first place due to the large number of members. Since the group has four frequent members of the Security Council, including Japan who has been elected six times in the post-Cold War period, this results in the largest shrinking of available time left for other members of a regional group. Consequently, the Asia Pacific Group has both the one member who have been elected most times to the Security Council (Japan, 12 times) and the largest share of members who have not served once (52 percent).

In contrast, the regional group with the best initial conditions for the average member to reach the Security Council is the WEOG. Not only has the group several permanent representatives, but it has also somewhat more seats in relation to the number of members than other regional groups. While the WEOG has a similar group of successful few as the other regional groups, there is a large group of states just behind this top-team, including Austria, Ireland,

Norway, and Sweden. The higher share of available time for each single member remains also after the successful few have gotten their share of years. There is a notable outcome of failed candidatures from countries with a high profile in UN-politics, including Canada, New Zealand, and Sweden, which attests to hard competition in contested slates. Still, only five states in the WEOG (19 percent) have not yet served in the Council. Overall, states within the WEOG are also resourceful in terms of wealth, even though they are small or medium-sized in terms of population.

Bibliography

Chapnick, Adam. *Canada on the United Nations Security Council: a Small Power on a Large Stage* (Vancouver, Toronto: UBC Press, 2019).

Dreher, Axel, Matthew Gould, Matthew D. Rablen and James Raymond Vreeland. 'The Determinants of Election to the United Nations Security Council'. *Public Choice*, 158 (2014), 51–83.

Ekengren, Ann-Marie, Fredrik D. Hjorthen and Ulrika Möller. 'A Nonpermanent Seat in the United Nations Security Council: Why Bother?'. *Global Governance: a Review of Multilateralism and International Organizations*, (26) (2020), 21–45.

Ekengren, Ann-Marie and Ulrika Möller. 'Campaigning for the prize: the Quests by Sweden and the Kingdom of the Netherlands for Security Council Membership, 2017–2018'. *The Hague Journal of Diplomacy*, 16 (2021), 1–26.

Hassler, Sabine. *Reforming the UN Security Council Membership: the Illusion of Representativeness* (London and New York: Routledge, 2013).

CHAPTER 4

Why Do States Want a Seat on the UNSC? Expectations between Different Types of States

Ann-Marie Ekengren, Fredrik D. Hjorthen and Ulrika Möller

1   Introduction

Why do UN member states seek representation on the Security Council? What opportunities do they expect to receive from holding a nonpermanent seat? Results from the previous chapter reveal how the Security Council elections contribute to the constitution of international hierarchy, through uneven access to political authority over time, as well as between different categories of members within regional groups. Given the highly competitive nature of the Security Council elections, why do states prioritize to embark on this political and diplomatic journey? According to a broader pattern of views among UN member states, they identify reasons and entertain expectations about opportunities to influence, to network and to improve on status. Generally, to influence is the most important stated reason for launching a candidature, but the expectation about actual influence is lower than the expectations about improving their network and their status as benefits from a term.[1]

In this chapter, we conduct a further exploration on why states take the decision to candidate, which – if the campaign turns out successful – results in a subsequent two-years term in the Security Council. The analysis relies on results from our phone survey with delegates, most often the Permanent Representatives (PR), at the permanent missions in New York. We investigate expectations on an elected term through 1) comparisons between states in different regional groups, and 2) comparisons of different types of states within regional groups. Members of the WEOG have higher expectations than non-WEOG members on the opportunity to exercise influence from a term, and bigger states have higher expectations than smaller states on this opportunity. Among sub-groups, the Nordic states display high expectations about the opportunities brough by an elected seat.

---

1   Ekengren et al. 2020.

2   Rationales of the Comparisons

To learn more about differences and similarities in states' expectations on an elected seat, we conduct comparisons that take into consideration: 1) regional group membership, 2) state size, and 3) subgroup coordination. First, we know from the results in previous chapters that the chances of becoming an elected member of the Security Council is affected by regional group membership and that size and wealth is important to the stratification of states based on the number of elected terms. In accordance with previous studies, regional membership matters due to the difference in size of the regional groups, and due to differences in their nomination procedures. However, our main finding in the previous chapter is the variation in how within-group dynamics between big and small states further reinforce unequal opportunities between members. Small states face the least favorable conditions in the Asia-Pacific Group, and the most favorable conditions in the WEOG. As consequence, a larger share of the members in the Asia-Pacific Group have never been members of the Security Council, while only a smaller share of the members in the WEOG lacks this experience.

In this chapter, we begin with a comparison between members of WEOG and members in other regional groups. Most states within the WEOG have been candidates and served as elected member, while the other groups have a more varied experience of being a candidate. We proceed with comparisons of categories within WEOG, as well as comparisons of sub-groups within the European context (i.e., WEOG and EEG). In the broader context, the Security Council elections are a striking example of how a few influential states have dictated institutional conditions of the current world order. Even if smaller states have increased their overall opportunities for IO participation, populous, and wealthy states have an advantage. State awareness of this pattern can have an impact on why they seek a SC candidature, as well as their views on what a term can bring. Within the regional WEOG context, with better opportunities for small states to run a candidature, we still suggest that it is valuable to assess whether there are differences between big and small state expectations. We suggest two theoretically substantiated specifications on possible effects from the size related disadvantages small states are facing. First, small states are less prone than big states to have high expectations on opportunities to exercise influence through a term in the Council and second, small states have higher expectations on status than on influence since this is a more available form of power to them.

We also suggest that it is relevant to focus on the Nordic countries, to examine whether they cluster as a group and whether their views correspond with the other small states or with the big states. The Nordic states are an example of UN members with a sense of community, with a historical record of coordinated policy, and with an established collaboration on turn-taking candidatures to the Security Council. Such a routinized pattern of collaboration based on a shared identity might shape their reasons for seeking a candidature, as well as their estimations on what a term can bring. Thus, we suggest that views might be similar among the Nordic states. To explore the relevance of a cooperative and coordinated approach in UN-politics, we will do a similar comparison with the Nordic-Baltic states (NB8), and big and small states, in the regional groups they belong, which is the WEOG and the EEG.

To sum up, we have singled out three types of comparisons to estimate states' expectations on a seat in the Security Council: First, we will compare the members of WEOG with members from other regional groups. Second, we will compare three sub-groups within the WEOG: big states, small states, and the Nordic states. Third, we will compare three sub-groups within the WEOG and the EEG: big states, small states, and the Nordic-Baltic states.

3   About the Telephone Survey

Between 25 September 2017 and 4 April 2018, we interviewed 53 diplomats representing their countries at the UN via telephone and 3 diplomats in person. The response rate was 27 percent. 19 states actively declined to participate, mostly based on state policy not to take part in studies like this. If these 19 states were not included in the population, the net response rate would be 32 percent. A further 32 states responded via email or over the telephone but were either unable to confirm a date or did not respond at all to follow-up requests to schedule an appointment. 28 responses were from European countries and 28 from non-European countries. Table 4.1 describes which countries took part in the telephone survey and hence what limitations we have for inferences. To our knowledge, this is the first phone survey addressed to the UN diplomatic community in New York. Previous studies to senior officials and diplomats within the EU have brought inspiration and useful guidance. The questions asked in the telephone survey is presented in Appendix 1 and the coding of the answers in Appendix 2.[2]

---

2   Johansson 2015; Aggestam and Johansson 2017.

TABLE 4.1   Responding countries to our telephone survey 2017–2018

Members of WEOG	Members of other groups
Andorra (WEOG)	Afghanistan (Asia-Pacific)
Australia (WEOG)	Argentina (GRULAC)
Austria (WEOG)	Bangladesh (Asia-Pacific)
Canada (WEOG)	Bosnia and Herzegovina (EEG)
Denmark (WEOG)	Botswana (African Group)
Finland (WEOG)	Brazil (GRULAC)
Germany (WEOG)	Cabo Verde (African Group)
Greece (WEOG)	Chile (GRULAC)
Iceland (WEOG)	Costa Rica (GRULAC)
Ireland (WEOG)	Croatia (EEG)
Italy (WEOG)	Cyprus (Asia-Pacific)
Lichtenstein (WEOG)	Djibouti (African Group)
Luxembourg (WEOG)	Egypt (African Group)
Malta (WEOG)	Estonia (EEG)
Netherlands (WEOG)	Guatemala (GRULAC)
New Zealand (WEOG)	Guyana (GRULAC)
Norway (WEOG)	Jamaica (GRULAC)
Portugal (WEOG)	Latvia (EEG)
Sweden (WEOG)	Liberia (African Group)
Switzerland (WEOG)	Lithuania (EEG)
	Maldives (Asia-Pacific)
	Mexico (GRULAC)
	Micronesia (Asia-Pacific)
	Mozambique (African Group)
	Nigeria (African Group)
	Slovakia (EEG)
	Slovenia (EEG)
	Pakistan (Asia-Pacific)
	Peru (GRULAC)
	Saint Lucia (GRULAC)
	Samoa (Asia-Pacific)
	Senegal (African Group)
	South Sudan (African Group)
	Ukraine (EEG)
	Uruguay (GRULAC)

TABLE 4.1   Responding countries to our telephone survey 2017–2018 (*cont.*)

Members of WEOG	Members of other groups
	Vanuatu (Asia-Pacific)

Note: The Western European and Other Group (WEOG), Eastern European Group (EEG), The Group of Latin America and Caribbean Countries (GRULAC). The table shows which countries our interviewees represent in the UN.

4   Comparing Members of the WEOG with Members of the Other Groups

The seats on the UNSC belong to five regional groups. The WEOG is fortunate to have three permanent members on the Security Council, and two non-permanent seats. WEOG differs from other regional groups by its frequent use of contested slates. However, while there is no formal rotation scheme, some informal mechanisms are at play that contribute to determine which states run for the SC. One example is the turn-taking order among the Nordic members, which means that a Nordic candidate will run during every second election for the seats assigned to the WEOG. The competition is made more challenging because, in addition to contested slates, most of the WEOG states have significant economic and diplomatic resources available, which leads to stiff competition.

To learn whether the WEOG countries differ from UN members more generally, we have explored the main reasons why states want a seat on the SC. We asked if the states wanted a seat to influence the agenda of the SC, if they wanted a seat to establish stronger relationships with other important actors, and if they wanted a seat to improve their status.

As Figure 4.1 shows, there is no obvious pattern among the WEOG countries (N = 19), while the distribution for the non-WEOG countries (N = 34) is considerably more concentrated towards middle values. The responses with the most positive expectations as well as the most negative expectations both belong in the WEOG. The median value is higher in the WEOG compared to the non-WEOG, with 6 and 5, respectively. The higher share of countries with first-hand SC experience in the WEOG compared to the non-WEOG might contribute to this pattern, in the sense that the responses reflect the different, ranging from very negative to very positive, experiences for single members on the opportunities to exercise influence as a member of the Council.

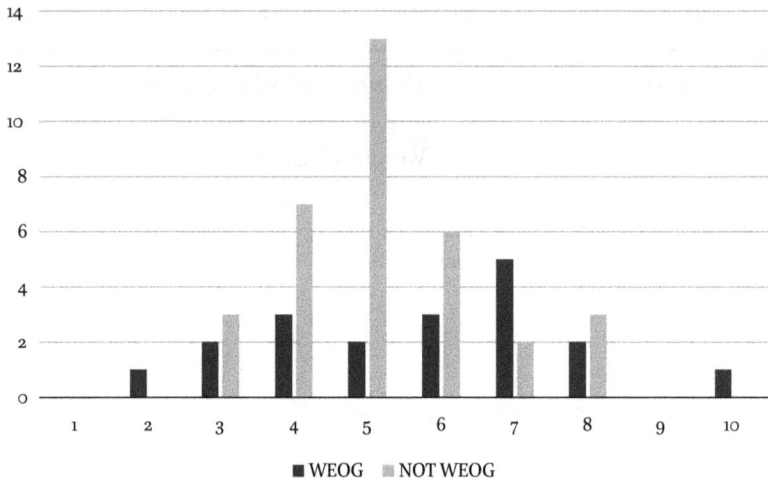

FIGURE 4.1   To what extent would your country be able to influence the agenda of
the sc, if you were elected? Comparison of responses between WEOG
and non-WEOG countries (N)
Note: The respondents were asked to respond on a scale from 1–10,
where 1 indicated to a very small extent and 10 indicated to a very
great extent

We asked the respondents to elaborate on the possible reasons for why they
believe their country could influence as an elected member of the Security
Council.

As Figure 4.2 shows, the most notable differences between the WEOG and
non-WEOG countries concern codes 5 and 6, which, respectively, map the
views that influence is often issue-specific, and that the agenda is mostly
determined by current affairs and circumstances. The WEOG countries were
notably less prone to mention reasons having to do with their influence being
issue specific. One possible explanation for this is that this view was most frequently mentioned by countries that had recently experienced conflicts or
were in regions often affected by conflict. Many members of the WEOG lack
this experience of recent military conflicts. When it comes to the difference
in the propensity to mention that the agenda is mostly determined by current
affairs, recurring items, etc., it might be that the WEOG members have more
sc experience. Both groups refer to the difference between permanent and
nonpermanent members on the opportunity to exercise influence (code 1),
and emphasize the presidency as a window of opportunity for nonpermanent
members to play a more significant role (code 4).

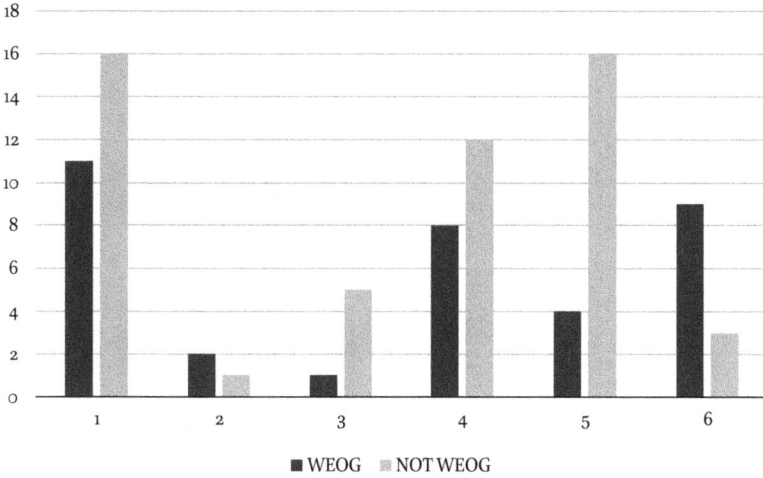

FIGURE 4.2 What might affect your possibility to influence the agenda when having
a nonpermanent seat? Comparison of responses between WEOG and
non-WEOG countries (N)
Note: The answers were coded using the following codes: 1. The
permanent members decide/are significantly more influential than
the NP members. 2. Difficult to build alliances in the SC. 3. We are a
small country/have limited resources. 4. Holding the presidency helps.
5. Influence is issue-specific (e.g., More influence regarding procedural
issues and debates; issues relating to own country or region). 6. Agenda
is mostly determined by current affairs/circumstances, or automatic/
recurring items (e.g., renewal of PKOs.)

Figure 4.3 shows that the WEOG countries (N = 19) have more positive views
on the possibility to establish stronger relationships with other countries as
elected members of the Security Council. The responses by the non-WEOG
countries (N = 34) are more scattered. The median value for the WEOG is 8
compared to 7 for the non-WEOG. We asked the respondents to elaborate on
different variables affecting their possibilities to network.

Next, we asked about the respondents' views on the possibility of elevating
their country's status in the global community.

As Figure 4.4 shows, the most notable differences between the WEOG and
non-WEOG countries concern the codes 2 and 5, which, respectively, emphasize that the nonpermanent seat makes you more interesting to others and
enables contacts with new countries. Non-WEOG countries seem to be more
positive about the opportunities provided by a seat in terms of making them
more interesting to others. One possible explanation for this difference is that

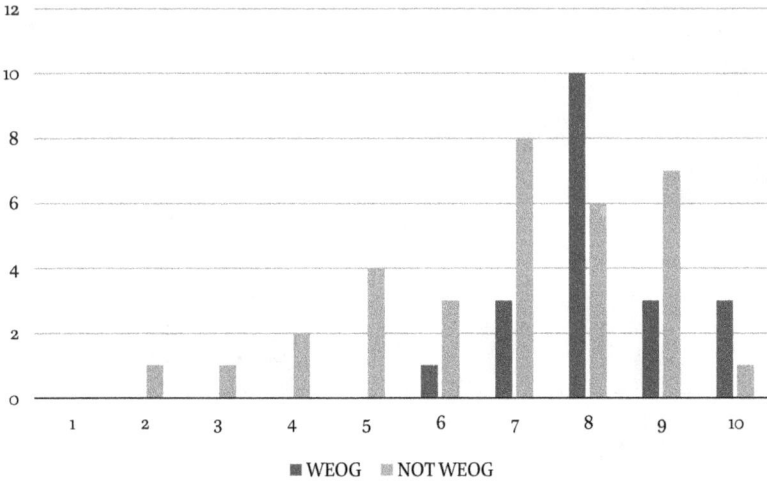

FIGURE 4.3 Would an elected seat improve your country's ability to establish
stronger relationships with other significant actors in global politics?
Comparison of responses between WEOG and non-WEOG countries (N)
Note The respondents were asked to respond on a scale from 1–10, where
1 indicated to a very small extent and 10 indicated to a very great extent

the WEOG countries believe that they are interesting to others also without a nonpermanent seat. However, the WEOG countries have more positive views regarding the idea that a seat would allow them to make contacts with countries that they had little contact with before, something that indicates that some WEOG states see a seat on the SC as useful for rather similar purposes as reported by non-WEOG countries, although in slightly different terms. A possible difference is that non-WEOG are more positive to the overall improved visibility, while the WEOG target specific countries when elected members of the Council. Both groups emphasize the relevance of close contacts with the permanent members (code 4).

As seen in Figure 4.5, both groups were reasonably positive towards a status increase because of a seat. There is considerable variation within both groups but the responses from the WEOG are clustered around the higher estimates. Members of the WEOG have an overall higher expectation on status-enhancing benefits from an elected seat, while members within other groups range from very modest to very high expectations regarding status. However, the median value is 7 for both groups. As with the previous questions, we asked the respondents to elaborate on their answers.

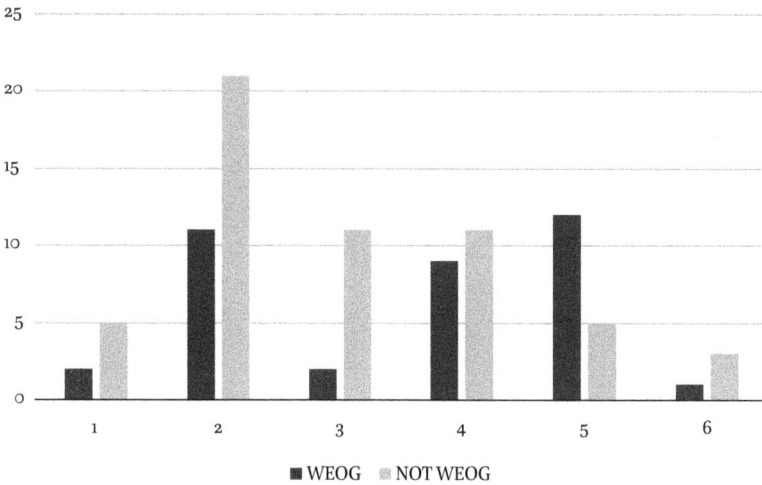

FIGURE 4.4 What might affect your possibility to establish stronger relationships
with other important actors through a nonpermanent seat on the
UNSC? Comparison of responses between WEOG and non-WEOG
countries (N)
Note: The answers were coded using the following codes: 1. Allows
you to represent your region. 2. Influence within the SC makes you
interesting to others. 3. Provides visibility for country/positions. 4. The
close contact with the P5 helps. 5. Enables contact with new countries
that you had little contact with before. 6. Other factors are more
important for establishing relationships

Figure 4.6 shows a notable difference regarding the propensity of states to
mention increased visibility and prominence (code 1). The non-WEOG countries are much more likely to mention this circumstance. This is similar to what
we found when analyzing the elaborated responses to the question on building relationships through holding a seat. As discussed above, it might be that
more WEOG states believe that they are already quite visible on the international scene, or do not think a seat on the SC is as important for this purpose.
Noteworthy, respondents in both groups pinpoint that enhancing status from a
nonpermanent seat is only temporary and conditioned by your achievements
and suggest that other factors are more important for gaining status (codes 3,
4 and 5).

To summarize the results from the comparisons between WEOG countries
and countries in other regional groups. The members of the WEOG have more
diverging views than non-WEOG countries on the opportunity to influence, but
cluster and leans towards positive estimates on the opportunities to network
and to gain/maintain status as an elected member of the Security Council. The

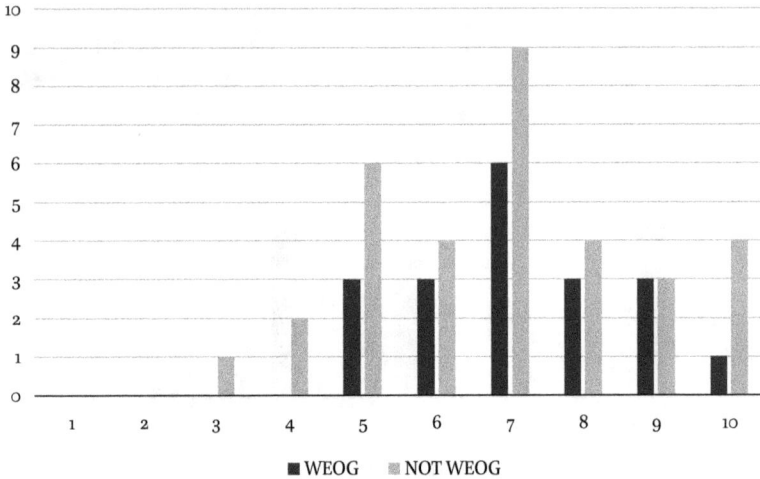

FIGURE 4.5   Would an elected seat elevate your country's status in the global
community? Comparison of responses between WEOG and non-WEOG
countries (N)
Note: The respondents were asked to respond on a scale from 1–10,
where 1 indicated to a very small extent and 10 indicated to a very
great extent

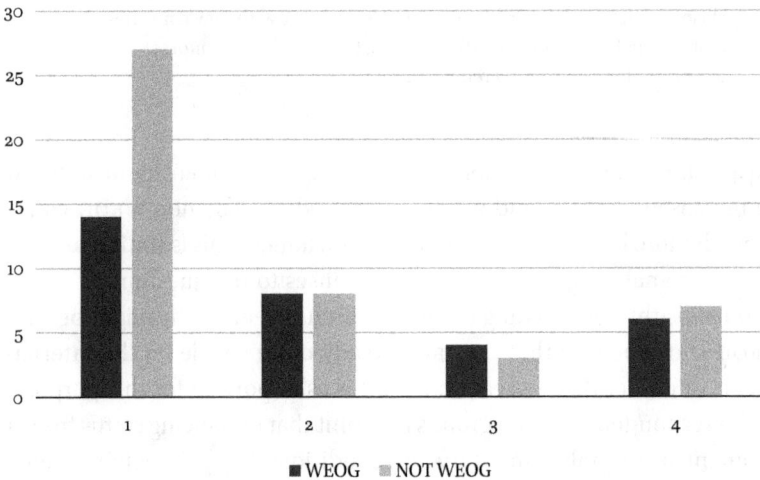

FIGURE 4.6   What would affect your elevated status from a nonpermanent seat on
the UNSC? Comparison of responses between WEOG and non-WEOG
countries (N)
Note: Elaborated answers to the question of the extent to which the
respondents think the status of their country in the global community
would be elevated if elected – were coded using the following
codes: 1. Because it increases visibility and prominence. 2. Yes, but only
temporarily/during or immediately before/after your tenure. 3. Depend
on how active you are on the SC/what you achieve. 4. Other factors are
more important for a country's status

median value is higher for WEOG countries on the opportunities to exercise influence and to network. The median value is similar for the two groups on the opportunity to gain status. Noteworthy in the elaborated answers is that non-WEOG countries emphasize the elected seat as a platform that brings visibility and makes you more interesting to others. Countries within the WEOG emphasize the elected seat as an opportunity to improve relationships with countries where contacts are otherwise limited.

5 Subgroups within the WEOG: Big, Small and Nordic

For the next step of our analysis, we have searched for patterns within the WEOG. Our theoretical point of departure is that we expect to find differences in foreign policy depending on state size. We have also paid special attention to the Nordic group. This section addresses the conceptualization of small states, as opposed to big ones, introduced in Chapter 2. To reiterate, our understanding builds on the combination of spatio-temporal considered identity and positional attributes that are relevant to the circumstance. As one of the detected determinants of success for SC elections, we suggest population size is the most relevant positional attribute to differentiate between larger and smaller European states.[3] We consider population as a proxy for the variation in economic and diplomatic capacities, i.e., possible size related advantages/disadvantages, between larger and smaller states. We define states with a population exceeding 12 million people as big, and states with less than 12 million people as small. This is, of course, a crude measure, but we believe that it is reasonable that we classify all Nordic countries as small states.

Our research objective is to investigate differences about the expected benefits from a seat in the Security Council between groups. In the context of their diplomatic coordination, including the turn-taking for candidatures, we will also examine whether the Nordic states cluster in their opinions, as an expression of a group identity with shared views and interests.

---

3 Dreher et al 2014.

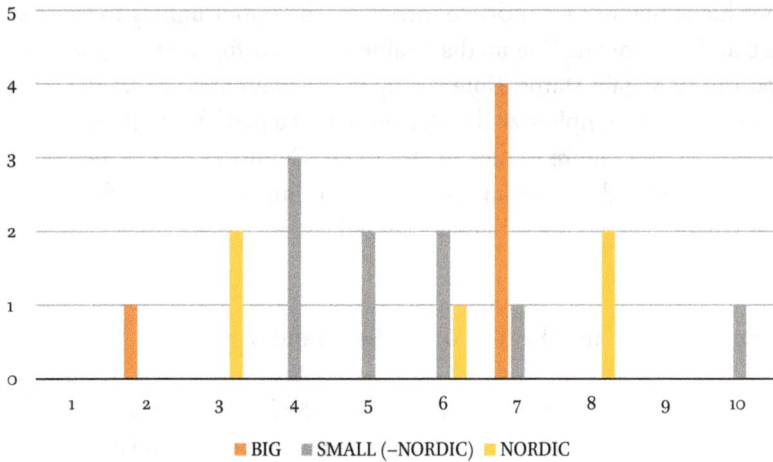

FIGURE 4.7 What might affect your possibility to influence the agenda when having a nonpermanent seat? Comparison of responses between big, small, and the Nordic countries, within the WEOG (N)
Note: The respondents were asked to respond on a scale from 1–10, where 1 indicated to a very small extent and 10 indicated to a very great extent

When asked if their country would be able to influence the UNSC agenda if holding a seat, it was clear that bigger WEOG states (N = 5, median score 7) generally had a more positive expectation than smaller states (N = 9, median score 5). Interestingly, even though the Nordic states are small, they have a more positive view on their possibilities to influence (N = 5, median score 6). However, the Nordic countries do not cluster together on one end of the scale, and the mean score is therefore difficult to interpret.

Turning next to their possibilities to build stronger relationships with other important actors, a slightly different pattern emerges.

When asked if their country would be able to establish stronger relationships with other actors, all three groups have expectations that are more positive. There seems to be an overall view of the nonpermanent seat as an opportunity for relationship building, networking, and communicating with others. Indeed, all three groups have a median value of 8. However, we can also see that the distribution differs markedly between the groups. While the big states (N = 5) are more clustered, the Nordic states (N = 5) are the most positive. Among small states (N = 10), the scores are more unevenly distributed.

Noteworthy, the Nordic states is the most positive group in this comparison. Several members of the group even express higher expectations than (any of) the big states. Small states are more modest in their estimations that a seat

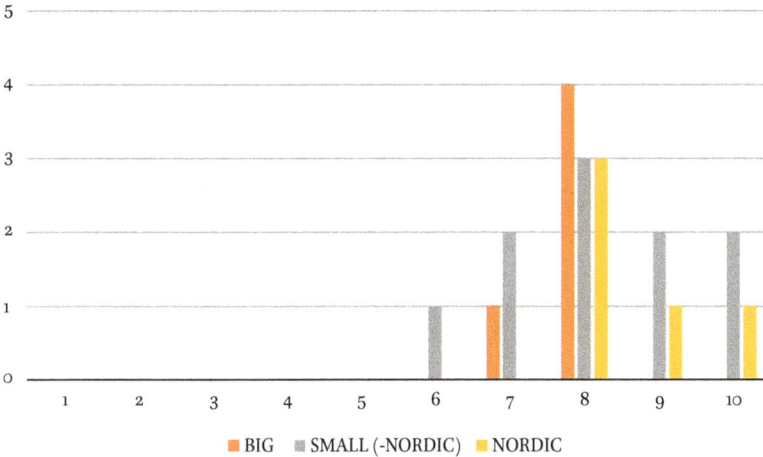

FIGURE 4.8 Would an elected seat improve your country's ability to establish
stronger relationships with other significant actors in global politics?
Comparison of responses between big, small, and the Nordic countries
within the WEOG (N)
Note: The respondents were asked to respond on a scale from 1–10,
where 1 indicated to a very small extent and 10 indicated to a very great
extent.

would lead to improved relationships with others. Either you are not interesting enough for others, or you will not be able to act in way that will facilitate
new contacts. One interpretation of this pattern is that the larger states have
sufficient opportunities to network also at the ordinary times when they are
not members of the Council, while the Nordic states see the value in an additional, although temporary, platform in their ongoing efforts to play a role in
world politics. The more modest expression by the other small states might
reflect their experience of size-related disadvantages in their efforts to establish a sufficient platform to maintain and to cultivate a constructive network.
From this experience, they are also modest in their expectations for the benefits a nonpermanent seat would provide.

Turning next to their possibilities to gain status, yet another pattern emerges.

Figure 4.9, on opportunities to gain status, reveals that the Nordic states
(N = 5, median score 7), and smaller states (N = 9, median score 7) have similar
expectations, and somewhat higher than the big states (N = 5, median score 6).
Answers for the group of big states are unevenly distributed and lean towards
a lower ranking compared with small states and Nordic states. One interpretation of this pattern is that small states indeed consider the nonpermanent
seat as an opportunity to stand in the international limelight, whereas big

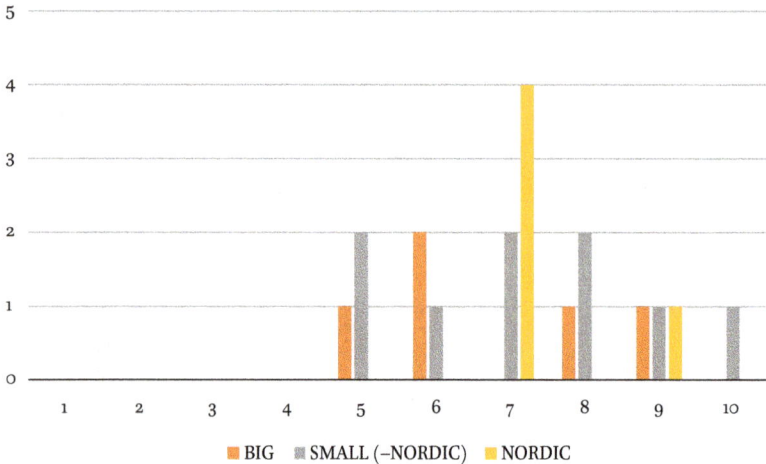

FIGURE 4.9   Would an elected seat elevate your country's status in the global
             community? Comparison of responses between big, small, and the
             Nordic countries within the WEOG (N)
             Note: The respondents were asked to respond on a scale from 1–10,
             where 1 indicated to a very small extent and 10 indicated to a very great
             extent.

states take part of world politics to an extent in accordance with their own
preferences also at ordinary times, and experience that their status already
appropriately reflects their current international standing. To a small state,
including the Nordic states, two years in the Council is a much greater opportunity to demonstrate skills and capacities that could positively elevate their
status, whereas big states already have access to platforms to demonstrate
their status-rewarding skills and capacities.

To summarize the main results of the comparisons between big, small, and
Nordic states within the WEOG: All groups have the highest expectations on
a nonpermanent seat when it comes to opportunities to network. Big states
have the highest expectations among the three groups on opportunities to
influence through a nonpermanent seat, whereas the small states, including
the Nordic states, have higher expectations on the status-enhancing effect of a
term in the Council. Notably, the Nordic states have higher expectations than
the other small states on the opportunities to influence, but they do not cluster
as a group on this issue. They are more coherent in their views on status, and
foremost on networking. The preliminary conclusions are that there are some
notable differences in expectations between big and small states, and that the

Nordic states to some extent cluster as a group. We will see if this conclusion stands after completing the next and final comparison of this chapter.

6 Subgroups within the WEOG and the EEG: Big, Small and NB8

We proceed in the analysis to examine the relevance of state size further, and to examine whether there is some clustering of views based on the diplomatic coordination among the Nord-Baltic (NB8) states also. NB8 coordination does not include a turn-taking order, as they belong to different regional groups. However, there is a routinized exchange of views and ideas, as well as explicit support for each other's candidatures.

Figure 4.10 on the opportunity to influence through a nonpermanent seat reveals an uneven distribution among all three groups of states. While there are instances of very low (big state) as well as very high (small state) expectations, most big states have higher expectations, most small states have lower expectations, and the NB8 are divided between high (> 5) and low (< 5) expectations. The median value is 7 for big states, and 5 for small states, including the NB8.

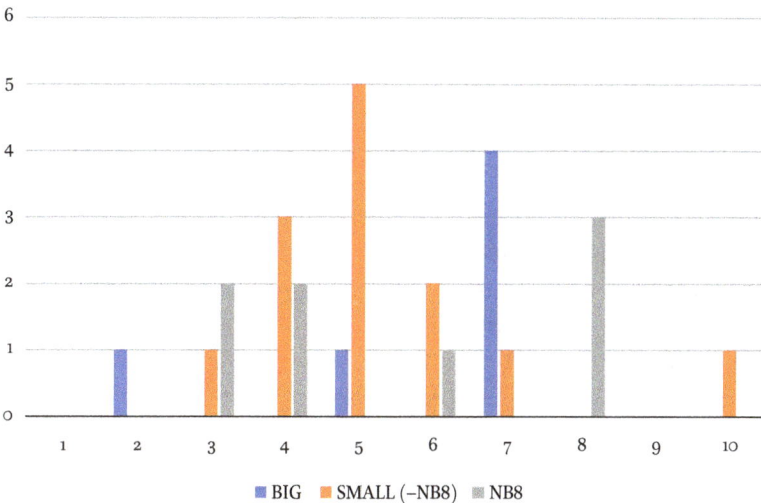

■ BIG ■ SMALL (−NB8) ■ NB8

FIGURE 4.10 What might affect your possibility to influence the agenda when having a nonpermanent seat? Comparison of responses between big, small, and the Nordic-Baltic countries, within the WEOG and the EEG (N)
Note: The respondents were asked to respond on a scale from 1–10, where 1 indicated to a very small extent and 10 indicated to a very great extent.

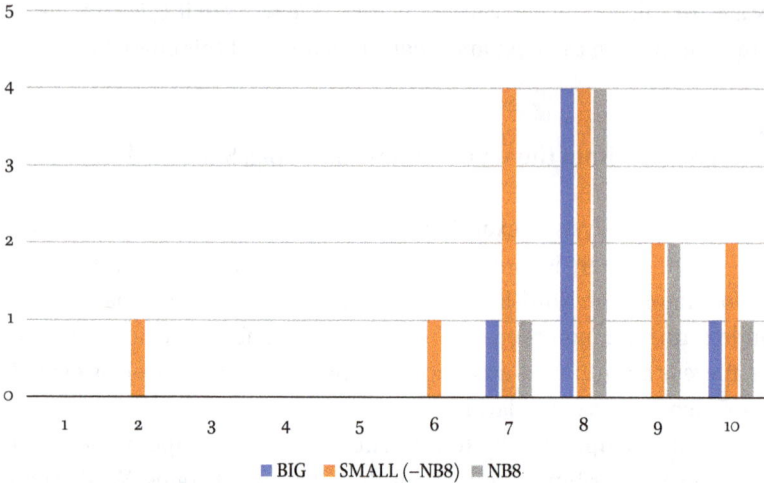

FIGURE 4.11 Would an elected seat improve your country's ability to establish
                  stronger relationships with other significant actors in global politics?
                  Comparison of responses between big, small, and the Nordic-Baltic
                  countries within the WEOG and the EEG (N)
                  Note: The respondents were asked to respond on a scale from 1–10,
                  where 1 indicated to a very small extent and 10 indicated to a very great
                  extent.

Figure 4.11 on the opportunity to establish contacts through a nonpermanent seat in the Security Council reveals the most uneven distribution among small states. The group of big states and NB8 are both more evenly distributed. All members of big states and NB8 also cluster within the higher expectations (> 5). However, the median value is 8 for all three groups.

Figure 4.12 on the opportunity to gain status through a nonpermanent seat reveals the most uneven distribution within the group of small states, which covers both the most negative and the most positive of all the responses. Big states and NB8 are both more evenly distributed and leaning towards the higher expectations. All members of NB8 cluster within the positive expectations (> 5). However, the median value is 6.5 for big states, and 7 for small states and NB8.

To summarize the main results of the comparisons between big, small, and Nordic-Baltic states within the WEOG and the EEG: All groups have the highest expectations on a nonpermanent seat when it comes to opportunities to network. Big states have the highest expectations among the three groups on opportunities to influence through a nonpermanent seat, whereas the small states, including the Nordic-Baltic states, have higher expectations on the

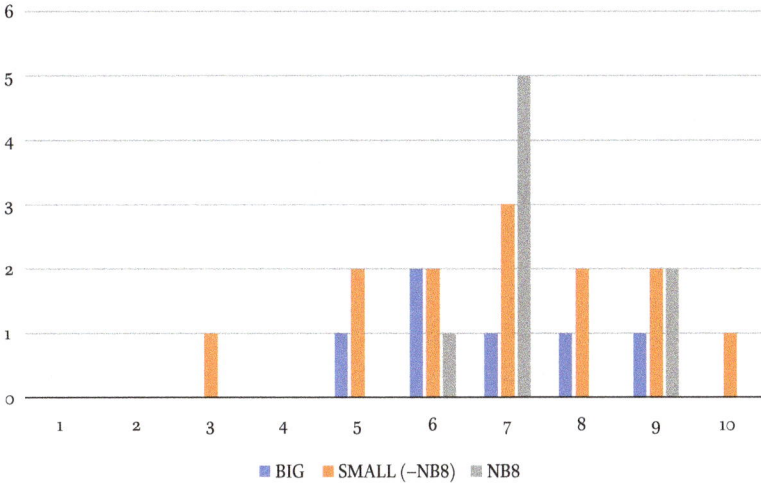

FIGURE 4.12 Would an elected seat elevate your country's status in the global community? Comparison of responses between big, small, and the Nordic-Baltic countries within the WEOG and the EEG (N)
Note: The respondents were asked to respond on a scale from 1–10, where 1 indicated to a very small extent and 10 indicated to a very great extent.

status-enhancing effect of a term in the Council. Like the responses for the Nordic states, the Nordic-Baltic states divide in their responses on influence, but cluster as a group in their views on network and status. The results of the comparison of big, small, and Nordic-Baltic states in the WEOG and the EEG lies in the similar direction as the previous results from the comparison of big, small, and Nordic states in the WEOG. These results support the conclusion that big states have higher expectations on the opportunities to influence through a nonpermanent seat, all states have high expectations on opportunities to establish useful relationships during a term in the Council, and a nonpermanent seat is more important as an opportunity to gain status for small states than for big states. The Nordic states, as well as the Nordic-Baltic states cluster in their views on networking and status, leaning towards positive expectations, but have diverging views on the opportunity to exercise influence. The Nordic states have somewhat higher expectations than the Nordic-Baltic states in this regard, which might reflect their longer history of an active and coordinated UN-politics. One possible effect of the extension of this coordination, the inclusion also of the Baltic countries, is that their views will become even more similar, and positive, over time.

7   Conclusion

The UN Security Council election is a procedure that constitutes international hierarchy through uneven access to political authority over time. This chapter has examined the more specified assessments by UN diplomats associated with a single candidature decision. We have focused on three power-enhancing benefits that an elected seat on the Security Council could lead to: influence, network, and status. We expect these benefits to imply reasons for countries' decisions to become candidates, and expectations on what a term on the Security Council will bring. Specifically, we have tried to find patterns of similarities and differences between groups of UN member states by comparing their answers from our phone survey. First, we have compared members of WEOG with members from other regional groups. Second, as sub-groups within the WEOG, we have compared big, small, and Nordic states. Thirdly, as sub-groups of WEOG and the EEG, we have compared big, small, and Nordic-Baltic states.

We have found some similarities and differences in all comparisons. Members of the WEOG have higher expectations than the non-WEOG countries on the opportunity to influence and to network. The highest expectations for both groups concern the opportunity to network, and the lowest to exercise influence. While the WEOG members have higher expectations on influence, the responses are scattered. There is no difference between groups on the status-enhancing effect. We consider international rank as a longitudinal feature rather than as a reason for specific candidatures, but we suggest that the widespread association between holding an elected term and status imply that states are well-aware of the hierarchized character of the electoral procedure.

The comparisons of big, small and subgroups (Nordic states, NB8) support the conclusion that big states have higher expectations on the nonpermanent seat as an opportunity to exercise influence, while small states, including the Nordic states, have higher expectations on the status enhancing effect of a term in the Council. This is an expected pattern given the overall disadvantages connected with smallness in world politics and the challenges facing a small, nonpermanent country in the Security Council in particular. All groups of states have similar, positive expectations on the opportunities to network as elected members. We see that the clustering of positive views among the Nordic states on network and status remains, also when we change subgroup from the Nordic states to the Nordic-Baltic states. The notable difference after the change of subgroup concerns their views on the opportunity to influence, which is more modest for NB8 than for the Nordic states. Actual differences in size and wealth between the Nordic states and the Baltics might be a contributing factor to this difference in perception.

The results for the Nordic states seem to reflect the scholarly, as well as political, views on members of the Nordic group as having high expectations and ambitions about their opportunities to contribute to shaping world politics. Relevant scholarly analysis includes the coining of Nordic states as norm entrepreneurs and the conclusion that these small states have an historical record of conducting foreign policy based on a middle-power identity.[4] We also know that this approach is politically recognized, sometimes in words of praise, but also with a sense of irritation. President Obama's public reference to Norway as a state that 'punches above its weight' attests to the former. The Wikileaks' publicized secret cable, sent in 2009 by the US embassy in Stockholm to the State Department in Washington, which describes the Swedish Foreign Minister Carl Bildt, as a 'Medium Size Dog with Big Dog Attitude', illustrates the latter.[5]

It is interesting that the result in this chapter reflects similar shared and positive views on the opportunities from an elected seat on basis of a group identity also for the Nordic-Baltic states. They express modest expectations on the opportunity to exercise influence though an elected seat, but their coordination significantly increases their chances of a more frequent representation in the Council given the circumstance that they belong to different regional groups.

Appendix 1 Interview Survey to UN Ambassadors/UN Staff

Before starting, I want to emphasise that your participation and the views you are about to share are of value to the study. I also want to remind you that you take part on an anonymous basis (all the answers are anonymised as soon as they have been coded for statistical analysis) and the interview is not being taped or recorded.

---

4 Ingebritsen 2002; Brommesson 2018.
5 de Carvalho and Neumann 2014; WikiLeaks. In the Swedish press this characterization – made available to the public by Wikileaks – was discussed as if it were a statement about the minister's personality. In the cabled report, however, Bildt stood for Sweden at large, namely 'a medium-size country (9.5 million [inhabitants], $350 billion annual GDP) that has some major power ambitions and capabilities'. After pointing out that Sweden maintained 'the world's 7th largest foreign aid program (nearly $5 billion), focused on Africa and the Middle East', the author of the report cited UN military deployment and a tradition of supplying the world with international civil servants to further substantiate this claim. Secret cable from US embassy Stockholm (Robert Silverman) to State Department, 29 Apr. 2009. See also Ekengren and Götz 2013.

Country: **Date:**

Click or tap here to enter text.   Click or tap to enter a date.

Q1a: As the first question, I would just like to verify the accuracy of the information we have. Since 1990, (country) has campaigned x time(s) and been elected x time(s),/but not been elected/, for a seat in the Security Council. Is this correct?

☐YES ☐NO

Not Correct? Verify times and year(s).

Click or tap here to enter text.

Q1b: As the first question, I would just like to verify the accuracy of the information we have. Since 1990, (country) has not campaigned for an elected seat in the SC. Is this correct?

☐YES ☐NO

Not Correct? Verify times and year(s).

Click or tap here to enter text.

Q2a: In your opinion, why is it of interest to your country to serve as an elected member of the SC? What are the main reasons behind the decision to campaign for a seat?

Open ended answer.

Click or tap here to enter text.

Q2b: In your opinion, would it be of interest to your country to serve as an elected member of the SC in the future? What are the main reasons for why your country has not campaigned for a seat so far?

Example of a common answer important to be aware of is that the regional group might not have nominated the country. Here it could it be interesting to know whether that country has actively sought nomination?

Open ended answer.

Click or tap here to enter text.

Q3: In general, and not only thinking of your own country, are there more reasons for why states seek an elected seat in the SC?

Open ended answer.

Click or tap here to enter text.

I will now proceed with additional questions related to influence. Before elaborating on your answers I want you to rank them on a scale from 1–10, where 1 is to a very small extent and 10 is to a very great extent.

Country: **Date:**

Q4: To what extent would your country be able to influence the agenda of the SC, if you were elected? Please answer on the scale from 1–10, where 1 is to a very small extent and 10 is to a very great extent.
Clarification if suitable/required: You could consider this question in the context of the veto-power of the permanent members, which would suggest very limited opportunity to influence, and yet, since we know that there are examples of elected members' influence, some opportunities are still available.
□1 □2 □3 □4 □5 □6 □7□8 □9 □10

Q4f: Could you please elaborate on why and how?
Click or tap here to enter text.

Q5: Would an elected seat improve your country's ability to establish stronger relationships with other significant actors in global politics? Please answer on the scale from 1–10, where 1 is to a very small extent and 10 is to a very great extent.
Clarification if suitable/required: You could consider the question in the context of the arenas that are open for UNSC members, such as meetings with other UNSC members (including the P5), or even meetings with other actors, depending on the particular questions that are being discussed.
□1 □2 □3 □4 □5 □6 □7□8 □9 □10

Q5f: Could you please elaborate on why and how?
Click or tap here to enter text.

Q6: Would an elected seat elevate your country's status in global community? Please answer on the scale from 1–10, where 1 is to a very small extent and 10 is to a very great extent.
Clarification if suitable/required: When we speak about 'status' we consider descriptions such as international prominence, reputation and leverage as synonymous. It is about possessing a certain credibility either overall, or limited to certain policy areas.
□1 □2 □3 □4 □5 □6 □7□8 □9 □10

Q6f: Could you please elaborate on why and how?
Click or tap here to enter text.

Q7: If you consider the campaigns for the elected seats conducted in recent years, are there any examples you would like to give as especially successful (in the sense of well-organized / skillfully conducted) campaigns?
Click or tap here to enter text.

Country: **Date:**

Q7f: Are there examples of not so well carried out campaigns also?
Click or tap here to enter text.

Q8: How would you describe the relationship between (country) and the UN?
Friendly? Unfriendly? Critical? Defender? Supporter? Reformer? Other
suggestion?
*We are now done with the substantive questions, and I just have three
'background'-questions left:*
First, what is your current position (at your UN office)?
Click or tap here to enter text.
Second, how long have you held your current position?
Click or tap here to enter text.
Finally, how long have you worked within the UN system?
Click or tap here to enter text.
Thank you so much for your time!

Appendix 2 Code Sheet for the Interview Survey

Country: **Date:**

Click or tap here to enter text.   Click or tap to enter a date.
*Q1a: As the first question, I would just like to verify the accuracy of the
information we have. Since 1990, (country) has campaigned x time(s) and been
elected x time(s),/but not been elected/, for a seat in the Security Council. Is this
correct?*
☐YES 1. ☐NO 2.
Not Correct? Verify times and year(s).
Click or tap here to enter text.

*Q1b: As the first question, I would just like to verify the accuracy of the
information we have. Since 1990, (country) has not campaigned for an elected
seat in the sc. Is this correct?*
☐YES 1. ☐NO 2.
Not Correct? Verify times and year(s).
Click or tap here to enter text.

Country:	Date:

Q2a: In your opinion, why is it of interest to your country to serve as an elected member of the SC? What are the main reasons behind the decision to campaign for a seat?

Open ended answer.

1. Influence the agenda/work of the UNSC. 2. Take responsibility/sense of obligation to contribute. 3. Stronger relationships with other actors/ networking. 4. Status-seeking/reputation/be seen in the international arena. 5. Achieve economic advantages/get something from the money/resources invested in the UN. 6. Opportunity to gain experience for the diplomatic corps/capacity building. 7. Country specific issues/politics (e.g. policy of running at regular intervals). 8. Other.

Q2b: In your opinion, would it be of interest to your country to serve as an elected member of the SC in the future? What are the main reasons for why your country has not campaigned for a seat so far?

Example of a common answer important to be aware of is that the regional group might not have nominated the country. Here it could it be interesting to know whether that country has actively sought nomination?

Open ended answer.

1. 1. No resources to do so. 2. No competence/insufficient personnel to do so. 3. The SC has not been the most important priority. 4. We know that we do not have the support. 5. Regional group rotation schemes.

Q3: In general, and not only thinking of your own country, are there more reasons for why states seek an elected seat in the SC?

Open ended answer.

1. Influence the agenda/work of the UNSC. 2. Take responsibility/sense of obligation to contribute. 3. Stronger relationships with other actors/ networking. 4. Status-seeking/reputation/be seen in the international arena. 5. Achieve economic advantages/get something from the money/ resources invested in the UN. 6. Opportunity to gain experience for the diplomatic corps/capacity building. 7. Country specific issues/politics (e.g. policy of running at regular intervals). 8. Reasons related to regional rotation schemes. 9. Other.

I will now proceed with additional questions related to influence. Before elaborating on your answers I want you to rank them on a scale from 1–10, where 1 is to a very small extent and 10 is to a very great extent.

Country: **Date:**

Q4: To what extent would your country be able to influence the agenda of the sc, if you were elected? Please answer on the scale from 1–10, where 1 is to a very small extent and 10 is to a very great extent.
Clarification if suitable/required: You could consider this question in the context of the veto-power of the permanent members, which would suggest very limited opportunity to influence, and yet, since we know that there are examples of elected members' influence, some opportunities are still available.
□1 □2 □3 □4 □5 □6 □7□8 □9 □10

Q4f: Could you please elaborate on why and how?
1. The permanent members decide/are significantly more influential than the NP members. 2. Difficult to build alliances in the SC. 3. We are a small country/have limited resources. 4. Holding the presidency helps. 5. Influence is issue-specific (e.g. More influence regarding procedural issues and debates; issues relating to own country or region). 6. Agenda is mostly determined current affairs/circumstances, or automatic/recurring items (e.g. renewal of PKOS, etc.).

Q5: Would an elected seat improve your country's ability to establish stronger relationships with other significant actors in global politics? Please answer on the scale from 1–10, where 1 is to a very small extent and 10 is to a very great extent.
Clarification if suitable/required: You could consider the question in the context of the arenas that are open for UNSC members, such as meetings with other UNSC members (including the P5), or even meetings with other actors, depending on the particular questions that are being discussed.
□1 □2 □3 □4 □5 □6 □7□8 □9 □10

Q5f: Could you please elaborate on why and how?
1. Allows you to represent your region. 2. Influence in the SC makes you interesting to others. 3. Provides visibility for country/positions. 4. The close contact with the P5 helps. 5. Enables contact with new countries that you had little contact with before. 6. Other factors are more important for establishing relationships.

Q6: Would an elected seat elevate your country's status in global community? Please answer on the scale from 1–10, where 1 is to a very small extent and 10 is to a very great extent.

Country: **Date:**

Clarification if suitable/required: When we speak about 'status' we consider descriptions such as international prominence, reputation and leverage as synonymous. It is about possessing a certain credibility either overall, or limited to certain policy areas.

□1 □2 □3 □4 □5 □6 □7□8 □9 □10

Q6f: Could you please elaborate on why and how?
1. Because it increases visibility and prominence. 2. Yes, but only temporarily/during or immediately before/after your tenure. 3. Depends on how active you are on the SC/what you achieve. 4. Other factors are more important for a country's status.

Q7: If you consider the campaigns for the elected seats conducted in recent years, are there any examples you would like to give as especially successful (in the sense of well-organized / skillfully conducted) campaigns?
1. Sweden 2. Luxembourg 3. Austria 4. Other
Q7f: Are there examples of not so well carried out campaigns also?
1. Finland 2. Iceland 3. Other

Q8: How would you describe the relationship between (country) and the UN?
1. Friendly supporter 2. Critical supporter 3. Reformer 4. Critical 5. Other suggestion?
We are now done with the substantive questions, and I just have three 'background'-questions left:
First, what is your current position (at your UN office)?
a. 1. Ambassador 2. Higher diplomatic position 3. Other
Second, how long have you held your current position?
1. 1–2 years 2. 3–5 years 3. 6–9 years 4. Longer
Finally, how long have you worked within the UN system?
1. 1–2 years 2. 3–5 years 3. 6–9 years 4. Longer
Thank you so much for your time!

Appendix 3 Percentages in Relation to Figures Presented in Chapter 4

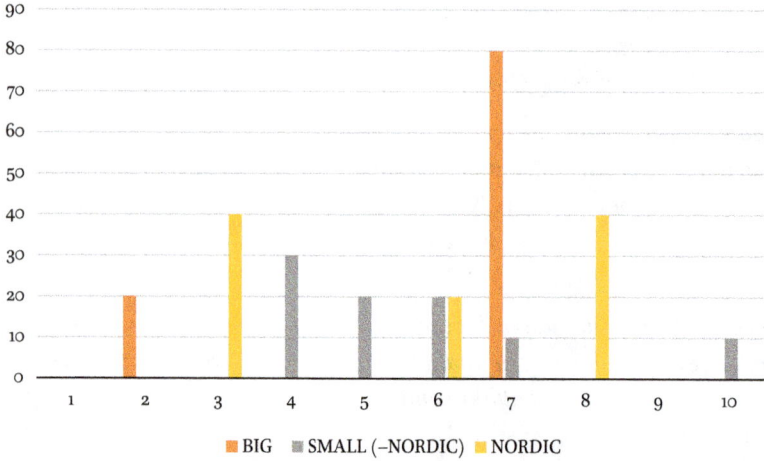

FIGURE 4.13 What might affect your possibility to influence the agenda if you held a nonpermanent seat? Comparison of responses between small, big, and the Nordic countries within the WEOG (percent)

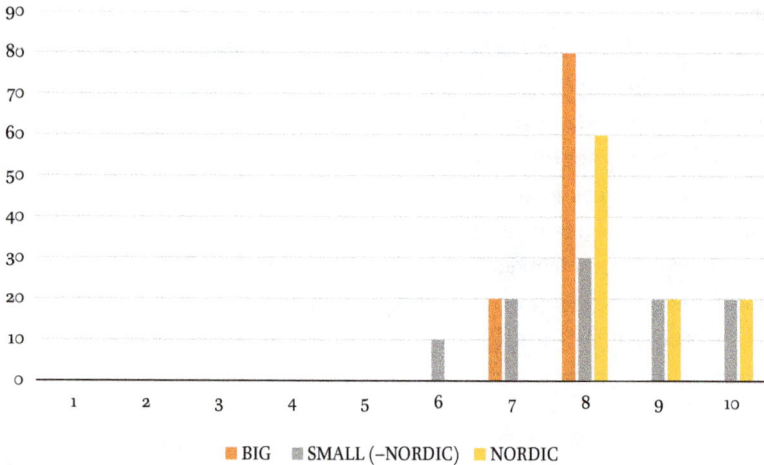

FIGURE 4.14 Would an elected seat improve your country's ability to establish stronger relationships with other significant actors in global politics? Comparison of responses between small, big, and the Nordic countries within the WEOG (percent)

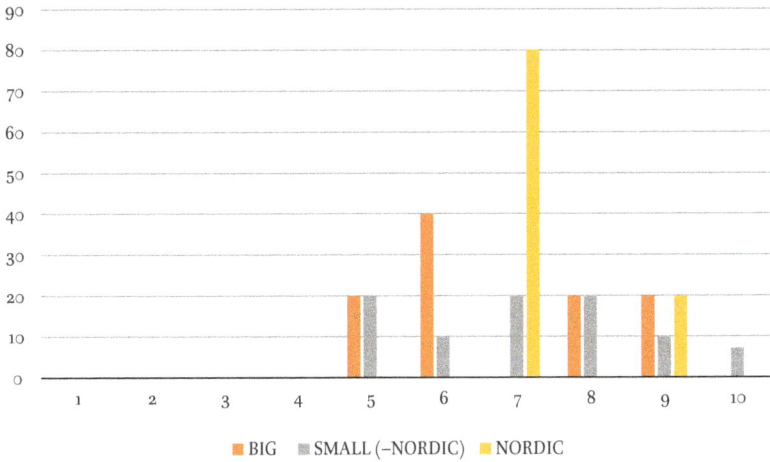

FIGURE 4.15 Would an elected seat elevate your country's status in the global community? Comparison of responses between small, big, and the Nordic countries within the WEOG (percent)

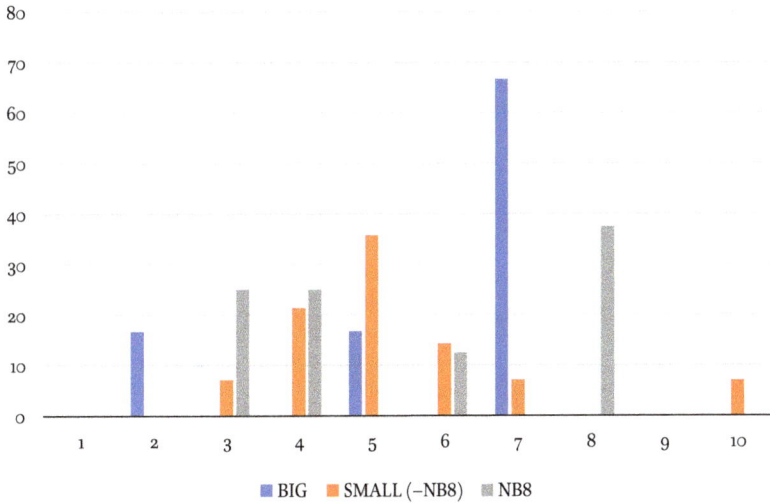

FIGURE 4.16 What might affect your possibility to influence the agenda if you held a nonpermanent seat? Comparison of responses between small, big, and the Nordic countries within the WEOG (percent)

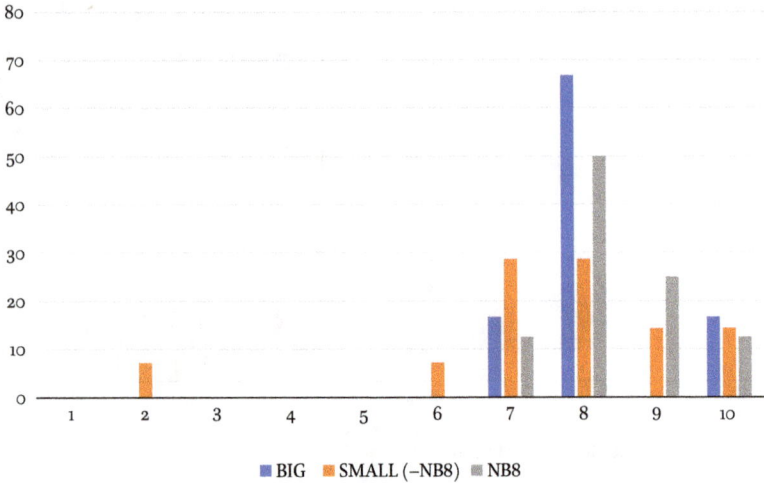

FIGURE 4.17 Would an elected seat improve your country's ability to establish stronger relationships with other significant actors in global politics? Comparison of responses between small, big, and the Nordic countries within the WEOG (percent)

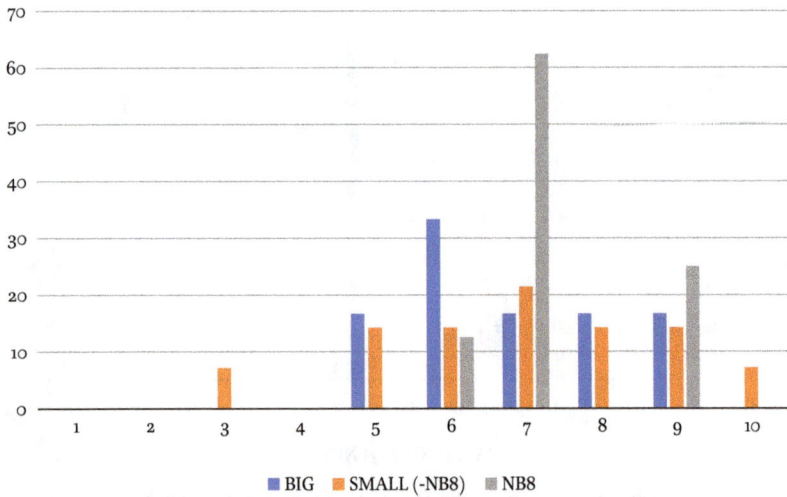

FIGURE 4.18 Would an elected seat elevate your country's status in the global community? Comparison of responses between small, big, and the Nordic countries within the WEOG (percent)

Bibliography

Aggestam, Lisbeth, and Markus Johansson. 'The Leadership Paradox in EU Foreign Policy'. *JCMS: Journal of Common Market Studies*, 55 (6) (2017), 1203–1220.

Brommesson, Douglas. 'Introduction to Special Section: from Nordic Exceptionalism to a Third Order Priority – Variations of "Nordicness" in Foreign and Security Policy'. *Global Affairs*, 4(4–5) (2018), 355–362.

De Carvalho, Benjamin, and Iver B. Neumann. *Small State Status Seeking: Norway's Quest for International Standing*. (London and New York: Routledge, 2014).

Dreher, Axel, Matthew Gould, Matthew D. Rablen and James Raymond Vreeland. 'The Determinants of Election to the United Nations Security Council'. *Public Choice*, 158 (2014), 51–83.

Ekengren, Ann-Marie and Norbert Götz. The One Per Cent Country: Sweden's Internalization of the Aid Norm. In Olesen, Thorsten B, Pharo, Helge and Paaskesen, Christian (eds.) *Saints and Sinners. Official Development Aid and its Dynamics in a Historical and Comparative Perspective*. (Oslo: Akademika, 2013).

Ekengren, Ann-Marie, Fredrik D. Hjorthen and Ulrika Möller. 'A Nonpermanent Seat in the United Nations Security Council: Why Bother?'. *Global Governance: a Review of Multilateralism and International Organizations*, (26) (2020), 21–45.

Ingebritsen, Christine. 'Norm Entrepreneurs: Scandinavia's Role in World Politics', *Cooperation and Conflict*, Vol. 37(1) (2002), 11–23.

Johansson, Markus. *Negotiations as Usual: Putting Domestic Constraints on the Table in the Council of the European Union*. PhD Thesis (University of Gothenburg, Department of Political Science, 2015).

Wikileaks https://wikileaks.org/ retrieved on the 5 of May 2023.

CHAPTER 5

Candidature Decisions: Six In-depth Examinations

Ann-Marie Ekengren, Ulrika Möller, Touko Piiparinen, Tarja Seppä, Anni Tervo, Baldur Thorhallsson, Jóna Sólveig Elínardóttir and Anna M. Eggertsdóttir

1 Introduction*

Why do UN member states seek representation on the Security Council? What opportunities do they expect from holding a nonpermanent seat? Results from the previous chapter underlined the relevance of state size and regional group-belonging for expectations associated with a candidature. The confidence about exercising influence is higher among representatives of big compared to small states, and among members of the WEOG compared to non-WEOG members. Among the power-enhancing benefits, representatives of small states have the highest expectations on a status-enhancing effect from the elected seat. Among small states, the Nordic states stand out as a somewhat more confident group on the expectations to exercise influence.

In this chapter, we are interested in the more fine-grained considerations associated with the candidature decision and related expectations about the opportunities from an elected term. The specific purposes are: 1) to find more details on the three main power-enhancing benefits, 2) to identify additional, related and/or alternative, main reasons for why states embark on the candidature journey, and 3) to detect whether there are similarities within the Nordic group in relation to the other WEOG countries. The analysis is conducted through a focus on actual candidature decisions by a few selected members of the WEOG. The main empirical source is interviews with senior officials and diplomats who were actively involved in the candidatures. In some of the cases, we combine results from the interviews with written sources. The cases are the same as the forthcoming comparisons between successful and unsuccessful campaigns: Iceland – Austria, Finland – Luxembourg, Sweden

---

* Ann-Marie Ekengren and Ulrika Möller are the main authors of the introduction and conclusion of the chapter, as well as the section on Sweden and the Netherlands. Touko Piiparinen, Tarja Seppä and Anni Tervo are the main authors of the section on Finland and Luxembourg. Baldur Thorhallsson, Jóna Sólveig Elínardóttir and Anna María Eggertsdóttir are the main authors of the section on Iceland and Austria.

– The Netherlands. We suggest that it is relevant to focus on members in the WEOG since the frequent use of contested slate in this regional group might sharpen the ideas and arguments for why an elected seat is worth prioritizing. This quality of distinct opinions should be even clearer as we now examine a specific candidature for each of the selected countries.

Specifications of the established reasons include that the expectation to exercise influence is associated with a commitment to the multilateral order and a perceived responsibility to maintain and to develop that order. We also suggest that a successful election and subsequent term not only elevates status but could have a confirmatory effect of statehood for the smallest states included in the comparison. New additions include considerations on how the candidature and elected term bring opportunity to competence building of the foreign services. We suggest that this reflects the views of a small state with high international ambitions, as one out of several possible ways to compensate for size-related disadvantages in world politics that is highly relevant for the Nordic states.

2   About the Interviews

Between January 2018 and June 2020, we interviewed many senior officials and high-ranking diplomats involved in the planning and execution of the candidatures of the six cases we examine. Most interviews took place face-to-face, in a setting chosen by the respondent. A few interviews took place over the phone, due to inability to overcome large distance of location. The interviews followed a semi-structured format, with a selected set of questions, but with a free format to discuss the questions in accordance with the respondents' experience and expertise. The average time for an interview was 45 minutes to one hour. We summarized the main content of interviews in a transcript. The interviewees are anonymous in the presentation since some of the interviewees have requested to stay anonymous and if we reveal the names of the other persons, it could be possible to identify others as well.

Previous single case studies have detected specific self-interested as well as value-laden purposes for a Security Council candidature. By examining a larger number of in-depth cases, we contribute through inference on the relevance of such specific purposes for a term, in relation to the relevance of the broader power enhancing benefits that our study already has revealed. Further, we also want to push the analysis further on the result from the previous chapter that the Nordic countries cluster on expectations to network and to gain status from an elected term. We will look for additional similarities among the Nordic states. We present the results pairwise, in the order of their election: Iceland and Austria in 2008, Finland and Luxembourg in 2012, and Sweden and the Kingdom of the Netherlands in 2016.

3   Iceland and Austria – Becoming Relevant versus Staying Relevant

Both Iceland and Austria referred to their small size as one of the reasons for running for a seat on the UNSC, for the term 2009–10. However, their approaches to, and motivations for the candidature were very different. Iceland sought a seat on the UNSC based on its ambition to seek status and become more internationally relevant. As a former empire, an ambition to maintain power and remain relevant motivated Austria.

We describe the driving factors behind Iceland's candidature decision through four themes. First, running for an elected seat on the UNSC was viewed as a matter of principle, a way to confirm Iceland's sovereignty, strengthen its status in the international arena, and shoulder its rightful duty to contribute to international politics. It was in this optimistic atmosphere, characterizing Icelandic society and economy, which the Icelandic Foreign Service grew substantially stronger in the 1990s. It underscored the general feelings and arguments that Iceland was now ready to bear increased responsibility on the international level, as well as within the UN.[1] As an example, in 2007 Prime Minister Geir H. Haarde described why Iceland had decided to run: "The decision to run mirrors a new vision of Iceland's position in international affairs and a new self-confidence and active engagement in foreign affairs. It entails a definition of Iceland as a strong, smaller state but rejects the identity of Iceland as a powerless micro-state. It does not mirror vanity but a natural revaluation and constant attempts to strengthen Iceland's position".[2]

The personal ambitions of politicians and individuals within the diplomatic corps were an important driving force behind the decision to campaign for a seat on the UNSC. This was reflected in public officials encouraging the Foreign Minister, Geir Hallgrímsson, already in the mid-1980s to start preparing for a possible UNSC candidature by becoming more active within the UN. This resulted in Iceland becoming a first-time member of the UN ECOSOC, which is considered an important prerequisite and preparatory element to running

---

1   Blöndal, 2006; Gestsson, 1998; Gísladóttir, 2007; Pétursdóttir, 2003; Sigfússon, 2001; Sveinbjarnardóttir, 2006; Sverrisdóttir, 2006; Árnason, 2007b; Ásgrímsson, 1998; Þórðardóttir, 2003.
2   Haarde, 2007.

for a seat on the UNSC. Moreover, Prime Minister Davíð Oddsson, and Foreign Minister Halldór Ásgrímsson were both encouraged by high-ranking public officials in the late 1990s to make Iceland's first run for a seat on the UNSC. One interviewee described the decision to run as being part of 'office politics: personal ambitions of individuals', referring to both the Foreign Minister in office as well as high-ranking public officials within the foreign service.[3] Iceland would once again become an ECOSOC member during the 1997–1998 period. Shortly thereafter, in 1998, the decision to move forward with the UNSC bid was made in government and announced to the public.

The domestic debate on the candidature expressed both high hopes and deep skepticism, as will be discussed in forthcoming chapter. Up to 1998, Iceland had never participated in the Nordic UNSC rotation, despite being a member of the UN for 50 years, as neither politicians nor civil servants considered Iceland ready. However, with the country's increased economic prosperity, the political atmosphere provided fertile ground for such an endeavor. Initially, the candidature was met with optimism as it was considered a timely event, confirming Iceland's sovereignty and increased status on the international level. Iceland had been hoping for an uncontested campaign, but its positive stance soon changed for the worse when Turkey announced its candidature in 2003, and it became clear that the campaign would be more expensive than initially expected. Doubts began to grow among Icelandic politicians concerning excessive financial resources being wasted on a, perhaps, lost battle, which resulted in the campaign slowly losing momentum and eventually being put on hold for almost an entire year between September 2004 and September 2005. The Foreign Minister, Davíð Oddsson, experienced strong pressure from his Nordic colleagues to proceed with the campaign, as it had been collectively agreed upon that Iceland would run the candidature, not only on their own behalf, but on behalf of all the other Nordic countries, and therefore discontinuation was not a justifiable option.[4] Iceland's continued campaign was announced in late September 2005 when Geir H. Haarde took office as Foreign Minister, and as it turned out, this changed both the momentum and tone of the campaign.

Second, the UNSC candidature was an important component in Iceland's efforts to demonstrate its international commitment to the US authorities, who had shown signs of decreasing interest in maintaining its economically beneficial military presence in Keflavik, as well as to the international

---

3 High-ranking official C, 2018.
4 Fréttablaðið, 2005a, 2005b; High-ranking official B, 2018.

community, in general.[5] The US military base was an essential component of Iceland's defense, a small state without its own armed forces (the only NATO member state without an army). Hence, Iceland's decision to run for the UNSC seat was part of its larger strategy to share the burden of international activities with its allies. Iceland hoped that by spending more resources on international operations, its long-term ally, the United States, would keep its defense commitments to the country and maintain its activities at Keflavik military base.

Third, the decision to become a UNSC candidate was partly justified as being economically feasible since it would create a venue to lobby for vital national interests and build relationships, which could prove economically beneficial.[6] In this regard, it was mentioned that during the campaign Iceland received visits from powerful people from around the world in connection with the campaign, who otherwise would not have come, such as the leader of the League of Arab States.[7]

Fourthly, a completely altered domestic, political, international, and geo-political environment paved the way for new foreign policy decisions and a much more active foreign policy for Iceland as a small state. Examples of this increased activity is the foundation of the Icelandic International Development Agency in 1981 and in Iceland joining the European Economic Area (EEA) in 1994. The first steps towards establishing the Icelandic Crisis Response Unit (ICRU) in the 1990s, when peace building and peacekeeping became an increasingly important part of the Ministry for Foreign Affairs' (MFA) international activities, is relevant also. Moreover, there was an increased willingness among Icelandic policymakers to contribute to world affairs within their field of expertise, rather than focusing solely on direct economic and security gains from overseas relationships.[8] Icelandic politicians were becoming more confident that they could have a say within regional and international institutions.

We identify four driving factors behind Austria's decision to run for a non-permanent seat. First, UNSC candidature and membership was seen as a way to remain relevant in the international system and demonstrate the country's foreign policy, its fields of expertise, and its vision. During Austria's 50 years of UN membership, Austrian authorities had put great emphasis on being a devoted and reliable member state, as well as an active member of the international community, known for its long history of work in the fields of international law, development co-operation, peacekeeping efforts, and mediation.

5   Bailes and Thorhallsson, 2006.
6   Benediktsson, 2008; Sverrisdóttir, 2006; Árnason, 2007a; Ásgrímsson, 2001, 2003a, 2003b.
7   High-ranking official B, 2018.
8   Thorhallsson, 2009.

Representatives of the Austrian government therefore linked UNSC candidature to the importance of being active and effective in international affairs in order to raise the country's profile and spread Austrian expertise and peacekeeping messages.[9] In the words of one high-ranking official: 'Austria is a small country and the SC is a good opportunity to be on stage. It is important to be a part of initiatives regarding security policies. Show the world that there are good politicians in Austria and good initiatives and Austria is not the kind of country that hides behind the trees, but is an active member of the international community'.[10] Peter Jankowitsch (ÖVP), former Foreign Minister, president of the UNSC during Austria's first period on the council, and special emissary of the third candidature, claimed that because of Austria's limited resources and strong emphasis on the EU, the country hardly existed to a large part of the world. According to him, the UNSC was the best platform for states to present their profile and demonstrate what they stand for. At that time Austria had few embassies in Africa, Asia, and the Pacific, and consequently in Jankowitsch's opinion, the UNSC was the ideal place to showcase Austria's effectiveness on the international stage.[11] In addition, the Austrian government, perhaps because of their identity as a reliable member state, saw the candidature as a service to the UN and the international community.[12] This is reflected in Foreign Minister Ursula Plassnik's words about the candidature being an act of respect for diversity and in recognition of the need for unity, a service rendered to the UN by a candidate that inspires confidence and evokes a sense of partnership.[13] Finally, in the words of one official, seeking membership within the UN's most important institution was 'for Austria an essential part of taking responsibility for the maintenance of peace and security. We wanted to prove that countries like Austria could have an impact on the work of the Security Council'.[14]

Secondly, the decision to campaign for a seat on the UNSC was based on national and regional security incentives. Austria's small state status, limited military capabilities, and declared neutrality were presented as explanations for Austria's steadfast dedication to the functioning of the multilateral system, the rule of law, and the primacy of international law,[15] thus making Austrian

---

9   Machreich, 2008a; News, 2005.
10   Interview E, 2018.
11   Machreich, 2008a.
12   High-ranking official F, 2018.
13   Bundesministerium, 2006; 2008a.
14   Interview G, 2018.
15   Plassnik 2007, 2008.

representation at the UNSC a rational policy to be sought on a regular basis: 'A small state is not a military power. But involvement in multilateral structures is the best security guarantee for countries like Austria, who are also not part of any military alliances. Therefore, it makes sense for us to have a seat on the Security Council every 20 years or so. Then you have to declare yourself, take position and responsibility"[16] Moreover, this was not considered a contradiction, to be both neutral and in possession of a seat on the SC, as the country had a clear foreign policy and showed consistent dedication to international law, human rights, and democracy.[17]

Thirdly, the candidature served the country's economic interests, founded on the work that had been done to establish Austria, and Vienna in particular, as a *security centre*. The economic significance of strong Austria-UN relations could not be ignored, as Deputy Chancellor Wolfgang Schüssel referenced in the Austrian Federal Council (the upper house of the Austrian parliament) in 1997, stating that it contributed billions to the country.[18] Austria is the only EU country to host a UN headquarters as well as e.g. the UN Office for Drug Control and Crime Prevention (ODCCP) and the International Atomic Energy Agency (IAEA). These were the pillars for Austria's campaign when stressing the importance of Vienna to global security, making the capital what they repeatedly referred to as a *security centre*. The Vienna-based OSCE headquarters was also mentioned on several occasions in this respect. Moreover, Austria lobbied for increased UN presence in Vienna throughout the campaign period. As an example of this, Foreign Minister Plassnik announced Austria's support for creating a new International Renewable Energy Agency, proposing Vienna as the location, as well as the creation of a new regime, placing all enrichment facilities under the control of the Vienna-based IAEA.[19]

Finally, it can be said that a seat on the UNSC was perceived as a way for Austria to work towards strengthening the EU's position in the UN, and thus Austria's status and role within the EU. The main point of departure in one of Plassnik's addresses at the UN General Assembly was the EU's *United in Diversity* slogan, thereby emphasizing the role of the EU in building peace on the European continent, how well it worked with the Austrian emphasis on the dialogue of cultures and religions, and how that slogan should also be the guiding principle in the work done by the UN.[20] Furthermore, Austrian authorities

---

16   Die Presse, 2007a.
17   Die Presse, 2007a; Interview F, 2018.
18   News, 2005.
19   Ferrero-Waldner, 2002, 2003; Fischer, 2005; Plassnik, 2005b, 2006, 2007, 2008.
20   Plassnik, 2006.

often highlighted the country's leading role in developing EU's competences, engagement, and relationships with the UN in the fields of peacekeeping, development aid, EU-Africa relations, and women's rights. It was also a way to show commitment to their EU partners by advocating for increased EU influence on the work of the UN, both within the Security Council, as well as the importance of the EU having a formal role on the UN's Peacebuilding Commission.[21] When Federal Council MP Harald Himmer asked Plassnik in 2005 about EU's chances of obtaining a seat on the UNSC, Plassnik replied that a mutual seat on the SC for the EU as a whole certainly was a long-term goal, and in her opinion, it was a logical conclusion for the EU to have a shared voice on the UN's decision-making level, and thereby intensify the common grounds on which they operated.[22] It can be argued that this was a way for Austria to win the support of their EU partners, as well as a way to establish itself as a 'regional power', with a global reference, and an expert in the field of security, which in turn strengthened their own status within the UN.

To summarize, Iceland maintained that despite being small, the country had grown strong and was therefore capable of assuming the responsibilities of serving on the Security Council. The candidature was a milestone in confirming Iceland's sovereign status and an attempt to climb the ranks in the international system. However, Austria's approach maintained that, due to its small state status and military weakness, it was important to support multilateralism and the rule of law with their expertise and experience through the UNSC. Thus, Austria's bid was a rational part of the country's security and foreign policy, a tactical move reflecting the status Austria should have and a necessary measure to maintain influence and remain relevant, internationally. This reflects a high level of confidence built on history and culture.

Both states emphasized the importance of assuming international responsibility as one of their reasons for running, but while Iceland was taking its first steps, Austria was confirming its continued engagement in multilateralism. Both had economic incentives for running, albeit quite different ones. Iceland was motivated by being able to maintain the US military base in Keflavík through demonstrating an increased commitment to international activities, as well as building relationships which could prove economically beneficial. Austria had direct economic interests in working towards an even clearer status as a *security centre* in Europe, proposing that Vienna assume an even broader role as a UN host country.

---

21   Bundesministerium. 2008b.; Plassnik, 2005b, 2007, 2008.
22   Parliament, 2005.

4   Finland and Luxembourg – Business-as-Usual versus Political Zeal

Both Finland and Luxembourg referred to a wish to take part in multilateralism as a motivation to run for a seat on the Security Council, for the term 2013–14. Having a seat on the UNSC is as an opportunity to develop a multilateral approach further. Multilateralism does not necessarily conflict with national interests,[23] but the ways in which the two countries presented and pursued their campaigns and motivations differed from one another.

We suggest that 'business as usual' captures Finland's motivation in the sense that it was essentially a technical rather than a political candidature. It was considered natural to run for the seat; the candidature was part of the Finnish UN policy, which, in turn, formed an integral part of the Finnish foreign and security policy.[24] The candidature was not questioned politically, not even by the opposition, nor was it much discussed publicly, as opposed to the campaigns in Sweden and Iceland.[25] The candidature was described as given to Finland, in a way, due to the Nordic rotation system of applying for a seat on the Security Council.[26] Running for the seat was self-evident, and the general assumption was that Finland would be elected, as it had been twice before during other contests.[27]

Further, this could be one reason for the significant lack of political commitment in the Finnish campaign.[28] This could not be interpreted as a lack of commitment to the candidature as such, on the contrary: it was considered important,[29] but there were different views of responsibilities attributed during the campaign, i.e. who should be in charge of campaigning, politicians or officials.[30]

Finland's 'business as usual'-approach is integrally related to the rotation system among the five Nordic countries; it was 'Finland's turn' to run for the candidature of the UNSC nonpermanent seat for the period 2013–2014. In this sense, the rotation became a motivation as such. As one interviewee mentioned, there was no reason for Finland to step away from the Nordic rotation.[31] If Luxembourg was campaigning to gain the membership to the UNSC,

---

23   See e.g. Brown 2016.
24   Interview 7.
25   Interviews 2; 4; 7; 12.
26   Interview 4.
27   Interview 2.
28   Interviews 2; 7; 11; 12.
29   Interview 1.
30   Interviews 2; 4; 7; 8.
31   Interview 11.

then Finland was campaigning because it had no reason not to, since it was its turn. Luxembourg had to provide a reason and motivation for running, whereas Finland would have had to provide a reason for not running, due to the Nordic rotation. Perhaps, what Finland was missing was a clearer, or additional, motivation to run.

In addition, the Nordic rotation system entailed a cautious and passive approach during the early stages of the process, as Iceland was still campaigning for its own candidature.[32] The planning of the campaign began in a steering group within the Ministry for Foreign Affairs of Finland, led by Ambassador Marjatta Rasi, before the establishment of the official unit for the campaign in 2008. Finland refrained from campaigning earlier because of Iceland's candidature. This partly explains a difficulty by Finnish interviewees to name the exact date of the candidature decision.[33] However, Finland publicly announced its candidature in 2002 and Luxembourg in 2001.[34]

This could partly explain why there was no such 'passion', zeal or energy in the later stages of the campaign, as were present in Luxembourg's campaign. However, Finland's campaigning efforts did accelerate towards the end of the competition.[35]

Finland and Luxembourg engaged both politicians and officials, as well as other stakeholders, but Luxembourg used politicians very skillfully and actively, thus showing that it was more politically committed to its candidature than Finland. As officials held the primary responsibility for the Finnish campaign, it could be described as a technical project and even bureaucratic in the sense that 'politics' was removed from the campaign, although the UNSC is essentially a *political* body which makes political decisions.[36] In addition, as the Security Council campaigns have gotten more competitive, the contributions of politicians and high-level politicians have become much more necessary.[37]

The interviewees also mentioned that developing multilateralism, as in being able to influence the UNSC agenda, was a motivation for Finland's candidature. Finland fluctuated between being a small state and a middle power, being 'greater than its size', as will be discussed further in Chapter 7: it had middle power ambitions (see also Ekengren and Möller in this chapter). Adopting

---

32   Interviews 12;8.
33   See Chapter 7 in this book.
34   Interview 3.
35   Interview 1.
36   Interviews 2; 11.
37   Interview 11.

a middle power status by stressing peacekeeping, peacebuilding, and mediation was perhaps somewhat unintentional. Even though many of the interviewees stressed that Finland was a small country, with one even saying that Finland has the soul of a small country, it became evident that Finland boasted additional qualities over those of a small state.[38]

It could also be argued that a nonpermanent seat on the Security Council would offer the chance to network, and this was already seen during the campaign process. Finland tried to connect with geographical areas and countries where contacts had not yet been established. However, with politicians more willing to travel, networking could have been done more effectively.[39] The task of networking was done successfully by the Finnish special envoy to the Caribbean, and extremely well by Luxembourg, which had four regional envoys compared to Finland's one.[40] In addition, Luxembourg's Foreign Minister Asselborn was extremely active and personally travelled to all continents except for Australia.[41]

For Luxembourg, the main motivation was to have a seat on the UNSC, for the first time in its history. Luxembourg was a founding member of the UN but had never held a seat on the UNSC. Luxembourg was a defender of the UN values, multilateralism, and equal sovereignty, which were also central to Luxembourg's foreign policy. The candidature showed Luxembourg's willingness to take part in defending international peace and security, and the country was willing to contribute to the functioning and values of the UN. Luxembourg also considered itself competent for the job, despite its small size.[42]

In Luxembourg, the candidature was viewed as a national project and a foreign policy priority.[43] There was little public debate regarding whether to run for the candidature, the government was committed, and the parliament was interested in the campaign and how it was proceeding. The campaign had limited financial resources, so it had to be well planned.[44]

Already in 2001, Luxembourg introduced its candidature, showing a firm intention of winning the seat and bearing the responsibilities it would entail.[45] Luxembourg's foreign policy values coincided with UN values: Luxembourg

---

38   Interview 2.
39   Interview 2.
40   Interviews 1; 2; 4; 7.
41   Interview 10.
42   Interview 6.
43   Interview 12.
44   Interview 10.
45   Interview 6.

had contributions to make on the substance and values of the UN and a desire to further develop the UN. Luxembourg also considered itself a bridge-builder and a voice for other small countries.[46] Luxembourg believed that it was possible for a small, engaged country to accomplish a lot on the UNSC, even in spite of its size, and Luxembourg would thus be capable of influencing the UNSC agenda.[47] The sculpture portraying a knotted gun, a gift previously given to the UN by Luxembourg, perfectly captures this idea of commitment to maintaining both international peace and security.[48] Finland had similar ideas but presented them a bit differently.

The political commitment was strong in Luxembourg, demonstrating a clear intention and motivation to win the seat. The campaign was well planned and dedicated. It showed the kind of determination that the Finnish campaign lacked.[49] Luxembourg also campaigned up to the very last minute, showing its strong will to win the seat, and nothing was taken for granted.[50] Finland did not consider it necessary to campaign after the first voting round.[51]

Luxembourg's campaign was especially personified by Foreign Minister Asselborn who used his personal contacts widely and wisely.[52] In addition to this, Ambassador Lucas, together with Foreign Minister Asselborn, were active and respected by their peers.[53] Networking also played an important role for Luxembourg, as other countries lacked knowledge about Luxembourg. Foreign Minister Asselborn and special envoys travelled extensively, and they were welcomed at the highest political level.[54] As opposed to the Finnish campaign, which took for granted that other countries already knew about its activities and achievements, the Luxembourg campaign took a more active approach.

To summarize, Finland and Luxembourg both believed they could influence the agenda of the UNSC and that they had the necessary confidence (see Ekengren and Möller in this chapter) to win a seat. Winning a seat at the UNSC would bring increasing possibilities to network and gain status e.g. through increased visibility. Both wanted to pursue normative goals and acknowledged that the seat would promote their national and strategic interests. National and global interests were thus not in conflict. The UNSC is an important place,

---

46   Interview 6.
47   Interview 10.
48   Interview 6.
49   Interview 2; 7.
50   Interviews 6; 10.
51   Interview 7.
52   Interviews 7;10.
53   Interview 2.
54   Interview 6.

where even nonpermanent members can have an impact on global politics and gain power.

5   Sweden and the Kingdom of the Netherlands – Comeback in UN-politics versus Playing the Established Role

Both Sweden and the Kingdom of the Netherlands referred to the opportunity to influence as a motivation to running for a seat on the Security Council for the term 2017–18, with emphasis on ambitions to contribute to the multilateral order. However, these ambitions were formulated from different positions: Sweden's decision reflected the Nordic turn-taking order, with a subsequent levelling up of ambitions for UN-politics from a new coalition government, whereas the Netherlands had an established and coherent view of the candidature as an appropriate step for national purposes, as well as with reference to the EU membership. We describe the driving factors behind Sweden's candidature decision through six themes.

1) *Influence*. Sweden's main reason to run for a seat revolved around the chance to hold sway in matters of grave importance for world politics.[55] The Security Council is referred to as the main organ where authoritative decisions could be made, and therefore it was deemed vital for Sweden to take part in the decision-making. The UN is viewed as representing a multilateral, liberal world order, and to be part of the decision making there was especially important for a small, liberal state aiming for a rule-based world order.[56] Sweden, like many of the other states, referenced being a small state when arguing for a campaign on the UNSC. However, Sweden's ambition was to have real influence, like any other state, and to be just as involved in the decision-making, and on equal terms, as more powerful states. This line of reasoning is not typical to small state behavior but reflects a small state with a medium-sized state identity, believingly capable of using a seat on the SC to make a difference.

2) *Status/prestige*. Sweden also argued more in line with expected small state behavior in terms of a seat leading to increased status and prestige.[57] Being elected was seen as a confirmation of a certain status level, and as a sign of a country's relevance. The status increase was believed to be more important for newer states.[58] An increase in status was considered

---

55   Interviews SWE 1; SWE 2; SWE 4; SWE 5; SWE 6.
56   Interviews SWE 1; SWE 4; SWE 9.
57   Interviews SWE 3; SWE 4; SWE 5; SWE 7.
58   Interview SWE 5.

fragile and in need of defence through committed work once elected.[59]
The ambition to construct a more expansive brand for Swedish foreign
policy was in line with this motivation.[60] Confirming a certain status
helped Sweden to gain both material and non-material objectives, as
in how Swedish identity was perceived and how trade agreements were
structured.

3) *Network.* Running a campaign for a seat, as well as having a seat, was
important for Sweden in terms of connecting with many different
actors.[61] It was believed that communication, the backbone of diplomacy, was refined through a campaign and the eventual winning of
a seat; Swedish diplomats and politicians talked to new actors, they
explained Sweden's commitment to the campaign, their UN policy, and
more general foreign policy. In addition, the hope was that if their campaign was successful, then other states would want to talk to Sweden,
since they would be deemed important, and Sweden would learn from
others during the talks.

4) *Improving the competence of state officials.* Several interviewees stressed
that one reason Sweden wanted a seat was to improve the competence
among the diplomatic corps.[62] In doing so, the state capacity would then
increase, which is important for success in other foreign policy areas.
A campaign for the UNSC could therefore be described as a training
camp for diplomats, which could prove useful in other competitive situ-
ations down the line.

5) *Turn-taking.* Another motivation for Sweden's election campaign,
although not a very prominent one, was the norm of Nordic rotation.[63]
Given the Nordic countries' ambition of a rotating candidature among
them, this was a viable, though rather unimportant, argument for the
Swedish candidature. It was important not to disappoint the other
Nordic countries, and the presence of a turn-taking norm certainly reinforced the decision to run a campaign, but ultimately, this was not the
reason Sweden wanted a seat. The hope of being influential was a more
compelling factor for the Swedes to campaign for a seat.

6) *Domestic reasons.* Last, but not the least, there were also domestic reasons for pursuing a seat. Politicians and diplomats acknowledged the

---

59   Interview SWE 7.
60   Interview SWE 11.
61   Interviews SWE 3; SWE 4; SWE 5; SWE 7; SWE 10.
62   Interviews SWE 1; SWE 3; SWE 9; SWE 11.
63   Interviews SWE 1; SWE 2.

gap on this issue between the left and the right in Swedish politics.[64] The Social Democrats wanted to embrace the UN more so than the parties on the right, like the Moderate Party. The Moderate Party wanted to embrace the EU more, and both parties had an interest in emphasizing this difference. This meant that the Social Democrats had a stronger incentive to work in favor of a candidature and future seat for Sweden. If Sweden could get a seat at the UN, then this was seen as positive for the Social Democrats as a party and would help them to further carve out and reinvigorate a distinctive foreign policy profile.

To proceed, we identified four different arguments in favor of the Dutch decision to run for a seat on the UNSC.

1) *Influence.* A seat was associated with a possibility to influence world politics, in a way that was not often the case for states outside the P5. It was believed that a seat on the UNSC could give the Netherlands the chance to promote policies regarding peacekeeping and sanctions, and to be a key player in relation to these issues in global politics.[65] Australia was a referred example of another state that managed to be influential in relation to a specific issue (Malaysian Airlines flight MH17, shot down over Ukraine). In relation to discussing the possibilities of influencing world politics, the acknowledgment of the UN as a firm defender of multilateralism, and a world order where multilateralism was an important value, was another important departure for the Dutch candidature.

2) *Status/prestige.* A seat would bring status to a certain country through increasing visibility.[66] As part of the Security Council, a country becomes more visible when important issues are discussed, and that was seen as important to how the country is viewed and evaluated by others.

3) *Network.* A candidature, as well as a seat, would increase a country's ability to connect with others.[67] The improved contacts you receive would be helpful even after a country has left the SC. The positive returns from having improved networks were believed to offer advantages beyond the issues discussed at the UNSC.

4) *Take responsibility/turn-taking.* Finally, we also find evidence that the Dutch decision to run a campaign for a seat on the UNSC was influenced by a wish to contribute to the present order, and to take responsibility

---

64   Interviews SWE 1; SWE 8.
65   Interviews NL 14; NL 15; NL 18.
66   Interviews NL 15; NL 16.
67   Interviews NL 14; NL 15; NL 16.

regarding difficult and important issues.[68] In a way, this argument is about sharing the responsibility with others and doing your part in the global community.

To summarize, both countries had many shared reasons for their respective candidatures. Both countries believed a seat would increase their influence and their commitments to a multilateral order. They believed that despite their size, they could still make a difference by taking part in the decision-making at the UNSC. Both states also believed a seat would increase their status, mainly through increased visibility, and that they could increase their communication and contact with others, as well as taking on the additional responsibility that would come along with a seat. Both the Swedish and the Dutch bids can therefore be viewed as ways to maintain their places in the global community and as ways of defending their roles as committed members of the UN.

The Swedish candidature would also enhance the diplomatic skills among the Swedish diplomatic corps. This argument was not brought up with the Dutch decision makers. On the contrary, the long campaigning was described as something that drained the different agencies of competent personnel.[69] Moreover, the Swedish candidature had a more pronounced domestic dimension than the Dutch one. A Swedish seat on the UNSC would more directly benefit the Social Democrats, and their desire to again emphasize the role of the UN in Swedish foreign policy.

6   Conclusions

The closer examinations of candidature decisions by six members of the WEOG, of which three belong to the subgroup of Nordic states, have provided further details on the power enhancing benefits of an elected seat as well as revealed additional reasons for why states embark on this political and diplomatic journey. In the context of how they clustered in the comparative analysis in the previous chapter, there are also interesting similarities between members of the Nordic group.

It is important to note that the expected benefits – influence, network, and status, occur frequently among the stated reasons for these candidatures. Despite the institutional obstacles that elected members face on the Security Council, a candidature may well rest on the expectations to influence

---

68   Interview NL 16; NL17; NL18.
69   Interview NL 15.

decision-making. The frequent elaboration on influence concerns possible contributions to maintaining and improving the multilateral order. Notably, none of the cases contains expectations of issue-specific and/or interest-based influence beyond the fact that a firmer multilateral order is advantageous to the security of small and medium-sized states. The degree to which a specific national interest is present in the ambition to exercise influence, there are different national profiles related to the multilateral order. For example, Austria and the Netherlands have the highest ambitions to contribute to international law. Overall, however, we identify mainly value-laden and normative goals among these states in their wishes to exercise influence as elected members. The idea that their commitment to a multilateral order also constitutes a responsibility to contribute by making themselves available for an elected term is another distinct feature. The results confirm status as particularly important for small states. The two smallest states in our study, Iceland, and Luxemburg, both viewed the candidature for an elected seat as an opportunity to display their capabilities and ambitions as (small) sovereign states (rather than a micro-state). Thus, an elected term in the Security Council would function as status recognition of the statehood of these smaller states. Among the other cases, there was also a widespread agreement that prestige was at stake in the competition for an elected seat. The utility of a candidature and a term in the Council for building new and improving current relationship is another distinct feature among cases. In terms of additional reasons, we suggest that the ambitions regarding the multilateral order, and the sense of obligation to make regular contributions as complementary as to why and how states want to exercise influence through a term in the Security Council. The Swedish reference to the candidature and term in the Council as an opportunity to competence building of the foreign services is an additional and instrumental purpose. We suggest that this reflects the views of a small state with high international ambitions, as one out of several possible ways to compensate for size-related disadvantages in world politics.

Finally, there are some shared features among the Nordic states. They share the consideration of the Nordic turn-taking order, but in different ways. For Iceland, it is a push-factor for launching a candidature, as the time is considered right. For Finland, and for Sweden, it contributes to viewing the candidature as an established part of foreign policy. In the Finnish case, this seems to have led to an overconfidence of the chances of electoral success also. In the Swedish case, the shift of government generates additional arguments for the relevance of a candidature. All three states consider the candidature as relevant to network and to gain status. Finland and Sweden share a positive view on their respective candidatures as an opportunity to exercise influence.

Notably, they share the greater confidence with the two states in the study who alter between the small state and middle power identity, Austria, and the Netherlands.

Bibliography

Árnason, Á. P. Speech 1 in Alþingi, 8 November, 2007a. *Utanríkismál, munnleg skýrsla utanríkisráðherra.* Retrieved from https://www.althingi.is/altext/raeda/135/rad2007 1108T123433.html.

Árnason, Á. P. Speech in Alþingi, 8 November, 2007b. *Utanríkismál, munnleg skýrsla utanríkisráðherra.* Retrieved from https://www.althingi.is/altext/raeda/135/rad2007 1108T154555.html.

Ásgrímsson, H. Speech in Alþingi, 5 November, 1998. *Skýrsla utanríkisráðherra um utanríkismál.* Retrieved from https://www.althingi.is/altext/123/11/r05103406.sgml.

Ásgrímsson, H. Speech in Alþingi, 29 March, 2001. *Skýrsla utanríkisráðherra um utanríkismál.* Retrieved from https://www.althingi.is/altext/126/03/r29105342.sgml.

Ásgrímsson, H. Speech in Alþingi, 13 November, 2003a. *Skýrsla utanríkisráðherra um utanríkismál.* Retrieved from http://www.althingi.is/altext/130/11/r13103236.sgml.

Ásgrímsson, H. Speech in Alþingi, 27 February, 2003b. *Skýrsla utanríkisráðherra um utanríkismál.* Retrieved from https://www.althingi.is/altext/128/02/r27105147.sgml.

Bailes, A. and Thorhallsson, B. Iceland and the European Security and Defence Policy. In Bailes, A., Herolf G., and Sundelius B., eds. *The Nordic Countries and the European Security and Defence Policy.* (Oxford: Oxford University Press, 2006).

Benediktsson, B. Speech in Alþingi, 8 April, 2008. *Utanríkis- og alþjóðamál, skýrsla.* Retrieved from https://www.althingi.is/altext/135/04/r08144314.sgml.

Blöndal, H. Speech in Alþingi, 16 November, 2006. *Utanríkismál, munnleg skýrsla utanríkisráðherra.* Retrieved from https://www.althingi.is/altext/133/11/r16113756.sgml.

Brown, Chris. *International Society, Global Polity. An Introduction to International Political Theory.* (London: Sage, 2016).

Bundesministerium. Plassnik: 'Kandidatur für UNO-Sicherheitsrat als Dienstleistung an der Weltorganisation'. 2008a, 26 September 2008. Retrieved from https://www .bmeia.gv.at/das-ministerium/presse/aussendungen/2008/plassnik-kandida tur-fuer-uno-sicherheitsrat-als-dienstleistung-an-der-weltorganisation/.

Bundesministerium. 2008b. *Austria and the United Nations, Official UNSC campaign brochure.* Federal Ministry for European and International Affairs.

Bundesministerium. Erklärung von Ursula Plassnik vor der 61. Tagung der Generalversammlung der Vereinten Nationen. 21 September, 2006. Retrieved from https://www.bmeia.gv.at/das-ministerium/presse/reden-und-interviews/2006 /erklaerung-von-ursula-plassnik-vor-der-61-tagung-der-generalversammlung-der -vereinten-nationen/.

Die Presse. Interview von Staatssekretär Dr. Hans WINKLER in der Tageszeitung 'Die Presse' vom 7. März 2007, 2007a. Retrieved from https://www.bmeia.gv.at/das-mini sterium/presse/reden-und-interviews/2007/interview-von-staatssekretaer-dr-hans -winkler-in-der-tageszeitung-die-presse-vom-7-maerz-2007/.

Ferrero-Waldner, B. Statement at UN General Assembly's 57th session, 7th plenary meeting. A/57/PV.7, 2002. Retrieved from https://documents-dds-ny.un.org/doc /UNDOC/GEN/N02/590/07/PDF/N0259007.pdf?OpenElement.

Ferrero-Waldner, B. Statement at UN General Assembly's 58th session, 12th plenary meeting. A/58/PV.12, 2003. Retrieved from https://documents-dds-ny.un.org/doc /UNDOC/GEN/N03/531/39/PDF/N0353139.pdf?OpenElement.

Fischer, H. Statement at UN General Assembly's General Assembly 60th session. A/ 60/PV.6, 2005. Retrieved from https://documents-dds-ny.un.org/doc/UNDOC/GEN /N05/511/78/PDF/N0551178.pdf?OpenElement.

Fréttablaðið. *Umsókn um aðild að Öryggisráði Sameinuðu þjóðanna ákveðin fyrir upphaf þings*. 6 September 2005a. Retrieved from https://timarit.is/page/3860409#page/no /mode/ 2up.

Fréttablaðið. Aðild að ráðinu ekki einkamál Íslendinga. 15 September 2005b. Retrieved from https://timarit.is/page/3861106#page/no/mode/2up .

Gestsson, S. Speech in Alþingi, 5 November, 1998. *Skýrsla utanríkisráðherra um utan- ríkismál.* Retrieved from https://www.althingi.is/altext/123/11/r05115036.sgml.

Gísladóttir, I. S. Speech in Alþingi, 8 November, 2007. *Utanríkismál, munnleg skýrsla utanríkisráðherra.* Retrieved from https://www.althingi.is/altext/135/11/r08103 150.sgml.

Haarde, G. H. *Staða Íslands í samfélagi þjóðanna.* 2007. Retrieved from http://www.for saetisraduneyti.is/radherra/raedurGHH/nr/2709.

Machreich, W.'Ich tippe auf Österreich und Türkei!'. Die Furche, nr. 38/08, 18 September, 2008a. Retrieved from https://www.genios.de/document?id=FURC__0700850820 670720690952008+09181831150004&src=hitlist&offset=0.

Machreich, W. Sympathie in Stimmen verwandeln. Die Furche, nr. 38/08, 18 September, 2008b. Retrieved from https://www.genios.de/document?id=FURC__0700850820 670720690952008+09181831150002&src=hitlist&offset=0.

News. Zum bereits dritten Mal: Österreich bewirbt sich um UN-Sicherheitsrats-Sitz für 2009/10. 9 of August, 2005. Retrieved from https://www.news.at.

Plassnik, U. Statement at UN General Assembly's 60th Session, 2005b. Retrieved from http://www.un.org/webcast/ga/60/statements/aus050920eng.pdf.

Plassnik, U. Statement at the General Assembly's 61st Session, 2006. A/61/PV.15. Retrieved from https://documents-dds-ny.un.org/doc/UNDOC/GEN/N06/530/05 /PDF/N0653005.pdf?OpenElement.

Plassnik, U. Statement at UN General Assembly's 62nd Session, 2007. A/62/PV.11. Retrieved from https://documents-dds-ny.un.org/doc/UNDOC/GEN/N07/521/21/PDF/N0752121.pdf?OpenElement.

Plassnik, U. Statement at UN General Assembly's 63rd Session, 2008. A/63/PV.11. Retrieved from https://documents-dds-ny.un.org/doc/UNDOC/GEN/N08/522/72/PDF/N0852272.pdf?OpenElement.

Parliament. *Reform der Vereinten Nationen: Beantwortung der mündlichen Anfrage durch Bundesministerin Dr. Ursula Plassnik.* 25 May 2005. Retrieved from https://www.parlament.gv.at/PAKT/VHG/BR/M-BR/M-BR_01427/index.shtml.

Pétursdóttir, S. Speech in Alþingi, 13 November, 2003. *Skýrsla utanríkisráðherra um utanríkismál.* Retrieved from https://www.althingi.is/altext/130/11/r13113922.sgml.

Sigfússon, S. J. Speech in Alþingi, 29 March, 2001. *Skýrsla utanríkisráðherra um utanríkismál.* Retrieved from https://www.althingi.is/altext/126/03/r29144426.sgml.

Sverrisdóttir, V. Speech in Alþingi, 16 November, 2006. *Utanríkismál, munnleg skýrsla utanríkisráðherra.* Retrieved from https://www.althingi.is/altext/133/11/r16103457.sgml.

Sveinbjarnardóttir, Þ. Speech in Alþingi, 16 November, 2006. *Utanríkismál, munnleg skýrsla utanríkisráðherra.* Retrieved from https://www.althingi.is/altext/133/11/r16163947.sgml.

Thorhallsson, B. 'Can Small States Choose Their Own Size? The Case of a Nordic State – Iceland'. In *The Diplomacies of Small States: Between Vulnerability and Resilience,* eds. Andrew F. Cooper and Timothy M. Shaw. (New York: Palgrave MacMillian 2009).

Þórðardóttir, S. A. Speech in Alþingi, 27 February, 2003. *Skýrsla utanríkisráðherra um utanríkismál.* Retrieved from https://www.althingi.is/altext/128/02/r27120644.sgml.

Interviews
Interviews with Finnish Diplomats or Diplomats from Luxembourg

Interview 1 2018, 9 March, Interviewer Anni Tervo.
Interview 2 2018, 15 March, Interviewer Anni Tervo.
Interview 3 2018, 6 April, Interviewer Anni Tervo.
Interview 4 2018, 4 April, Interviewer Anni Tervo.
Interview 5 2018, 5 April, Interviewer Anni Tervo.
Interview 6 2018, 6 April, Interviewer Anni Tervo.
Interview 7 2018, 26 March, Interviewer Anni Tervo.
Interview 8 2018, 19 April, Interviewer Anni Tervo.
Interview 9 2018, 3 May, Interviewer Anni Tervo.
Interview 10 2018, 21 May, Interviewer Anni Tervo.
Interview 11 2018, 27 June, Interviewer Anni Tervo.
Interview 12 2018, 29 June, Interviewer Anni Tervo.

Interviews 1–13 with Swedish Diplomats

SWE Interview 1 2017, 28 November, Interviewer Ann-Marie Ekengren.

SWE Interview 2 2017, 5 December, Interviewer Ann-Marie Ekengren.

SWE Interview 3 2017, 5 December, Interviewer Ann-Marie Ekengren.

SWE Interview 4 2017, 15 December, Interviewer Ulrika Möller.

SWE Interview 5 2018, 22 January, Interviewer Ann-Marie Ekengren.

SWE Interview 6 2018, 5 February, Interviewer Ann-Marie Ekengren.

SWE Interview 7 2018, 6 February, Interviewer Ann-Marie Ekengren.

SWE Interview 8 2018, 6 February, Interviewer Ann-Marie Ekengren.

SWE Interview 9 2018, 26 February, Interviewer Ann-Marie Ekengren.

SWE Interview 10 2018, 27 March, Interviewer Ann-Marie Ekengren.

SWE Interview 11 2018, 27 March, Interviewer Ann-Marie Ekengren.

SWE Interview 12 2018, 6 April, Interviewer Ulrika Möller.

SWE Interview 13 2019, 3 June, Interviewer Ulrika Möller.

Interviews 14–18 with Dutch Diplomats

NL Interview 14 2018, 2 May, Interviewer Ulrika Möller.

NL Interview 15 2018, 19 December, Interviewer Ulrika Möller.

NL Interview 16 2019, 19 March, Interviewer Ulrika Möller.

NL Interview 17 2019, 2 April, Interviewer Ulrika Möller.

NL Interview 18 2019, 3 June, Interviewer Ulrika Möller.

Interviews A-F with Icelandic and Austrian Diplomats

Interview public official A 2018, 14 February, Interviewer J. S. Elínardóttir.

Interview public official B 2018, 15 February, Interviewer J. S. Elínardóttir.

Interview public official C 2018, 19 February, Interviewer J. S. Elínardóttir.

Interview public official D 2018, 19 February, Interviewer J. S. Elínardóttir.

Interview public official E 2018, 19 June, Interviewer A. M. Eggertsdóttir.

Interview public official F 2018, 22 June, Interviewer A. M. Eggertsdóttir.

Interview G Gísladóttir, I. S. 2018, 21 February, Interviewer J. S. Elínardóttir.

Interview H Haarde, G. H. 2018, 20 February, Interviewer J. S. Elínardóttir.

Interview Plassnik, U. 2018, 17 September, Interviewer A. M. Eggertsdóttir.

CHAPTER 6

Competing Small Powers: Austria versus Iceland on the UNSC

Baldur Thorhallsson, Jóna Sólveig Elínardóttir and Anna M. Eggertsdóttir

1 Introduction

In the 2008 election for nonpermanent seats on the UNSC, three candidates competed for the two WEOG seats for the term 2009–10: Iceland, Austria, and Turkey (or Türkiye). Up to 1998 Iceland had never, in its 52 years of UN membership, participated in the Nordic UNSC rotation. Austria however, had already served twice on the UNSC, first during 1973–1974 and then again in 1991–1992. Nevertheless, the elections in 2008 were the first time that Austria had to fight for a seat. Austria declared the intent to seek a seat in 1999 and Turkey in 2003.

This chapter offers a comparative analysis on the similarities and differences between Iceland's and Austria's campaigns. With departure in the framework presented in Chapter 2, we focus specifically on how the two campaigns were carried out, and why Austria was more successful than Iceland in its undertaking. Accordingly, we investigate the extent to which these two states demonstrated contributions, claimed competence, and emphasized ideational commitment during the campaign period. Which of these three logics were most important to them and how were they combined differently in the campaigns? Our comparison points especially at differences between the two campaigns as regards to features associated with claiming competence and proving ideational commitment. Iceland's lack of political leadership, and its small foreign service, proved to be impediments against Austria's united political elite and larger foreign service with greater resources. Iceland running its campaign on a traditional ideational Nordic ticket, focusing mainly on soft security issues, was also somewhat of a disadvantage since Austrian campaign had all that, along with hard security and defence matters, to boot.

While both Iceland and Austria can be defined as small states, especially compared with their larger European neighbouring states, such as Germany and the United Kingdom, there are important differences between the two states. For example, there is a considerable difference in the states' assets 'in possession', according to their ability to demonstrate contributions. Iceland

© BALDUR THORHALLSSON ET AL., 2024 | DOI:10.1163/9789004687110_007

sought status and was attempting to become relevant in the international system. In contrast, Austria, a former empire, was attempting to maintain its relevance and the influence it had secured in the post-war period. Although Iceland's foreign service had been growing for some years before the decision to run was made, its size and financial resources were nevertheless far inferior to the Austrian foreign service, its level of expertise much more limited, and the reach of its diplomatic corps more restricted. Moreover, the historical background and developments, affected by their geographic realities, need to be factored in. Iceland's history is one of a somewhat poor and isolated dependency which did not gain sovereignty from Denmark until 1918, whereas Austria is a former empire in the heart of Europe. These facts marked the states' campaign messages and their ability to advance their campaign arguments in a credible and convincing way.

This chapter is structured in the following manner: First, we will outline the most important characteristics of the campaign processes in terms of key-actors, organization, and activities. Second, an analysis of the core messages of the two different campaigns will be conducted. Third, we will examine the domestic debates surrounding the campaign, both in the media and national parliaments of the two states. Finally, building on our three different logics, an estimation of both successes and failures of the respective campaigns will be offered before the concluding remarks.

This chapter builds on extensive research into reports from the Icelandic and Austrian ministries for foreign affairs, published, unpublished, and confidential; promotional materials from the campaigns; newspaper and other media coverage in both countries; Icelandic foreign affairs' literature; reports from the New York-based think tank *Security Council Report*; speeches by politicians in the Austrian and Icelandic national parliaments and the UN General Assembly, and finally, on nine in-depth interviews with former ministers for foreign affairs and public officials in both countries.

2   Important Characteristics of the Campaign Processes: Key Actors, Organization, and Activities

Four characteristics stand out when it comes to the Icelandic campaign processes and can serve as evidence as to how the country managed to demonstrate contributions, and to some degree failed to claim competence according to the theoretical framework we laid out in Chapter 2.

First, the Icelandic campaign was solely organized and driven by Icelandic public officials. Political involvement in the strategic campaign planning, in of the choosing of key messages, and in the running of the campaign was very limited. This is mirrored by the fact that no politician, other than the Minister for Foreign Affairs (there were five different ministers during the campaign period), had any formal engagement with the campaign. The President of Iceland at the time, Ólafur Ragnar Grímsson, was proactive in the last years, but he had no formal affiliation with the campaign itself. This resulted in weak political ownership of the campaign which, despite cross-party support in the beginning, would render the campaign vulnerable to domestic criticism in 2004–2005. The criticism was primarily related to financial costs, which arose after Turkey announced its candidature in 2003, while Iceland – like Austria – had been hoping for a much cheaper, clean slate election. With Turkey's candidature it was clear that all candidates would have to invest in costlier campaigns if they hoped to win a seat. This led to a stir among the Icelandic public and political debate with the Minister for Foreign Affairs, Davíð Oddsson, contemplating the withdrawal of Iceland's candidature.[1]

Second, although the decision to run was made in 1998 and we can see some campaign preparations, the actual campaign was not launched with any real dynamism until 2006–2007, when Ingibjörg Sólrún Gísladóttir took office as Foreign Minister. With her leadership it was considered important to have a more targeted strategy. Iceland would focus specifically on working closely with its Nordic partners and decided to target the small state votes in the UN, in particular the small states in the UN sub-group, the Forum for Small States and the Small Island Developing States (SIDS). The campaign highlighted Iceland's main areas of expertise, such as the sustainable use of natural resources and gender equality, as well as Iceland's recent history, referring to Iceland's fast development from being one of the world's poorest countries to being one of the most prosperous. Thus, small island developing states in the Pacific and Caribbean, and challenges they face due to global warming, became a focus area, which also included financial support through a special development fund. Moreover, the 53 African states in the UN were targeted, where Iceland could contribute, thanks to its experience as a former, poor dependency.[2] Although most interviewees agreed that Iceland's rising ODA levels were important for the campaign, other perspectives were also presented: 'Those who are voting are not intellectually motivated. The island states and poor states just want money', said one Icelandic public official.[3] In fact, there were examples of developing states asking Icelandic representatives

---

1 Hauksson, J. 2005; Oddsson, D. 2005a; Oddsson, D. 2005b.
2 Utanríkisráðuneytið 2009a.
3 Public official C. 2018; Public official D. 2018.

whether Iceland would be able to match the contributions of Iceland's competitors. Asked whether Iceland's low level of ODA had negative effects on the campaign, one public official said:

> Yes, states in our focus groups asked questions. It could be that they weren't convinced that we could deliver what we said we would. For instance, Turkey gave two modern fire-trucks to a certain state, and they asked us, "What are you going to do?" One Permanent Representative for a small state in the Mediterranean said that Austria had donated three fishing boats, "Could you deliver the same?" We said that we could not, we were only 300 thousand, but that we would speak up for their cause and emphasized that we had a similar way of thinking and common interests.[4]

Third, the administration was able to build serious momentum for the Icelandic campaign, threatening the position of both Turkey and Austria. In fact, shortly before the elections, the think tank *Security Council Report* described the competition between the states as being 'hot' and predicted that it marked a return to contested elections in the WEOG.[5] The Icelandic campaign team was able to engage and motivate important political figures outside of the Icelandic government to fight for Iceland's bid, and to engage their Nordic partners to fight for Iceland's cause, organizing activities in New York, both formal and informal, and both inside and outside the UN institutions. According to Icelandic public officials, their mapping of support, based on declarations of backing and vote exchange agreements, was in Iceland's favour in the months before the financial crisis hit Iceland.

Fourth, Iceland's lack of experience and expertise in the UNSC's main fields of work, combined with the fact that the country had never held a seat on the council before, would work to its disadvantage both domestically as well as internationally. Domestically, the fact that Iceland was competing against strong, much larger candidates who both had extensive diplomatic relations and experience in the UNSC's fields of work, affected the level of confidence with which Icelandic political leaders would tackle domestic disputes and doubts over the issue. This was made even more difficult to tackle by the fact that the campaign had thus far been organized and run solely by public officials, making the political elite vulnerable and ill-equipped to argue for the

---

4   Public official D. 2018.
5   Security Council Report 2008.

continuation of the campaign. Internationally, the lack of experience and expertise was also a challenge. Iceland was a new, unknown player with little more than its Nordic identity and good intentions. This would prove insufficient when Iceland became the first state to be hit by the 2008 international financial crisis and nearly its entire financial sector and economy collapsed overnight, on 6 October 2008, just two weeks before the UNSC elections. On 8 October, the British government decided to use its anti-terrorism legislation to freeze the assets of Icelandic banks operating in Britain and based on EU/EEA rules, demanded full compensations for its citizens who had lost their investments in banks' savings schemes. This led to the infamous so-called 'Icesave dispute' between Britain and the Netherlands, on the one hand, and Iceland, on the other. Moreover, Britain engaged in diplomatic attacks on Iceland's bid for the UNSC as a means of pressuring the Icelandic government to comply. As a result, the Icelandic Permanent Representative in New York had to make rounds to fight propaganda spread by his British counterpart who was making rounds to Commonwealth-, island -, and African states, as well as the EU member states at the UN, saying that Iceland was unreliable and that states should not vote for a country that broke the rules and regulations.[6]

The targeted approach by British diplomats hit the Icelandic campaign especially hard, since Iceland had invested heavily in these countries during the campaign, as a former dependency and a small state with a lot to offer in terms of expertise in the sustainable use of natural resources, like fisheries, geothermal energy, and environmental protection. Iceland had also worked hard at establishing itself as the candidate for small states' interests, promising to initiate monthly 'de-marginalization briefings' for the Small Island Developing States' (SIDS) partners during the two year term.[7] Subsequently, the Nordic states began to distance themselves from Iceland within the UN and later denied the country loans within the IMF framework to counter the effects of the economic crisis until the Icesave dispute was resolved.[8] In addition, at the height of the economic crash, the Icelandic government publicly hinted that it was considering a loan from the Russian government.[9] Icelandic diplomats in New York later claimed that these reports caused significant damage to the campaign, creating anxiety among NATO allies and post-Soviet states.[10] Iceland did not have the diplomatic resources to fight back.

---

6   Haarde, G. H. 2018; Public official B. 2018; Public official D. 2018; Utanríkisráðuneytið 2009a.
7   Utanríkisráðuneytið 2009b.
8   Public official B. 2018; Strauss-Kahn, D. 2009.
9   US Embassy in Iceland 2008.
10   Utanríkisráðuneytið 2009b.

Like Iceland, Austria's campaign was not launched until after Turkey announced its intention to run in 2003. The Austrian campaign did not become part of the government agenda until 2005, even though it had already been decided in 1998 and announced in February 1999. According to an Austrian public official, 'the first part of the campaign is to collect support in the traditional manner with reciprocal agreements and classic diplomatic relations. But the general feeling was that it did not make sense to do big things 10 years in advance, because of changes in government and ambassadors.'[11] Another official agreed with this, saying: 'We want to reach the people that are responsible for the decisions and therefore we did not start sooner.'[12] This is a different view to the one presented by Icelandic high-level officials who were mostly of the opinion that it would have been better to start much earlier.

In contrast to the Icelandic campaign, the Austrian one demonstrated that strong domestic political involvement and the competence of high-level individuals do play an important part in enhancing the success of a campaign when used strategically. From the moment it was launched in 2005, the Austrian candidature had strong political engagement and there was little to no domestic opposition to the candidature, neither among politicians nor among the media. Federal Chancellor Wolfgang Schüssel said that all efforts would be made to achieve this particular goal and Peter Jankowitsch (ÖVP), former Minister of Foreign Affairs who had served during Austria's first term on the UNSC and was well-respected, and Herbert Scheibner, Chairman of the FPÖ parliamentary group and National Council (the lower house of the Austrian parliament) member, were named as special emissaries of the candidature, assigned with lobbying for Austria's seat on the UNSC.[13] Foreign Minister Ursula Plassnik also played an important role, appearing to some extent as a spokesperson or face of the candidature, as she held office throughout the entire campaign. Austrian authorities also highlighted the country's good personal and working relationship with public UN personnel, such as former Secretary-General Kofi Annan and the then current Secretary-General Ban Ki Moon.[14]

In terms of demonstrating contributions, the Austrian candidature proved highly successful in presenting itself as the 'good' UN member by consistently showing how it had led by example in all its UN-related work, within the UN and the EU, but also independently. This was done by giving concrete examples of Austrian contributions to multilateralism, peacekeeping missions, rising levels

---

11   Public official F. 2018.
12   Public official E. 2018.
13   News 2005.
14   Bundesministerium 2007a; Bundesministerium 2008c.

of ODA, and special, Austria-led initiatives, often of a regional nature. In fact, although the Austrian foreign service used its diplomatic presence around the world, the emphasis was more pronounced in the regions where Austria's presence was weaker: '[Y]ou have to focus on places where your diplomatic relations are thinner, in our case we had to focus on Africa, it's impossible to win without support from Africa. Also the Caribbean states and the Pacific islands,' said one public official.[15] To this end, a special Africa division was established within the Ministry of Foreign Affairs,[16] a Memorandum of Understanding on Caricom-Austrian Cooperation on climate change was signed,[17] and meetings were held with numerous UN state groups,[18] thereby carrying out Foreign Minister Plassnik's wishes to make the advantages of Austria's membership on the UNSC clear from every regional context.[19]

Moreover, Austrian representatives began the campaign by catering specifically to small states, either by identifying Austria as a small state or grouping small- and medium-sized states together during the campaign.[20] However, towards the end of the campaign Austria was represented as a medium-sized state in order to appeal to other medium-sized states. In the beginning, we find direct references to Austria as a small state, such as when State Secretary Winkler says that 'as a small state, we have an interest in the functioning of the multilateral system, we should also be represented in the most important body of the collective security system.'[21] During a debate in the Austrian Parliament, Plassnik says that 'the appropriate accessibility of small and medium-sized states to the Security Council is important to us', thus grouping small and medium states together.[22] Again, shortly before the elections, Plassnik is quoted as saying that Austria is seen by many as a 'reliable representative of the medium-sized UN members', but that it is also small enough to have sympathy within the category of countries that have fewer than 10 million inhabitants.[23] After the elections, Plassnik confirms that she regards Austria as

---

15   Public official F. 2018.
16   Turkey had apparently also set their eyes on Africa votes and had, as part of their candidature campaign, presented plans of increasing development aid in Africa and opening 15 new embassies in the continent by the end of 2009.
17   Bundesministerium 2008g. Caribbean Community (CARICOM) consists of 15 Caribbean states, the majority of which is also a member of the Alliance of Small Island States (AOSIS).
18   Bundesministerium 2008e.
19   DerStandard.at. 2008a.
20   Bundesministerium 2008d; Bundesministerium 2008e; Machreich, W. 2008a.
21   Die Presse. 2007a.
22   Plassnik, U. 2005a.
23   Bundesministerium 2008f.

a medium-sized state when she says: 'If we do not want to leave the shaping of the world to the big, middle states like Austria must be prepared to take on concrete responsibility.'[24] Ultimately, seeking membership to the most important institution of the UN was an essential way for Austria to take responsibility for the maintenance of peace and security. It was a way to prove that states like Austria could have an impact on the work of the Security Council, no matter their size.[25]

Although Austria had a firm policy in place to not to engage in what was termed 'vote purchasing',[26] one public official claimed that the Austrian authorities:

> developed a system of retreats, where we invited people to Austria, to Alpbach. We did not directly request people's votes but tried to focus on mutual interests. So the focus was not on the campaigning, we did not even mention that we were campaigning, but tried instead to highlight our profile, amongst others our peacekeeping work and the rule of law.[27]

Moreover, Austrian authorities made a tactical decision to create reciprocity agreements for UN votes, promising their support to states in other UN elections in exchange for their UNSC vote.[28] They did not, however, attempt to secure support for a possible second or third round of votes.[29] This can be interpreted as a sign of confidence.

Austria and Iceland have several similarities in their approaches. Both states were able to establish relationships, strengthen their networks, and secure support from other states by demonstrating their contributions to the UN. Both engaged in vote exchange, promised support for initiatives, and made efforts to appeal to states through means that could be classified as 'vote purchasing,' as both tried to financially support special initiatives, substantially increase development aid donations and participation in peacekeeping missions. Moreover, as was mentioned above, Austria was able to invite delegations from target countries to special retreats in Austria. Iceland's diplomatic and financial resources were much more limited than its competitors', which meant that

24   Bundesministerium 2008b.
25   Plassnik, U. 2018.
26   Machreich, W. 2008b.
27   Public official F. 2018.
28   Machreich, W. 2008a.
29   Public official F. 2018.

Austria could act more autonomously and did not require diplomatic support from neighbouring states.

Both states engaged in regional campaigning efforts, focusing specifically on Africa and small (island) and developing states. In their attempt to cater to diverse groups of states, both Iceland and Austria used size-related arguments, thereby using their size to their advantage, although Iceland's purview was limited to small states whereas Austria could credibly cater to small and medium-sized states. On top of that, Austria's reach was much broader due to its relatively strong foreign service and diplomatic missions. In addition, Austria, with its positive UN track record, could build its campaign on what it had already done and achieved, thereby further demonstrating its contributions to the UN, whereas Iceland was a new, unknown player with little more than its good intentions and Nordic identity.

As for being able to claim competence, the two states differ somewhat. Although this was the first time Austria had to campaign for a seat, it had already served twice on the UNCS, the candidature enjoyed an enlightened domestic consensus making domestic campaigning unnecessary, unlike Iceland's campaign with its very limited political involvement and volatile domestic support. On a positive note, Iceland was able to make up for this, to some extent, with its uncontroversial role in the UN and engagement of important Nordic political and diplomatic figures known for their good reputation and competent diplomacy. The Icelandic campaign team's good run towards the end was, however, not enough when the financial crisis and the Ice-save dispute hit Iceland, causing a great loss of international credibility.

3   Messages of the Campaigns

In Iceland, the fine tuning of the campaign messages seems to have been developing over some time, although almost all the main points had already been formed by 2003. Iceland's core campaign message and thereby its way of providing ideational commitment to the UNSC candidature, was that as a first-time candidate and as a small state with an identity rooted in the history of a former dependency which now boasted a flourishing economy through responsible use of its natural resources and promotion of gender equality, could and should have an elected seat at the UNSC table.[30]

---

30   Utanríkisráðuneytið 2009b; Gísladóttir, I. S. 2018; Public official A. 2018; Public official C. 2018; Public official D. 2018.

Iceland further established its commitment to UN values by underscoring its ability to understand the challenges that developing countries and former colonies faced by focusing on the country's recent transition from foreign rule and poverty to independence and prosperity. In its efforts to reach out to the developing and island states, Iceland's expertise in marine affairs and its use of clean, renewable energy was highlighted as proof of its commitment to sustainable development as well as its sustainable use of natural resources. This would also be augmented by development aid contributions to the Small Island Fund, intended for states belonging to the Small Island Developing States (SIDS) grouping.[31]

Highlighting the country's small state status was a key element, as most UN members are small states and therefore face many similar challenges. This, and the fact that Iceland was a Nordic country – not an EU member state – and the fact that Iceland does not have an army, also enabled Iceland to be perceived as a more neutral state. Also, Iceland promoted the principle of gender equality, women's empowerment and their participation in conflict resolution and peacebuilding as key pillars in its campaign.

More 'traditional' themes were also present in Iceland's campaign. These included emphasizing the state's strong and long-standing UN commitment, as well as its contributions to peacekeeping missions and reconstruction in war-torn areas. Respect for basic human rights, the promotion of democracy, the fight against poverty, respect for international law, the promotion of fundamental human rights and democracy, as well as Iceland's firm support for the reorganization of the UNSC, were all themes that were presented alongside the country's focus on the importance of counterterrorism, trade liberalization, disarmament, and the non-proliferation of WMDs. In these last two focus areas, however, Austria had a clear advantage in terms of its abilities for initiatives, as well as expertise.

In Austria, four key campaign themes emerged as evidence of the country's ideational commitment towards the UN. First, the official motto and main emphasis for Austria's candidature was the strengthening of a rules-based international system and the rule of law,[32] with the latter being described by the Foreign Minister as the backbone of Austria's candidature.[33] The campaign underscored the country's vision of the importance of the UN's continued role in international affairs when it came to securing peace and promoting

---

31   Utanríkisráðuneytið 2009b; Gísladóttir, I. S 2018; Haarde, G. H. 2018; Public official B. 2018; Public official D. 2018; Iceland Review 2008.
32   Parlament 2007b.
33   Plassnik, U. 2006.

multilateral cooperation. Accordingly, Austria's long tradition of international cooperation was highlighted, especially its effective multilateralism in the practice of and engagement with the rule of law.

Secondly, Austria's previous contributions to and active engagement in shaping the UN's work became one of the focal points of its campaign, focusing specifically on how Austria had led by example in many policy fields within the UN. A particular focus was placed on disarmament and non-proliferation, environmental and energy affairs, on combating terrorism, and on how Austria had and would continue to lead by example in these areas. The country's close relationships with important UN figures, such as former Secretary-General Kofi Annan and the then current Secretary-General Ban Ki Moon, were emphasized in order to indicate that the country was at the heart of the UN. For instance, Austria's official campaign brochure included an address from Kofi Annan on the subject of the close relationship between the UN and Austria, praising Austria's contributions to the UN.[34] Moreover, the close relationship between Austria and Ban Ki Moon was underscored in an address given by the Minister for Foreign Affairs on the occasion of Moon's formal visit in February 2007.[35] This formal visit would be highly criticized by the Icelandic campaign team, who said that it demonstrated inappropriately favorable treatment toward Austria by the UN Secretary-General.[36]

Thirdly, Vienna, one of the EU's few headquarters, was portrayed as 'a fully-fledged centre of competence for issues related to safety and security' focusing especially on nuclear safety, disarmament, combating drugs, crime, and human trafficking, as well as the promotion of industrial development and the application of outer space technologies.[37] The campaign's claim was that Austria's long tradition of international work enabled it to develop extensive expert knowledge in these fields. These traits were reflected in numerous international meetings on UN-related issues hosted in Vienna.

Fourthly, the country's contributions to international peacekeeping missions and development aid were emphasized, highlighting the number of Austrian civilians who had participated in peacekeeping missions around the world. Moreover, the country's role in developing the EU's competence, engagement, and relationship with the UN in these fields was underscored. Austria's relatively high ODA levels were also mentioned, along with promises of increased contributions in the future. The country's regional activities were

---

34   Bundesministerium 2008a.
35   Bundesministerium 2007a.
36   Utanríkisráðuneytið 2009a.
37   Bundesministerium 2008a.

stressed in this regard, each time offering concrete examples of Austria's contributions, with a special focus on women, peace, and security.[38]

Although there are commonalities in the countries' campaign messages, and thereby their ideational commitments to UN values and principles, such as promises of rising ODA levels, contributions to peacekeeping, focus on states' respective fields of expertise and experiences, their regional standing, women's rights and empowerment, and disarmament and non-proliferation, there are still important differences when it comes to the states' ability to demonstrate their respective contributions and thus, their credibility. While Austria was able to showcase its strength and abilities in fields directly related to the work of the UN, and the UNSC specifically, with concrete examples, Iceland was confined to trying to 'sell' their smallness as a strength and a reason to be elected. Austria's campaign showcased the country's strong international and internal competence and commitment to the work and overarching goals of the UN, demonstrating explicitly how the country works at securing effective engagement and contributions of the EU for both peacekeeping missions and development aid, the good working relationship Austria had with the UN Secretary Generals and, finally, how Austria had been willing and able to lead by example in its work. Thus, Austria could demonstrate the way in which it had contributed, both financially and ideologically, with human resources and expertise.

Iceland, however, had little to show aside from their promises, their Nordic partners' track record, and their domestic performance in soft-security fields that related, albeit only partially, to the work of the UNSC, such as gender equality and the sustainable use of natural resources. And although the country's level of contributions to peacekeeping missions had been on the rise in the decade before the elections, the levels were incomparable to Austria's level of peacekeeping engagement. In addition, Iceland's ability to allocate resources to its campaign were much more limited.

4   Domestic Debate

The domestic debate in Iceland can be divided into three periodical phases. The first phase occurred before 2003, and was marked by optimism and a generally positive, albeit very limited, debate regarding Iceland's decision to run. As already discussed in Chapter 3, the campaign was thought to be a timely

---

38   Bundesministerium 2008a.

event, confirming Iceland's sovereign and independent status in the international arena. Iceland was establishing itself as a nation among nations and could play an important role.[39] However, there was also a clear focus on what could be gained from having a seat, namely that Iceland would be in a better position to safeguard its vital national interests.[40] This was the case both in parliament and in the media.

The second phase was marked by a rising scepticism beginning with Turkey's decision, in 2003, which would entail increased financial resources and limit Iceland's chances of succeeding substantially,[41] as well as Iceland being put on the list of the US's *Coalition of the Willing*.[42] Growing scepticism reached new heights when discussions about the excessive costs of the campaign were adopted by the Foreign Minister, former Prime Minister, Davíð Oddsson in 2005.[43] In general, the campaign was considered an expensive endeavour, rendered even more expensive with Turkey's candidature. It was seen as destined to fail since Iceland now had no chance of winning. Iceland was therefore cautioned to prioritize its resources into its real fields of its expertise, such as marine and environmental affairs, human rights and gender equality.[44]

The third phase, characterized by an increased public awareness and interest in the campaign, marked a return to optimism,[45] despite the strong hold sceptical voices continued to have on one of Iceland's biggest newspapers.[46] Interestingly, there is little to no mention of Iceland's possibilities to safeguard its national interests through its UNSC membership. Instead, the focus was placed on creating venues for social debate about Iceland's position in an ever more globalized international world, its role in this new reality, what it entailed to be a responsible member of the international society, and what Iceland could and should contribute to it. This contribution could be expertise in the fields of gender equality, human rights and environmental, marine and

---

39   Blöndal, H. 2006; Gestsson, S. 1998; Pétursdóttir, S. 2003; Sigfússon, S. J. 2001; Sveinbjarnardóttir, Þ. 2006; Sverrisdóttir, V. 2006; Árnason, Á. P. 2007b; Ásgrímsson, H. 1998; Þórðardóttir, S. A. 2003.

40   Benediktsson, B. 2008; Sverrisdóttir, V. 2006; Árnason, Á. P. 2007a; Ásgrímsson, H. 2001; Ásgrímsson, H. 2003a; Ásgrímsson, H. 2003b.

41   Oddsson, D. 2005a; Oddsson, D. 2005b.

42   Egilsson, G. S. 2003; Friðgeirsson, Á. 2003; Halldórsdóttir, K. 2003; Ingadóttir, Á. 2003; Sigfússon, S. J. 2003; Skarphéðinsson, Ö. 2003.

43   Oddsson, D. 2005a; Oddsson, D. 2005b.

44   Grétarsdóttir, G. L. 2007; Jónasson, Ö. 2006; Jónsson, G. M. 2007; Mbl 2005; Þórðarson, S. 2006.

45   Fréttablaðið 2006; Sigurðsson, D. L. 2006; Sigurðsson, D. L. 2007.

46   Morgunblaðið 2006; Morgunblaðið 2007.

energy affairs, as well as speaking up, based on experience, for smaller and more vulnerable states in the UN.

This change in approach reflects the general change in sentiment in Iceland about the country's abilities to be an active member in the international arena and a realization of the benefits of being active on the international stage. It is yet another sign of Iceland's pivot from limited resources and reactiveness, towards a more open and prosperous society.

Political discussions about Austria's UNSC campaign from the time leading up to the candidature announcement until the elections in the General Assembly were rather limited. The limited debate that took place focused on two specific issues during the campaign as well as Austria's standing within the UN. First, the use, or rather supposed misuse, of funds intended for development aid to buy votes. Second, a series of debates regarding the connection between Austria's candidature and the country's military intervention in Chad. Third, the discussions about the importance of Vienna as a host city for the EU's only UN headquarters and Austria's image as a devoted UN member.

On the matter of the possibility of development cooperation resources being misused for candidature purposes, an issue brought forward by the Austrian opposition party, the Greens, Foreign Minister Plassnik (ÖVP) denied the possibility that certain developing countries were promised gifts, financed with development cooperation funds, in exchange for their vote.[47] These allegations were also firmly denied by the Austrian Ministry of Foreign Affairs (MFA), who claimed that the country's strategy for this campaign would be to establish deep and long lasting relationships with UN member countries.[48]

On a similar note, an oral inquiry was made as to whether the Austrian federal army's operations in Chad were a prerequisite for Austria's seat on the UNSC, thus echoing concerns, also voiced by the Green Party and BZÖ,[49] that Austria did not meet any requirements for the mission.[50] Moreover, the mission was considered too dangerous in addition to not being consistent with Austria's neutrality.[51]

Strengthening both Vienna as a UN headquarters site, and the country's image as a reliable and devoted member of the UN was also a matter of interest to the Austrian parliament, and a major candidature motivation, already discussed in Chapter 3. When asked about Austria's ability to accommodate

---

47   DerStandard.at. 2007; Parlament; Parlament 2007c.
48   DerStandard.at. 2008b.
49   Parliament 2007a.
50   Die Presse 2007b.
51   OE24 2007.

additional UN organizations, Foreign Minister Plassnik replied that bringing attention to Vienna's importance as UN headquarters, and increasing cooperation with the UN, especially in the fields of security, disarmament, and arms control, was a major focus of hers when meeting with the UN's high officials. Since Vienna was the only UN HQ location within the EU, as well as accommodating the Organization for Security and Co-operation in Europe (OSCE) HQ, it was clear that Austria's interests matched those of the UN.[52]

It is interesting to note that there seem to have been few, if any, doubts about whether Austria *should* run for a seat on the UNSC, even after Turkey entered the bid, meaning that Austria would have to allocate financial resources to campaign for a seat. The candidature enjoyed full, cross-party support throughout the campaign period and there seems to have been very limited domestic debate on the issue.[53] This may be why there was no need for domestic campaigning, which in turn may also be connected to the fact that Austria had already served on the UNSC twice before. Moreover, it may reflect a mature self-identity when it comes to participation in international cooperation.

Reflective of its history as a former empire, which was able to exert influence and even force, Austria has a culture of viewing itself as internationally relevant. This is not the case for Iceland, which was mostly under foreign rule until the twentieth century. In fact, Iceland's colonial identity was a particularly important point that was emphasized in both its international and domestic campaigns, as previously stated. When Turkey decided to run, and it became apparent that the three states would need to finance campaigns to stand a chance of winning a seat on the UNSC, the reactions in the two countries were very different. It can be argued that Turkey's decision revealed the weakness of Iceland's identity as a participant in the international arena, as well as a lack of confidence among some of the most powerful members of the political elite in Iceland's cause. These political hesitations would spark intense media coverage in Iceland, whereas Turkey's candidature never gained any real traction in the Austrian public debate. It is therefore safe to conclude that the matter became a highly political issue in Iceland, whereas in Austria it enjoyed both political and public consensus.

---

52   Plassnik, U. 2005a.
53   Public official E. 2018.

5   Estimating Successes, Failures, and Lessons Learned

To provide a clearer understanding of how Iceland and Austria applied and combined the three logics of our theoretical framework in Chapter 2 (demonstrating contributions, claiming competence, and proving ideational commitment), this section will focus on possible successes and failures of the two campaigns. For this purpose, we find it helpful to divide the estimations of success into three categories: international campaigning efforts, New York campaigning efforts, and national campaigning efforts. Failures, on the other hand, will not be categorized in the same detailed manner, as the two states' campaigns differ to the extent that in Austria's successful case it is more appropriate to talk about lessons learned rather than failures.

6   Successes

The Icelandic Foreign Service was quick to realize the importance of seeking expert advice on how to plan and conduct its campaign and what pitfalls to avoid from both the Nordic countries and Ireland.[54] Contextualized with the theoretical framework, it can be said that during the final two years of the campaign Iceland managed to demonstrate its contributions by actively engaging with Nordic partners' foreign services, claiming some level of competence by showcasing support from high-level Nordic politicians in the campaign efforts. Engaging the other Nordic foreign services compensated for the limited human resources within the Icelandic foreign service. Another important trait of the international campaign was the decision to channel its attention and resources into developing states, small states, and small island developing states, thereby adding to the element of ideational commitment. This helped focus and sharpen the message of the campaign, in that (island) Iceland could easily relate to the specific challenges that poor, developing states and former colonies faced, being that Iceland had been in the same situation relatively recently. Moreover, Iceland could – based on its own experiences – contribute expertise and newfound financial resources to help these states face these challenges. Finally, engaging important political personalities would prove useful in both the international campaign and in New York. For instance, the President of Iceland wrote personalized letters to every UN member state. Three letters, asking for support for the Icelandic candidate, were sent in the

---

54   Utanríkisráðuneytið 2002.

names of Nordic leaders, i.e. letters from the Nordic Prime Ministers, Foreign Ministers and Development Ministers, to their colleagues in the UN member states. This had never been done before.[55]

The Icelandic Foreign Service was also successful in their lobbying efforts in New York. It was decided to increase Iceland's participation within the work of different UN bodies in New York. This would raise the Icelandic profile and show that Iceland was serious in its efforts to be an engaged and serious UN member. Moreover, the decision to use Iceland's presence in New York to establish formal political relationships with almost every single UN member state would create important ties between the Icelandic Permanent Representative and other UN members' Permanent Representatives and show that Iceland wanted to hear every UN member's point of view, which would also be helpful during the international campaign. This was important since, for some states, the Permanent Representative is the one who decides which way to vote. In addition to this, during the final days leading up to the election, Jan Eliasson, the former Swedish Minister for Foreign Affairs, Deputy Secretary-General of the United Nations, and President of the United Nations General Assembly from 2005–2006, and former Danish Foreign Minister Niels Helveg Petersen, contributed to Iceland's campaign by participating in meetings and events in New York.[56] Moreover, the Nordic permanent missions organized events, thus underscoring that Iceland's candidature was a Nordic endeavour.[57] Cultural events that had been planned in New York helped raise the bar of the Icelandic campaign, increasing visibility, and drawing attention to the country and thus reminding people that Iceland was a candidate.

The decision in 2006/7 to place additional focus on national campaigning efforts was an important one for Iceland, and arguably an indicator of claiming competence in an attempt to prove its leadership skills. The decision would secure sufficient public support for the candidature, necessary for the government to be able to campaign effectively without having to channel important efforts into answering what could otherwise have become domestic political reservations about the purpose of the candidature and whether it was considered a reasonable financial priority. Moreover, it was a tactical move to prove to the outside world that Iceland was serious in its efforts to become a responsible and valuable UNSC member. This was not deemed necessary in Austria.

When it came to demonstrating contributions, Austria was highly successful in drawing attention to its own assets and strengths, internationally. One

55   Public official B. 2018; Utanríkisráðuneytið 2009a.
56   Public official C. 2018.
57   Utanríkisráðuneytið 2009a.

of the pillars of the Austrian campaign was its ability to build on the country's own experiences and expertise that directly related to the work of the
UNSC, thus giving the impression of being an experienced, reliable, and overall
'good' UN member and international actor. This added to Austria's ability to
appeal to both small- and medium-sized states within the UN and having an
extended diplomatic network around the world. In short, these components
inspired confidence. Austria was able to demonstrate its expertise, in both traditional working fields of the UNSC, i.e., hard security and defence matters, as
well as with the so-called soft security issues such as climate change, poverty
eradication, multiculturalism, and gender equality. Austria did this by bringing
attention to different institutions and agencies, hosted in Vienna, that work in
the field of security and defence, as well as to special initiatives and Austrian
support measures with softer security issues. The UN HQ was oftentimes mentioned along with the International Atomic Energy Agency, the Commission
for the Comprehensive Nuclear-Test-Ban Treaty, and the UN Office on Drugs
and Crime Prevention, as well as the OSCE. Moreover, Austria emphasized
its ability to lead by example and take on new initiatives, bringing attention
to the fact that Austria had ratified all 13 UN conventions and protocols on
combatting terrorism. In addition, during the campaign, Austrian authorities
promoted an international legally binding ban on cluster munitions, leading by example by passing a national legislation in 2007 which completely
outlawed the weapon. The country subsequently signed the Convention on
cluster munitions.[58] Moreover, Austria's track record of being active in peacekeeping (deploying thousands of personnel on peacekeeping missions), as
well as contributing millions of euros to the UN's World Food Programme,
and taking independent, financial action against starvation and poverty, supported their campaign and added to their ideational commitment within our
theoretical framework. Austria also emphasized gender equality, advocating
for increased awareness on the issue within the UN and among UN members,
as well as showing leadership within the EU during their presidency in 2006
by making it a priority to recruit and deploy women to EU peace missions.
Austrian authorities also supported a 'dialogue among civilizations' through
conferences and other private and EU initiatives, building on their image as a
regional partner with an ideal geographical location to promote such dialogue.

The fact that there was consistent, cross-party domestic support for the
campaign was also important since it enabled Austrian authorities to focus all
their efforts on international campaigning and campaigning in New York. This

---

58   Bundesministerium 2007b.

domestic stronghold may have been further strengthened by the recruitment of strong domestic political figures who possessed a good UN track record, to lead the campaign efforts. Another successful aspect of the campaign was Austria's ability to highlight the country's strong UN relationship through their good connection with UN Secretary Generals, Kofi Annan and Ban Ki-Moon, as already stated. This arguably increased the country's international credibility and influence during the campaign and, furthermore, falls into the category on claiming competence within our theoretical framework.

Moreover, the fact that Austria had already served twice on the UNSC and that Austria's 'participation in international peace missions was not only a sign of Austria's solidarity but also deeply embedded in their self-image', to quote Foreign Minister Plassnik, also provided the campaign with a sound ideological basis, according to the importance of providing a campaign with ideational commitment.[59] All of the above supported the campaign efforts in New York where a lot of emphasis was put on bilateral meetings with different regional and religious organizations, alliances of small states, as well as on hosting numerous cultural activities. This was further complemented by inviting delegations from certain countries on special retreats to Austria during the campaign period. Moreover, according to one interviewee, Austria, like Iceland, looked to the successful campaign methods used by Ireland for the 2001–2002 UNSC term in their planning.[60]

After evaluating campaign successes from three angles, international campaigning efforts, New York campaigning efforts, and national campaigning efforts, we can see that both the Icelandic and Austrian campaigns utilized all three of our campaign logics combined, although their campaigns differed in their successes in numerous aspects. Both states were successful in building regional and size-related relationships, as well as in engaging strong and internationally renowned personalities in their campaigns, but while Iceland successfully engaged their Nordic partners in their campaign (as tradition dictated in the Nordic rotation), Austria benefitted from its widespread and firmly rooted diplomatic network and relations, making it much less reliant on others. Similarly, whereas Iceland was successful in building domestic consensus and support for its UNSC candidature after a difficult period of conflict over whether to continue the campaign, Austria, who had already served twice on the UNSC, as well as having a longstanding culture of international engagement, did not need to focus any energy on domestic campaigning. Austria was

59   Bundesministerium 2007.
60   Public official F. 2018.

moreover successful in recruiting important, domestic political figures to lead the campaign efforts whereas Iceland's campaign was mainly driven by public officials. Finally, whereas Austria could build on expertise, nurtured over a long period of time, in both traditional, 'hard' security matters as well as in different, 'softer' security matters, Iceland's expertise lay mainly in the field of soft security matters. These softer security matters were less obviously related to the work of the UNSC, and Iceland had a history as a small state and former, poor dependency. Arguably, this provided Austria with an advantage in terms of contributions, competence, and credibility of ideational commitment.

7   Failures and Lessons Learned

One of the core weaknesses of the Icelandic campaign was that it lacked a strong and decisive political engagement and leadership. This could be the reason why in the years leading up to 2003 the public debate rendered the campaign an easy target for domestic scepticism and negative criticism in 2003–2005, which in turn made campaigning highly problematic for public officials abroad in 2004–2005. From a theoretical point of view, this left the Icelandic campaign characterized by a lack of, and struggle to claim competence, as it relied heavily on Nordic political support to add merit to its candidature when domestic support was not nearly as tangible.

Moreover, the national campaign was launched too late, either due to the lack of political leadership or simply because it was not considered necessary. The lesson learned would be that a national campaign and a general political consensus about the candidature is no less important than campaigning internationally. Active engagement of both the government and the MPs is important. The establishment of a good working relationship with the media and the creation of a venue for open meetings and seminars answering questions about the campaign, its costs, and benefits are important factors in building nationwide public awareness and trust. These are essential factors in securing sufficient political support for the campaign throughout the campaign period.

The tardy launch of the actual campaign also meant that lobbying specific target groups and fine-tuning the campaign messages to them, specifically, came too late, resulting, for instance, in the loss of potential votes among the Pacific Island states. This might have been avoided if effective organization of campaign efforts between the Nordic partners' administrations (MFAs and embassies around the world) had been secured earlier in the process. Unfortunately, it was not realized until the last two years of the campaign. The key lessons learned are that campaigning activities should begin as soon as possible after a decision to run has been made, at least for small states with limited resources. These activities should include strategic campaigning both nationally and internationally, ensuring strong, sustainable political leadership and thereby sufficient political support at home, which in turn makes credible lobbying and effective vote hunting easier.

Taking all of this into account, it is still difficult to say whether these changes would have made the necessary difference, considering the detrimental effects of the international financial crisis, the collapse of the Icelandic economy, and the ensuing diplomatic attacks on Iceland by Britain, along with talks about a possible bailout from Russia. However, it is evident that the process of running as a candidate for a UNSC seat was a steep but valuable learning curve for the Icelandic administration, the Ministry for Foreign Affairs, and the political elite, in particular.

While Austria was able to conclude a successful campaign with features from all three campaign logics combined, the process of having to campaign was nevertheless a learning process that produced some results in terms of a newfound knowledge on how best to conduct a campaign. A public official mentioned two lessons, specifically: First, over the campaign period the campaign team learned the importance of focusing 'more on the interests of regions where we had no diplomatic relations.'[61] In addition, that it was important to demonstrate vested interests in softer security matters, such as sustainable development and environmental programmes. This was mentioned in relation to the country's campaigning efforts in the Pacific islands and the Caribbean states.

It appears that both states became aware of the importance of targeting specific regions and that the campaign messages needed to be adjusted to the needs of these states. However, whereas Austria became aware of the importance of specifically targeting states where their diplomatic resources were scarce, this was hardly a discovery for Iceland. For Iceland, it was obvious from the very start, with its limited diplomatic network, that it would need to both collaborate extensively with its Nordic partners to approach regions and states where it had little to no representation and that it would also need to establish formal political relationships with every UN member. The latter had only been done to a very limited degree before the UNSC campaign. Like Austria, however, the way in which to approach these states, that is focusing on topics such as sustainable development and the environment, and how to present these topics, was not obvious until later in the campaign. It is fair to assume that it

---

61   Public official F. 2018.

may have been easier for Austria to adapt to this 'late discovery' than it was for Iceland, with the latter suffering far greater size-related limitations, such as scarce human resources and budgetary restraints.

As was revealed in the section on successes, Austria was able to successfully engage domestic political actors, while the Icelandic campaign was primarily driven by public servants. Austria's advantage in this respect is mirrored in the fact that there was no need for domestic campaigning efforts due to their longstanding culture of international engagement, stemming, inter alia, from their history and geographic realities as centrally located country in the middle of Europe. Moreover, it seems that the active involvement of politicians as promoters of the campaign from the very beginning may also have ensured that the whole of the Austrian government was part of the team from very early on. They shared the responsibility of getting Austria elected from the very start, whereas keeping the ownership of the campaign within the MFA, as was mostly the case in Iceland, may have stunted their success in this regard.

While Icelandic and Austrian officials seemed to disagree as to whether or not it was important to start the campaign or campaign preparations as early as possible after the decision to run had been made, this may be because a smaller state like Iceland needs more time to prepare the actual campaigning activities and coordinate with its Nordic colleagues. For a self-sufficient and experienced foreign service like the Austrian one, which also enjoys political and public support for international engagement and activities, this is not the case. Moreover, the fact that domestic campaigning would be necessary in Iceland to ensure stable support for the endeavour throughout the campaign period, would also require a longer working period on the campaign.

8   Concluding Remarks

One point of departure for this analysis has been that whereas Iceland saw the adventure of seeking an elected seat on the UNSC as a pursuit of status, for Austria it was more a question of maintaining the power of their former, continental empire. It was nothing new for the Austrian political elite and their bureaucracy to seek (increased) regional and international power. In fact, it can be argued that while Iceland's candidature was an attempt to *become* internationally relevant, for Austria it was more a question of *remaining* relevant.

In their quest for status, Iceland saw the prospect of an elected seat on the UNSC as a historic milestone, being that it was the first time that the former dependency attempted to become a member and, at that point in time, it was by far the largest individual project the MFA had envisaged in its relatively short history. Icelandic diplomats and politicians saw membership in the UNSC as a way to enhance the country's status amongst states around the world and in international organizations, as discussed in Chapter 3. Furthermore, Iceland's hopes of a new and enhanced status in world affairs was reinforced by the optimism that it would bring about economic benefits in the long run and give the country a chance to contribute to the international debate within its fields of expertise. Icelandic diplomats and a large portion of the political elite were changing their political discourse concerning the small state's ability to have an active role and a say in international organizations. They were, however, not confident in the new approach. Thus, the endeavour became an important bone of contention in Icelandic political debate. Politicians were split on the candidature, which led to a domestic debate about the financial costs, and whether it was even logical to prioritize the candidature for a small state like Iceland, which arguably had little experience in the main fields of work of the UNSC. Concerns were raised about whether Iceland would be able to act independently and have a say in the council. Moreover, the fact that the Icelandic campaign was solely organized and driven by Icelandic public officials, with very limited political involvement in the strategic campaign planning, management, or choices of key messages, resulted in weak political ownership of the campaign. This, despite cross-party support in the beginning, would render the campaign vulnerable to domestic criticism in 2004–2005 and would ultimately damage it abroad.

In Austria, however, the candidature seemed to be more self-explanatory and self-evident. Austria was seeking influence in the most powerful international body that deals with matters of global security and defence. In terms of claiming competence, the like-minded Austrian political elite was confident about the country's status and its international role to play, as well as its ability to influence the international system. In addition, they defined Austria as a medium-sized state, rather than a small state, in an attempt to secure the country's interests. The UNSC was the place to be for Austria. There was no debate as to whether or not Austria should run for a seat. Apparently, it was quite obvious to everyone that it should. This mirrors the differences between the two states had regarding national self-perception and identity, at the time. It was perceived as only natural that Austria should strive to be a relevant international actor, whereas in Iceland the debate continued, indicating, arguably, a justified feeling of inferiority.

The Austrian campaign proved highly successful in demonstrating what the country had to offer by consistently bringing attention to their capabilities and strengths, thereby further establishing Austria as a 'good' UN member. During the campaign period, Austria benefitted from, and was able to build on, its extensive diplomatic network, developed over decades and centuries. They drew upon their experiences in the work of the UNSC as a former two-time member on the council, their expertise in numerous hard and soft security related fields of work of the USNC, as well as their ability to cater credibly to both small- and medium-sized states. Austria was able to allocate important financial resources to the campaign, evidenced by numerous independent initiatives and the fact that they were able to invite target states' delegations to special retreats in Austria. In addition, throughout the campaign they were able to build their campaign messages on concrete examples of what they had already done, what they were doing, and what they were going to do, thus reinforcing their ideational commitment and credibility. Iceland, however, was unable to build its campaign on anything more than its Nordic identity and prospects, supported by its ability to reach remarkably high levels of prosperity after becoming independent. The latter argument suffered substantial damage towards the end of the campaign period with the financial crisis and the diplomatic crisis concerning Iceland's relations with Britain and the ensuing discussions about a possible bailout by Russia. These had detrimental effects on the country's international credibility. Moreover, Iceland's financial resources and administrative capacity were very scarce which in turn meant that they had to rely heavily on their Nordic partners.

Nevertheless, despite the fact that Iceland was not elected in 2008, it can be argued that the long-term effects of the UNSC candidature were much more limited in Austria than in Iceland. Some direct effects of the UNSC candidature and campaign on the Icelandic administrative system were the establishment of political and diplomatic relationships around the globe and the expertise gained within the MFA about the workings of the UN. Moreover, it was a unique training exercise in effective international campaigning, communications, collaboration, and lobbying efforts for Icelandic diplomats. The campaign also created a motivation for Iceland to become even more active in international affairs, thus opening up the domestic debate of Iceland's role in the world. The effect was that the debate about international relations in Iceland transformed from being mainly about what Iceland could gain from international relations to what and how the country could contribute to international affairs. This would be one of the most important outcomes of the venture. The risks are that the eventual failure of the campaign, in part due to the international financial crisis and British diplomatic aggression, may discourage similar major foreign policy decisions that are made in the future, at least for some years to come, perhaps leading to stagnation within at least some fields of the foreign service. That being said, with the continued, accelerated renewal of the Icelandic political elite, and the fact that there will always be ambitious civil servants and foreign ministers, it is more likely than not that ambitious individuals and teams will endeavour to go on ambitious adventures. An example of this is the fact that in late June 2018, Iceland decided to run for a seat on the UN Human Rights Council, thus offering to replace the vacancy left by the United States following its decision to withdraw its membership on 19 June. A few days later, Iceland, the only candidate for the seat, was elected to serve on the Council until 31 December 2019.[62] Following a generally successful membership term on the Council and an alleged prioritization of human rights as part of Iceland's foreign policy agenda, Iceland has announced its candidature for a seat on the UN Human Rights Council for the term 2025–2027.

Although there are many similarities in the way in which Austria and Iceland viewed, planned, and conducted their campaigns, there are also important inherent historical, cultural, geopolitical, and size-related differences, which had an effect on how they decided and were able to conduct their respective candidatures. These variables inevitably marked how the three campaign logics of our theoretical framework appear in the campaigns, and in the end, also affected the final result of the UNSC election. Although, theoretically, the two states have several similarities in their approaches, in as much they were able to demonstrate contributions by focusing on their assets and strengths, enhancing their networks, and securing support from other states, albeit to a different extent largely due to the countries' historical and geographical realities; Austria is a former empire in the heart of Europe, and Iceland is a former dependency on the edge of the earth. The differences between the two candidatures become clearer when looking into features of claiming competence and proving ideational commitment. Iceland's lack of political leadership and its small foreign service proved to be impediments against Austria's united political elite and larger foreign service with greater resources, causing Iceland to struggle to claim competence. In terms of ideational commitment, Iceland was also at somewhat of a disadvantage to Austria, running its campaign on a traditional ideational Nordic ticket, focusing mainly on soft security issues, whilst the Austrian campaign had all that, along with hard security and defence matters, to boot. For the Icelandic campaign, the logic of demonstrating contributions therefore seems to have been the one logic that proved the most important and successful. Austria, on the other hand, managed to combine all three campaign logics (demonstrating contributions, claiming competence, and proving ideational commitment) to their advantage.

---

62   OHCHR 2018.

Bibliography

Árnason, Árni Páll. Speech 1 in Alþingi, 8 November, 2007a. *Utanríkismál, munnleg skýrsla utanríkisráðherra.* Retrieved from https://www.althingi.is/altext/raeda/135 /rad20071108T123433.html.

Árnason, Árni Páll. Speech in Alþingi, 8 November, 2007b. *Utanríkismál, munnleg skýrsla utanríkisráðherra.* Retrieved from https://www.althingi.is/altext/raeda/135 /rad20071108T154555.html.

Ásgrímsson, Halldór. Speech in Alþingi, 5 November, 1998. *Skýrsla utanríkisráðherra um utanríkismál.* Retrieved from https://www.althingi.is/altext/123/11/r05103406.sgml.

Ásgrímsson, Halldór. Speech in Alþingi, 29 March, 2001. *Skýrsla utanríkisráðherra um utanríkismál.* Retrieved from https://www.althingi.is/altext/126/03/r29105342.sgml.

Ásgrímsson, Halldór. Speech in Alþingi, 13 November, 2003a. *Skýrsla utanríkisráðherra um utanríkismál.* Retrieved from http://www.althingi.is/altext/130/11/r13103236 .sgml.

Ásgrímsson, Halldór. Speech in Alþingi, 27 February, 2003b. *Skýrsla utanríkisráðherra um utanríkismál.* Retrieved from https://www.althingi.is/altext/128/02/r27105147 .sgml.

Benediktsson, Bjarni. Speech in Alþingi, 8 April, 2008. Utanríkis- og alþjóðamál, skýrsla. Retrieved from https://www.althingi.is/altext/135/04/r08144314.sgml.

Blöndal, Halldór. Speech in Alþingi, 16 November, 2006 *Utanríkismál, munnleg skýrsla utanríkisráðherra.* Retrieved from https://www.althingi.is/altext/133/11/r16113756 .sgml.

Bundesministerium. Plassnik, Ursula. 'Solides österreichisches Engagement in internationaler Friedensarbeit'. 31 October, 2007. Retrieved from https://www.bmeia.gv .at/das-ministerium/presse/aussendungen/2007/plassnik-solides-oesterreichisc hes-engagement-in-internationaler-friedensarbeit/.

Bundesministerium. Plassnik, Ursula. 'Bestätigung der Bedeutung Wiens als UNO-Amtssitz'. 2007a. Retrieved from https://www.bmeia.gv.at/das-minister ium/presse/aussendungen/2007/plassnik-bestaetigung-der-bedeutung-wiens-als -uno-amtssitz/.

Bundesministerium. Plassnik, Ursula. 'Signifikanter Bewussteinsschub für ein Verbon Streumunition'. 2007b. Retrieved from https://www.bmeia.gv.at/das-minister ium/presse/aussendungen/2007/plassnik-signifikanter-bewussteinsshub-fuer-ein -verbot-von-streumunition/.

Bundesministerium. *Austria and the United Nations, Official UNSC campaign brochure.* Federal Ministry for European and International Affairs, 2008a.

Bundesministerium. Plassnik, Ursula zur UNO-Wahl 'Beeindruckender Vertrauensbeweis der internationalen Staatengemeinschaft'. 2008b. Retrieved from https: //www.bmeia.gv.at/das-ministerium/presse/aussendungen/2008/plassnik-zur -uno-wahl-beeindruckender-vertrauensbeweis-der-internationalen-staatengemei nschaft/.

Bundesministerium. Plassnik, Ursula. 'Ein Stück Österreich in der UNO'. 2008c. Retrieved from https://www.bmeia.gv.at/das-ministerium/presse/aussendungen /2008/plassnik-ein-stueck-oesterreich-in-der-uno/.

Bundesministerium. Plassnik, Ursula. 'Kandidatur für UNO-Sicherheitsrat als Dienstleistung an der Weltorganisation'. 26 September 2008d. Retrieved from https: //www.bmeia.gv.at/das-ministerium/presse/aussendungen/2008/plassnik-kandida tur-fuer-uno-sicherheitsrat-als-dienstleistung-an-der-weltorganisation/.

Bundesministerium. Plassnik, Ursula. 'Sind verlässlicher UNO-Partner und Teilhaber'. 2008e. Retrieved from https://www.bmeia.gv.at/das-ministerium/presse/ausse ndungen/2008/plassnik-sind-verlaesslicher-uno-partner-und-teilhaber/.

Bundesministerium. Plassnik, Ursula. 'Zuversicht für den österreichischen Sicherhei-tsratssitz'. 2008f. Retrieved from https://www.bmeia.gv.at/das-ministerium/pre sse/aussendungen/2008/plassnik-zuversicht-fuer-den-oesterreichischen-sicherhe itsratssitz/.

Bundesministerium. Winkler, Hans. 'Österreichische Expertise als Exportprodukt für die Karibik'. 2008g. Retrieved from https://www.bmeia.gv.at/das-minister ium/presse/aussendungen/2008/winkler-oesterreichische-expertise-als-export produkt-fuer-die-karibik/.

Caribbean Community (CARICOM) consists of 15 Caribbean states, the majority of which is also a member of the Alliance of Small Island States (AOSIS).

DerStandard.at. Plassnik, Ursula. wirbt für Österreichs Sicherheitsrats- Kandidatur. 2008a. Retrieved from https://derstandard.at/3322724/Plassnik-wirbt-fuer-Oeste rreichs-Sicherheitsrats--Kandidatur.

DerStandard.at. Topfenstrudel für die Südsee. 2008b, 14 July 2008. Retrieved from https://derstandard.at/3410744/Topfenstrudel-fuer-die-Suedsee.

DerStandard.at. Schulbusse für den Sicherheitsrat. 2007, 26. September 2007. Retrieved from https://derstandard.at/3046357/Schulbusse-fuer-den-Sicherheitsrat.

Die Presse. Interview von Staatssekretär Dr. Hans WINKLER in der Tageszeitung "Die Presse" vom 7. März 2007, 2007a. Retrieved from https://www.bmeia.gv.at/das-mini sterium/presse/reden-und-interviews/2007/interview-von-staatssekretaer-dr-hans -winkler-in-der-tageszeitung-die-presse-vom-7-maerz-2007/.

Die Presse. Tschad-Einsatz: Sicherheitsrat einberufen. 2007b, 2 November 2007. Retrieved from https://diepresse.com/home/politik/innenpolitik/340673/Tscha dEinsatz_Sicherheitsrat-einberufen.

Egilsson, Gunnar Smári. Túristar í öryggisráðinu. Fréttablaðið, 2003, 23 July p. 12.

Fréttablaðið. Fjölmörg ríki heita stuðningi. Fréttablaðið, 23 September, 2006 p. 1. Retrieved from http://timarit.is/view_page_init.jsp?issId=272521&pageId=3916816.

Friðgeirsson, Ásgeir. Speech in Alþingi, 13 November, 2003. Skýrsla utanríkisráðherra um utanríkismál. Retrieved from https://www.althingi.is/altext/130/11/r13144 116.sgml.

Gestsson, Svavar. Speech in Alþingi, 5 November, 1998. *Skýrsla utanríkisráðherra um utanríkismál.* Retrieved from https://www.althingi.is/altext/123/11/r05115036.sgml.

Grétarsdóttir, Guðfríður Lilja. Speech in Alþingi, 8 November, 2007. *Utanríkismál, munnleg skýrsla utanríkisráðherra.* Retrieved from http://www.althingi.is/altext/raeda /135/rad20071108T144532.html.

Halldórsdóttir, Kolbrún. Speech in Alþingi, 13 November, 2003. *Skýrsla utanríkisráðherra um utanríkismál.* Retrieved from https://www.althingi.is/altext/130/11 /r13145442.sgml.

Hauksson, Jóhann. Stefnan tekin á öryggisráðið. Fréttablaðið, 17 September 2005, p. 10. Retrieved from http://timarit.is/view_page_init.jsp?issId=270825&pageId=3861267.

Iceland Review. Iceland Launches Fund for Island States, 25 September 2008. Retrieved from https:// www.icelandreview.com/news/iceland-launches-fund-island-states/.

Ingadóttir, Álfheiður. Speech in Alþingi, 13 November, 2003. *Skýrsla utanríkisráðherra um utanríkismál.* Retrieved from https://www.althingi.is/altext/130/11/r13142352 .sgml.

Jónasson, Ögmundur. Speech in Alþingi, 6 April, 2006. *Utanríkismál, munnleg skýrsla utanríkisráðherra.* Retrieved from https://www.althingi.is/altext/132/04/r06112 752.sgml.

Jónsson, Grétar Mar. Speech in Alþingi, 8 November, 2007. *Utanríkismál, munnleg skýrsla utanríkisráðherra.* Retrieved from https://www.althingi.is/altext/raeda/135 /rad20071108T134621.html.

Machreich, Wolfgang. Sympathie in Stimmen verwandeln. Die Furche, nr. 38/08, 18 September, 2008b. Retrieved from https://www.genios.de/document?id=FURC__07 0085082067072069095200⁨8⁩+0918183115000⁨2⁩&src=hitlist&offset=0.

Machreich, Wolfgang. 'Ich tippe auf Österreich und Türkei!'. Die Furche, nr. 38/08, 18 September, 2008a. Retrieved from https://www.genios.de/document?id=FURC__07 0085082067072069095200⁨8⁩+0918183115000⁨4⁩&src=hitlist&offset=0.

Mbl. Kostar um milljarð. 24 January 2005. Retrieved from https://www.mbl.is/greinas afn/grein/840910/?_t=1535655478.59.

Morgunblaðið. Staksteinar. *Morgunblaðið,* 23 September, 2006 p. 8. Retrieved from http://timarit.is/view_page_init.jsp?issId=284804&pageId=4141141.

Morgunblaðið. Staksteinar. *Morgunblaðið,*15 December, 2007 p. 10. Retrieved from http://timarit.is/view_page_init.jsp?issId=286070&pageId=4177775.

News. Zum bereits dritten Mal: Österreich bewirbt sich um UN-Sicherheitsrats-Sitz für 2009/10. 9 August 2005. Retrieved from https://www.news.at/a/zum-mal-oesterre ich-un-sicherheitsrats-sitz-2009-10-118888.

Oddsson, Davíð. Speech 1 in Alþingi, 29 April. Utanríkismál, munnleg skýrsla utanríkisráðherra. 2005a. Retrieved from http://www.althingi.is/altext/raeda/131/rad2005 0429T103643.html.

Oddsson, Davíð. Speech 2 in Alþingi, 29 April. Utanríkismál, munnleg skýrsla utanríkisráðherra. 2005b. Retrieved from https://www.althingi.is/altext/raeda/131/rad 20050429T162809.html.

OE24. Österreich schickt Elite-Einheit in den Tschad. 6 November, 2007. Retrieved from https://www.oe24.at/oesterreich/politik/Oesterreich-schickt-Elite-Einheit-in -den-Tschad/186826.

Parlament. Einsatz des österreichischen Bundesheeres im Tschad als Vorleistung für den nicht permanenten Sitz Österreichs im UN-Sicherheitsrat (30/M). 2007a. Retrieved from https://www.parlament.gv.at/PAKT/VHG/XXIII/M/M_00030/index .shtml.

Parlament. Kandidatur Österreichs für den UN-Sicherheitsrat (1509/AB). 2007b. Retrievedfromhttps://www.parlament.gv.at/PAKT/VHG/XXIII/AB/AB_01509/index .shtml.

Parlament. Kandidatur Österreichs für den UN-Sicherheitsrat (1546/J). 2007c. Retrieved from https://www.parlament.gv.at/PAKT/VHG/XXIII/J/J_01546/index.shtml.

Pétursdóttir, Sólveig. Speech in Alþingi, 13 November, 2003. *Skýrsla utanríkisráðherra um utanríkismál*. Retrieved from https://www.althingi.is/altext/130/11/r13113922 .sgml.

Plassnik, Ursula. Speech in Parlament, 722nd session, 2005a. Retrieved from https: //www.parlament.gv.at/PAKT/VHG/BR/BRSITZ/BRSITZ_00722/SEITE_0024.html.

Plassnik, Ursula. Statement at the General Assembly's 61st session. A/61/PV.15, 2006 Retrieved from http://www.un.org/en/ga/search/view_doc.asp?symbol=A/61/PV.15.

Security Council Report. 'Special Research Report No. 2: Security Council Elections 2008'. 29 August, 2008. https://www.securitycouncilreport.org/research-reports/.

Sigfússon, Steingrímur Jóhann. Speech in Alþingi, 29 March, 2001. *Skýrsla utanríkisráðherra um utanríkismál*. Retrieved from https://www.althingi.is/altext/126/03 /r29144426.sgml.

Sigfússon, Steingrímur Jóhann. Speech in Alþingi, 13 November, 2003. *Skýrsla utanríkisráðherra um utanríkismál.* Retrieved from https://www.althingi.is/altext/130/11 /r13115913.sgml.

Sigurðsson, Davíð Logi. Töluvert meiri bjartsýni ríkir um framboð Íslands. *Morgunblaðið*, 9 October, 2006 p. 44. Retrieved from http://timarit.is/view_page_init.jsp?issId=284 849&pageId=4142521.

Sigurðsson, Davíð Logi. Meira en 100 loforð um stuðning. *Morgunblaðið*, 31 May, 2007 p. 2. Retrieved from http://timarit.is/view_page_init.jsp?issId=285549&pageId =4162623.

Skarphéðinsson, Össur. Speech in Alþingi, 13 November, 2003. *Skýrsla utanríkisráðherra um utanríkismál.* Retrieved from https://www.althingi.is/altext/130/11 /r13110800.sgml.

Strauss-Kahn, Dominique. *Letter from IMF Managing Director to Open Civil Meetings.* 13 November, 2009. Retrieved from www.imf.org/external/np/vc/2009/111209.htm.

Sveinbjarnardóttir, Þórunn. Speech in Alþingi, 16 November, 2006. *Utanríkismál, munnleg skýrsla utanríkisráðherra.* Retrieved from https://www.althingi.is/altext/133/11/r16163947.sgml.

Sverrisdóttir, Valgerður. Speech in Alþingi, 16 November, 2006 *Utanríkismál, munnleg skýrsla utanríkisráðherra.* Retrieved from https://www.althingi.is/altext/133/11/r16103457.sgml.

US Embassy in Iceland. Icelandic Economic Crisis, time for USG to get involved? 2008. Retrieved from https://wikileaks.org/plusd/cables/08REYKJAVIK225_a.html.

Utanríkisráðuneytið. *Framboð Íslands og þátttaka í Öryggisráði Sameinuðu þjóðanna 2009–2010 – Trúnaðarmál [Iceland's Candidature and Participation in the UN Security Council 2009–2010 – Confidential].* Utanríkisráðuneytið. Reykjavík, 2002.

Utanríkisráðuneytið. Skýrsla um framboð Íslands og kosningabaráttu til sætis í öryggisráði Sameinuðu þjóðanna, 2009–2010 [Report on Iceland's bid for a seat in the UN Security Council]. 2009a. Retrieved from https://www.stjornarradid.is/media/utanrikisraduneytimedia/media/PDF/Lokaskyrsla_um_oryggisradsframbodid_2008.PDF.

Utanríkisráðuneytið. *Iceland's campaign for election to a non-permanent seat on the United Nations Security Council, 2009–2010* [Unpublished report], 2009b.

Þórðardóttir, Sigríður Anna. Speech in Alþingi, 27 February, 2003. *Skýrsla utanríkisráðherra um utanríkismál.* Retrieved from https://www.althingi.is/altext/128/02/r27120644.sgml.

Þórðarson, Sigurjón. Speech in Alþingi, 16 November, 2006. *Utanríkismál, munnleg skýrsla utanríkisráðherra.* Retrieved from https://www.althingi.is/altext/133/11/r16144936.sgml.

Interviews

Interviews A-F with Icelandic and Austrian Diplomats

Interview public official A 2018, 14 February, Interviewer Elínardóttir, Jóna Sólveig.

Interview public official B 2018, 15 February, Interviewer Elínardóttir, Jóna Sólveig.

Interview public official C 2018, 19 February, Interviewer Elínardóttir, Jóna Sólveig.

Interview public official D 2018, 19 February, Interviewer Elínardóttir, Jóna Sólveig.

Interview public official E 2018, 19 June, Interviewer Eggertsdóttir, Anna Margrét.

Interview public official F 2018, 22 June, Interviewer Eggertsdóttir, Anna Margrét.

Interview Gísladóttir, Ingibjörg Sólrún, 2018, 21 February, Interviewer Elínardóttir, Jóna Sólveig.

Interview Haarde, Geir, 2018, 20 February, Interviewer J Elínardóttir, Jóna Sólveig.

Interview Plassnik, Ursula, 2018, 17 September, Interviewer Eggertsdóttir, Anna Margrét.

CHAPTER 7

Greater Than Its Size? Comparing Finland's and Luxembourg's Campaigns to the Security Council

Touko Piiparinen, Tarja Seppä and Anni Tervo

1 Introduction

In the 2012 election for nonpermanent seats in the Security Council, three candidates competed for the two WEOG seats for the term 2013–14: Finland, Luxembourg, and Australia. After two rounds of voting in the UN General Assembly's session on October 18, 2012, the GA selected Luxembourg and Australia, against the expectations of many practitioners and observers who had predicted that Finland would be selected in the very first round. Before these candidatures, Finland had served twice on the UNSC (1969–1970; 1989–1990) and Luxembourg, although a founding member of the UN, had never been a member of the UNSC. Australia, Luxembourg, and Finland received 140, 128 and 108 votes respectively in the first round, and in the second round, Luxembourg received 131 votes against Finland's 62 votes. This poses the important and intriguing question why Finland lost, and Luxembourg won, contradicting predictions?

This chapter offers a comparative analysis on the similarities and differences between Finland's and Luxembourg's campaigns. With departure in the framework presented in Chapter 2, we focus specifically on how the two campaigns were carried out, and why Luxembourg was more successful than Finland in its undertaking. Accordingly, we investigate to which extent these two states demonstrated contributions, claimed competence, and emphasized ideational commitment during the campaign period. Which of these three logics were most important to them and how were they combined differently in the campaigns? Our comparison points especially at differences between the two campaigns as regards to coherence between demonstrated contributions and competence claims and attests to the relevance of political dedication to convincingly claim competence and prove ideational commitment. While Finland's actual contributions to the UN system had hit an historical all point low, undermining a message that displayed middle power pretensions, Luxembourg created a convincing and coherent image of itself as a competent small state. Secondly, the Finnish defeat can also be attributed to

© TOUKO PIIPARINEN ET AL., 2024 | DOI:10.1163/9789004687110_008 the weaker commitment of political decision makers, negatively affecting the strength of the campaign as regards to the competence and skills in relation to Luxembourg's campaign.

The domestic settings were quite different in these two countries for the campaigning period. Throughout its campaign, Finland[1] had six different official governments[2] with five different people serving as prime ministers. Within the six governments, of which one lasted only 69 days, Finland had four[3] ministers for foreign affairs throughout the campaign season. As there were six governments, five prime ministers, and four ministers for foreign affairs, there were bound to be inconsistencies within foreign politics and the Security Council campaign.

Luxembourg,[4] however, had three different governments[5] throughout its campaign season with only one Prime Minister, Jean-Claude Juncker. For the entire period of campaigning, Luxembourg had only two Foreign Ministers, Lydie Polfer and Jean Asselborn, and Minister Asselborn served as the Foreign Minister for most of the campaign period. The governmental consistency gave Luxembourg stability not only in its policies and politics, but also in its campaign efforts.

This chapter discusses Finland's and Luxembourg's Security Council campaigns, how they were carried out, and what kind of similarities and differences can be detected between them. The theoretical framework was presented in Chapter 2 and the discussion in this chapter follows that framework, namely how these two states demonstrated their resourcefulness and contributions, how they claimed competence, and how they showed ideational commitment to be a good and reliable member state of the United Nations. The description of the two candidatures covers campaign organisation, key-participants, activities, message, and domestic debate.

There were differences between the two countries in how they attempted to demonstrate their resourcefulness to the rest of the UN membership.

---

1   See Valtioneuvosto/Statsrådet 2020.
2   Governments, named after the Prime Ministers: Lipponen II (15.4.1999–17.4.2003), Jäätteenmäki (17.4.2003–24.6.2003), Vanhanen (24.6.2003–19.4.2007), Vanhanen II (19.4.2007 –22.6.2010), Kiviniemi (22.6.2010–22.6.2011), Katainen (22.6.2011–24.6.2014).
3   Ministers for Foreign Affair: Erkki Tuomioja (25.2.2000–17.4.2003; 17.4.2003–24.6.2003; 24.6.2003–19.4.2007), Ilkka Kanerva (19.4.2007–4.4.2008), Alexander Stubb (4.4.2008– 22.6.2010; 22.6.2010–22.6.2011), and Erkki Tuomioja (22.6.2011–24.6.2014).
4   See The Luxembourg Government 2020.
5   Governments, named after the Prime Ministers and vice-/deputy Prime Ministers, who were also Ministers of Foreign Affairs: Juncker/Polfer (7.8.1999–31.7.2004), Juncker/Asselborn I (31.7.2004–23.7.2009), Juncker/Asselborn II (23.7.2009–4.12.2013).

There were also differences in how they wanted to showcase their 'UN CV'. Luxembourg emphasised communicating about its present and future contributions to the UN system while Finland concentrated on the historical record of Finnish peacekeeping. However, there was a common denominator: both countries tried to demonstrate their basic administrative capacities and competencies, internal and external, to defend and promote effective multilateralism despite being small states. Finland, perhaps unintentionally, showed some elements of a middle power image through its campaign. There were also differences between these two countries as to how they provided ideational commitment, especially relating to human rights, gender equality and implications for global justice. This chapter also discusses campaign processes and structures of both countries and draws conclusions on the lessons learned and unlearned when comparing these two UNSC campaigns utilising the theoretical framework.

This chapter draws on in-depth interviews of twelve Finnish and Luxembourgian officials and ministers. These interviews provide empirical data drawing upon the experiences of those involved with campaigns, providing comparative analysis and information of structural factors in the campaigns of the two countries. Most of the interview requests were accepted without hesitation but some prospective interviewees declined interviews. In addition, the campaign brochures and other relevant material were used to contextualise the interviews.

2   Campaign Processes, Organisation, and Key Participants

Regarding the campaign process, among the three candidates of the WEOG, Luxembourg was the first to enter the competition in 2001,[6] followed by Finland in 2002.[7] Australia joined the race in 2008. However, Finland did not start campaigning actively until 2008, seven years after Luxembourg began campaigning, which gave Luxembourg a significant head start. Luxembourg took full advantage of its earlier start, actively garnering support from other UN member states, securing pledges and agreeing on vote exchanges well before Finland actively entered the competition.[8] UN member states proved willing to give their support to Luxembourg early on.[9] In fact, this could have

---

6 Interview 6.
7 Interviews 3; 10.
8 Interview 12.
9 Interview 10.

been the case for Finland as well: one interviewee noted that some countries had tried to exchange votes with Finland in the early stages of the race, but Finland had not responded.[10]

The hold-up of Finland's campaign was caused by the rotation arrangement between the five Nordic countries. Because of this, Finland was obliged to refrain from official campaigning before the previous Nordic candidate – in this case Iceland – had completed its campaign. This occurred in 2008 when Iceland lost its bid.[11] Many of the interviewees maintained that Finland started its campaign too late[12] including the planning of the budget and main themes of the campaign.[13]

The early planning of the Finnish campaign began in a steering group and in the unit for UN affairs at the Ministry for Foreign Affairs (MFA) of Finland, before a separate unit for the Security Council campaign was established in 2008. However, during Iceland's candidature, until 2008, Finland refrained from actively discussing its own campaign in bilateral discussions with other UN member states, as this would have undermined the credibility of the Nordic support to Iceland's campaign.[14] The MFA also attempted to engage politicians in the campaign so that they would bring up Finland's candidature in their meetings with foreign counterparts.[15]

One interviewee criticised Finland's cautious and passive approach in the early stage of campaigning, especially in regard to acquiring reciprocal voting pledges and vote exchanges.[16] It was estimated that at least ten member states would have been willing to vote for Finland, but they had already made a deal of reciprocal vote exchange with one of Finland's rivals before Finland replied to their offer for reciprocal support. Interestingly, all the offers for reciprocal support were internally submitted to the political level for decision in the early stage of campaigning, which slowed down decision-making and negotiation processes.[17] One interviewee believed that reciprocal vote exchanges should have been prioritised at least one year earlier, and easy votes should have been collected as early as possible.[18]

---

10   Interview 1.
11   Interviews 2; 4; 7; 12.
12   Interviews 1; 7; 12. Only one interviewee stated that Finland began campaigning early enough (Interview 11).
13   Interview 12.
14   Interview 8.
15   Interview 11.
16   Interview 12.
17   Interview 1.
18   Interview 1.

Finland's campaigning efforts accelerated towards the end. A new phase was launched in spring 2012, and the campaign intensified toward the autumn and culminated in the final six weeks.[19] At that point, the focus was on deepening existing contacts and reinforcing pledges of support that had already been made in the course of the previous four years.[20] One interviewee, however, pointed out that the campaign would have had a more effective peak in the end, had it been led by politicians in a more vigorous manner.[21] Unlike Luxembourg, Finland lacked a so-called plan B, i.e. a plan to get votes in the second round in case Finland failed in the first round of voting – as it actually did. This was a clear omission or mistake albeit not a decisive one, as one interviewee mentioned.[22]

Luxembourg was able to start its campaign already in 2001,[23] and its campaign was very determined and dynamic.[24] Even from the Finnish perspective, Luxembourg proved highly dedicated to win the elections.[25] Luxembourg started to campaign more actively in 2008,[26] and its campaign efforts continued until the very last minute, even with those countries that had already pledged their support to Luxembourg.[27] Before the announcement of the results of the first round of voting, during the counting period, Luxembourg deployed all members of its delegation to the General Assembly to participate in campaigning efforts, thanking those representatives of member states who had already pledged their support to Luxembourg and attempting to convince those who were uncertain to vote for them.[28]

Luxembourg's perseverance until the very last minute was seen as a considerable asset[29] and could be interpreted as showing significant diplomatic skills. Luxembourg effectively implemented their plan B, in a striking contrast to Finland, which did not even have such a plan. The inaction of the Finnish campaigners may have partly been caused by the fact that Luxembourg was close to being elected together with Australia, already in the first round, and Finland was therefore unlikely to succeed in the second round. However, since

---

19   Interview 1.
20   Interview 2.
21   Interview 7.
22   Interview 2.
23   Interviews 2; 6; 7.
24   Interview 2.
25   Interview 7.
26   Interview 6.
27   Interview 10.
28   Interview 10.
29   Interview 10.

there was no plan to get votes in case of a second round of voting, another potential explanation is that Finland was overconfident of being elected already in the first voting round.

The above findings demonstrate that the important factor affecting the election outcome in terms of the campaign process was Luxembourg's head start, which can be attributed to the Nordic rotation but also to Finland's inaction in the beginning. Even though the Nordic rotation was still considered a useful means of rallying support,[30] the rotation cycle was widely viewed as too dense.[31]

Regarding campaign structures, both Finland and Luxembourg had relatively small campaign organisations with limited financial resources.[32] Finland had a budget of two million euros for 2010–2012 and Luxembourg one million euros for 2011–2012.[33] In comparison, Australia's campaign budgeted 25 million USD[34] for a five-year period.[35] In addition to substantial campaign funds, Australia had a large campaign organisation,[36] which included the Governor-General of the Commonwealth of Australia, the prime minister, and special representatives of the prime minister. Australia also employed several special representatives to Africa alone.[37] Australia's outreach thus far surpassed Finland's and Luxembourg's networks. Finland had neither any special representatives of the prime minister nor special representatives designated to Africa.

As previously mentioned, the planning of the Finnish campaign began in a steering group chaired by Ambassador Marjatta Rasi. The members of the steering group were initially heads of units and other MFA officials. Political decision-makers also occasionally participated in it. The outcomes and decisions of the group's meetings were subjected to the government's Foreign Affairs Committee for approval, which could take a long time and sometimes slowed down decision-making related to the campaign. The group planned the means and tools of campaigning, as well as the campaign messages.[38] It also produced guidance papers for the campaign and discussed regional issues.[39] Its overall

---

30   Interview 7.
31   Interviews 2; 7.
32   Interviews 7; 10; 12.
33   Excluding additional staff costs.
34   Including all costs.
35   International Peace Institute (IPI) 2013, 14–15.
36   For Australia's campaign, see Carr 2014.
37   Interview 2.
38   Interview 12.
39   Interview 11.

aim was to make the campaign a common initiative for the entire MFA and to engage the MFA's different departments in the campaign.[40] When a separate unit (known by the Finnish acronym POL-TN) was established and started to work on the campaign in May 2009, the steering group was shut down. Foreign Minister Alexander Stubb had asked Ambassador Pasi Patokallio to reorganise the campaign, and he reported directly to Minister Stubb, and later on to his successor Erkki Tuomioja.[41] One interviewee maintained that the actions taken by the new organisation should have started many years earlier, given the aforementioned hindrances of the first organisation.[42]

POL-TN consisted of five people, altogether. Ambassador Patokallio, who was leading the team, requested his colleague, Ambassador Kari Kahiluoto, to join. Ambassador Patokallio was also named the Special Representative of the Foreign Minister, which allowed him to meet with representatives of UN member states at a higher political level. In addition, POL-TN included a desk officer, a trainee and a secretary.[43] Ambassadors Patokallio and Kahiluoto divided the responsibilities of the campaign between themselves so that Ambassador Patokallio was in charge of most of the travels abroad, especially for bilateral meetings with the representatives of other governments, while Ambassador Kahiluoto was responsible for national activities and matters related to international and regional organisations.[44] While Ambassador Patokallio did most of the planning for the campaign, the Permanent Representative of Finland to the UN, Ambassador Jarmo Viinanen, was in charge of campaign activities in New York. Ambassador Viinanen was in close contact with the permanent representatives of other UN member states, and the campaign was prioritised in his meetings.[45]

Besides POL-TN, there was also a separate unit for UN affairs at the MFA, which had existed before any of the campaigning efforts began. Because of the earlier organisational restructuring of the MFA's departments, the unit for UN affairs had been placed under global affairs instead of political affairs. The unit for UN affairs was involved in beginning and coordinating the campaign, but many interviewees believed that the campaign needed more support from the Department for Political Affairs at the time.[46] The unit for UN affairs was

---

40   Interview 12.
41   Interview 2.
42   Interview 1.
43   Interview 2.
44   Interviews 1; 2; 7.
45   Interviews 1; 2.
46   Interview 12.

later located under that department. POL-TN, in turn, was formed under the Department for Political Affairs to begin with, although it was responsible for reporting directly to the Foreign Minister, not to the head of the department. The unit also had a separate budget and separate offices from the department.[47]

Finnish campaign messages were integrated in different ministerial and parliamentary visits and meetings in foreign countries, and the campaign was brought up in all the relevant reports of ministers.[48] The Permanent Mission of Finland to the UN was responsible for contacting the representatives of UN member states in New York. However, all Finnish embassies were assigned a role in the campaign: they were to inform POL-TN of relevant developments and to take instructions from it, as needed. Early on, the heads of missions were asked by Ambassador Patokallio to prepare proactive campaign strategies for each country they covered and to provide up-to-date information and analysis of the state of support, or the lack of it, for the Finnish candidature on a regular basis. They were also tasked with reporting on the campaign activities of Australia and Luxembourg.[49] However, former ambassadors were not utilised for the campaign, even though some of them offered their help and support to the campaign team,[50] which could be considered another potential shortcoming of the Finnish campaign's process and structure.

Luxembourg's campaign organisation, unlike Finland's, remained somewhat intact throughout the campaign. During the first years, the campaign work was managed by the Ministry of Foreign and European Affairs. The campaign was institutionally located under the Directorate of Political Affairs, where Ambassador Sylvie Lucas worked as the director from 2004 to 2008. During that time, the campaign was coordinated by Ambassador Lucas from Luxembourg, until she was appointed as Permanent Representative to the UN. Once she left for New York in 2008, it was decided that she would continue coordinating the campaign from New York. After that, most of Luxembourg's campaign work was managed and executed from New York[51] whereas Finland's campaign continued to be led from Helsinki for the entire duration of the campaign.

The concentration of Luxembourg's campaign planning in New York constituted a wise strategic move in light of Luxembourg's limited diplomatic network.[52] Most of Luxembourg's embassies were located in Europe, not in those

---

47   Interview 2.
48   Interview 4.
49   Interviews 2; 7.
50   Interview 11.
51   Interviews 6; 10.
52   Interview 6.

areas that were most relevant for the campaign such as Africa and the Pacific.[53] Luxembourg's embassies were informed of the campaign, but they were not actively campaigning. In New York, however, Luxembourg was able to reach all the UN member states. In this context, Luxembourg also made a tactical decision that Ambassador Lucas would not be travelling to summits or bilateral meetings to conduct the campaign but instead focused her work to New York.[54] There, Ambassador Lucas took up visible and high-level positions in major organs of the UN, notably the Presidency of the Economic and Social Council, the Chair of the Guinea Configuration of the Peacebuilding Commission, and as facilitator in some negotiations when asked by the President of the General Assembly.[55] Using these strategic and tactical moves to focus the campaign efforts on New York, Luxembourg was able to effectively compensate for some of the disadvantages related to its smaller embassy network compared to its rivals Finland and Australia.

Luxembourg's small New York-based campaign team planned the priorities, key targets, and momentums of campaign actions and later defined critical gaps in Luxembourg's outreach.[56] It produced virtually all campaign materials, including brochures and leaflets, in-house at the Permanent Mission of Luxembourg to the UN. The campaign trips of ministers and special envoys were also partly organised from there.[57] Besides Ambassador Lucas, the core campaign team included Véronique Dockendorf and Marc Weydert, who were also working for the Permanent Mission to the UN. The Deputy Permanent Representative, Ambassador Jean Olinger, was also actively involved[58] when he was in New York for five years, beginning in 2005.[59] Ambassador Olinger coordinated the travels of Luxembourg's special envoys in the campaign, helped the ambassadors with multiple accreditations to carry out the campaign, and organised internal matters. He also met with his peers and discussed the campaign in his capacity as the Deputy Permanent Representative.[60] In 2010, Ambassador Olinger returned to Luxembourg and continued campaigning from there with a UN desk officer. A small team was considered an advantage,

---

53   Interview 3.
54   Interview 6.
55   Interview 6.
56   Interview 10.
57   Interviews 6; 10.
58   Interview 6.
59   Interview 10.
60   Interview 10.

since it was always clear what each member was doing, and the campaign message remained cohesive.[61]

3   Messages of the Campaigns

Finland and Luxembourg attempted to demonstrate their resourcefulness to the rest of the UN membership in different ways. While Luxembourg decided to put an emphasis on communicating about its present contributions to the UN system, the Finnish campaign focused on the historical record of Finnish peacekeeping. Although the track record, or 'UN CV', of Finland's engagement in peacekeeping over the previous decades has been good, one interviewee pointed out that Finland's strategy to highlight its past performance in peacekeeping during the campaign became self-defeating and detrimental to its cause, since the message was essentially backward-looking.[62] UN member states had hoped to receive a more future-oriented account or vision of what the Finnish membership at the Security Council, including its one-month Presidency of the Council, would actually entail in multilateral and bilateral terms.[63]

In comparison, Australia was able to demonstrate its resourcefulness consistently by drawing upon its country's image as a middle power.[64] Australia harnessed votes from other UN member states by signalling its greater capacity to promote their interests at the Security Council because of its greater resources, as compared to its rivalling smaller states Finland and Luxembourg.[65] In this way, Australia effectively used its greater size to its advantage.

The analysis of the campaign brochures published by the Finnish and Luxembourgian governments confirms the above observations.[66] Finland's brochure concentrates on reviewing 'the golden history' of Finnish peacekeeping with the clear aim of demonstrating its credibility and resourcefulness in the field of peace and security, arguing, for example, that since 1956 Finland has deployed more than 50,000 people to 30 peacekeeping operations.[67] At

---

61   Interview 6.
62   Interview 7.
63   Interview 7.
64   On the term 'middle power', see for example Robertson 2017; Carr 2014; Ungerer 2007.
65   Interview 2.
66   Finland to the UN Security Council in 2013–2014; Luxembourg and the United Nations 2013 – 2014.
67   Finland to the UN Security Council in 2013–2014, 4.

the same time, however, the brochure lacks updated statistics of contemporary Finnish contributions to UN peacekeeping.

The statistical analysis of UN peacekeeping shows that Finland contributed only a handful of troops to UN peace operations during and prior to the 2012 elections. The number of Finnish troops deployed in UN operations dropped to a low point in 2011, when it had between 21 and 25 peacekeepers deployed between January and December 2011. The average number of Finnish blue helmets in the field during the critical years of campaigning was 43 (2008), 88 (2009), and 53 (2010).[68] The low level of Finnish contributions to UN peace-keeping stands in contrast to the image it promoted of itself as a committed and pioneering country in the field of UN peace and security. However, the number of Finnish UN peacekeepers did rise during the second half of 2012, reaching 200 in October 2012.[69]

These observations also raise a question: why did the Finnish campaign pri-oritise peacekeeping in the first place? The Finnish campaign message, which highlighted peacekeeping, appears somewhat misguided and unconvincing considering Finland's actual contributions, outlined above.

A distinct feature, which sets Luxembourg's campaign message in its bro-chure apart from the Finnish one, is its focus on up-to-date statistics and numer-ical evidence of its current contributions to the UN system. It also highlights Luxembourg's major financial contributions to UN peacekeeping, in addition to its sustained troop contributions to UN and EU operations. Its significance is impressive, considering the small size of its army (approximately one thousand soldiers).[70] Luxembourg's brochure vividly shows that its contributions to the UN regular budget and to the UN peacekeeping budget rank among the highest ones of all UN member states when measured *per capita*. It also reveals that Luxembourg ranks among the top donors to various UN agencies and programs in absolute terms, including, for example, to the Central Emergency Response Fund, where Luxembourg ranks the 13th major donor in absolute terms.[71]

Luxembourg's brochure also unapologetically highlights its generous ODA (official development assistance) appropriations to poorer countries, which amounted to 1.05 percent of Gross National Income in 2010: 'Today, Luxembourg comes 2nd among the countries that exceed the United Nations target of 0.7% of Gross National Income in official development aid',[72] the brochure states. In

---

68   Global Policy Forum 2019; United Nations Peacekeeping 2019.

69   Global Policy Forum 2019.

70   Interview 10.

71   Luxembourg and the United Nations 2013–2014.

72   Luxembourg and the United Nations 2013–2014.

comparison, the Finnish brochure states that, 'The Finnish Government will ensure that its development co-operation appropriations take Finland towards the level of 0.7 percent of gross national income set by the United Nations'.[73] Finnish ODA appropriations did increase through 2014, but never reached the target level of 0.7 percent of GNI. One interviewed official from Luxembourg made an indirect jab at the Finnish campaign by stating that Luxembourg did not need to 'play with the figures', making pledges (or excuses) to poorer countries, saying that its ODA contributions would rise to a certain level in a certain timeframe, since Luxembourg could unambiguously confirm its *actual* level of 1.05 percent ODA support that was already provided. The interviewee regarded the high level of Luxembourg's ODA support as a major contributing factor to its success in the election.[74]

Most Finnish interviewees downplayed Finland's lower ODA support and its diminished peacekeeping contributions as having a negative impact on the campaign. They emphasised that neither point was ever raised in discussions with representatives of other UN member states during the campaign.[75] The interviewees also rationalised that neither factor contributed to Finland's defeat,[76] because the major cuts in the Finnish ODA support were made only after the October 2012 election.[77] Moreover, Finland was still connected with the group of Nordic countries and thus received 'tug assistance' from its fellow Nordic countries with much higher levels of ODA contributions.[78] One interviewee pointed out that ODA and peacekeeping contributions were raised as overall themes in domestic discussions. However, in discussions with UN member states the votes were never conditional on Finnish ODA contributions or on peacekeeping contributions.[79] Another interviewee assessed retrospectively that greater contributions would probably have had a positive impact on the election result[80] as these issues under discussion were also highly reputational issues.

The Finnish campaign depicted Finland as 'greater than its size' and as a middle power pioneer, major contributor and norm-entrepreneur on peacekeeping and mediation, which, however, stood in stark contrast to its actual,

---

73   Finland to the UN Security Council in 2013–2014.
74   Interview 10.
75   Interviews 1; 2; 5.
76   Interviews 2; 5.
77   Interviews 4; 5.
78   Interview 1.
79   Interview 7.
80   Interview 4.

reduced number of contributions to UN peace and security. In addition to the low number of blue helmets, the level of mediation interventions undertaken by the Finnish government also remained relatively low. Still, in 2010 Foreign Minister Alexander Stubb and the Ministry for Foreign Affairs announced their vision to make Finland a 'great power of mediation'.[81] In particular, the Finnish campaign actively promoted two thematic issues of UN policy, peacekeeping and mediation.[82] These signalled some elements of a middle power image of Finland, despite the fact that Finland actually belonged to the Forum of Small States – an informal grouping of small countries at the UN, established in 1992 – coupled with the fact that its senior officials likened Finland more to the group of small states, rather than middle or great powers. Plainly rendered, Finland signalled a somewhat contradictory country image and identity.

The depiction 'greater than its size' was never explicitly announced in Luxembourg's campaign. In fact, Luxembourg consistently attempted to build an image of itself as a small state, organising events and participating actively in the Forum of Small States at the UN,[83] which – alongside *la Francophonie* – constituted an important platform, reference point and stakeholder group for Luxembourg. However, the depiction 'greater than its size' perfectly characterised Luxembourg's country image at the practical level. The interviewees from Luxembourg pointed out that its relatively high ODA contributions were used during the campaign to illustrate and confirm Luxembourg's commitment to effective multilateralism and to the UN system. Luxembourg was thus able to effectively demonstrate its active solidarity and responsibility to other UN member states by referring to its actual ODA contributions and other contributions.[84]

The interviewees also mentioned that, according to the UN Charter, itself, one of the main criteria for a state to be elected to the Security Council is its contribution to the maintenance of the principles of the UN. Luxembourg also firmly supported the UN's holistic approach to peace and security, in which development, security, human rights, and the rule of law are interlinked. Luxembourg has consistently contributed more than 0.7 % of its GNI to ODA since 2000, and one percent since 2009, which constituted one of Luxembourg's long-held policies derived from the coalition agreement of successive governments. This demonstrates how the consistency and continuity

---

81   See for example Ministry for Foreign Affairs of Finland 2010; Mäkinen 2013.
82   One interviewee pointed out that mediation was an emerging priority for Finnish UN policy at the time, while peacekeeping had been a more permanent feature (Interview 7).
83   Interview 6.
84   Interviews 6; 10.

of Luxembourg's government policy contributed to its successful election result.[85]

However, some interviewees pointed out that when constructing bilateral relations and trying to get pledges for votes, some counterparts wanted to know what they could receive in return for their vote, either as a means of bilateral support of some kind, or as political usefulness once Finland would be on the Security Council.[86] Many interviewees referred to exchanging votes, in general, but asking for additional support in exchange for a vote was also portrayed. Generally, most interviewees considered close and functional bilateral relationships to be crucial.

In terms of demonstrating contributions, Luxembourg also possessed one crucial asset compared to Finland and Australia, namely its unique access to la Francophonie and the French-speaking world, at large. As the only French-speaking country among the three candidates, Luxembourg was perceived to have a special understanding of the issues francophone countries faced, and it could rely on support provided by member states of la Francophonie.[87] Luxembourg engaged actively with la Francophonie,[88] hosting events and working as an active member of the organisation,[89] as well as actively reaching out to other French-speaking countries.[90]

The Nordic network could not provide the same *extent* of support to Finland as the other two networks – la Francophonie and the Commonwealth – could give to Finland's rivals Luxembourg and Australia respectively, but the *depth* of support provided by the Nordics to Finland was certainly the greatest. The other Nordic countries brought up Finland's candidature in their meetings with foreign representatives in developing countries.[91] They also agreed to support Finland's campaign especially in areas where its own embassy network was inadequate, including in West Africa, where Finland did not have embassies, except for Abuja, Nigeria.[92] In practice, however, that kind of support remained limited.[93]

---

85   Interviews 6.
86   Interviews 1; 2.
87   Interview 6.
88   *La Francophonie* was established in 1970 to promote co-operation between French speaking countries. At the time of writing there were 58 members and 26 observers in the organization, which amounts to up to one third of the entire UN membership. See for example Organisation internationale de la Francophonie.
89   Interview 6.
90   Interview 10.
91   Interview 7.
92   Interviews 1; 2; 7; 12.
93   Interview 7.

Both la Francophonie and the Commonwealth were loyal supporters of Luxembourg and Australia respectively, and their internal solidarity was strong.[94] Finnish interviewees estimated that France also gave strategic support to Luxembourg, along with certain other French-speaking countries[95] even though as a permanent member of the Security Council, France never publicly voices its support of any candidate country.[96] Finland, however, did not receive support from any great power.[97]

In contrast to Luxembourg, Finland came up short when reaching out to French-speaking countries, as well as, to a certain extent, to Portuguese-speaking countries.[98] While Finland was supported by all the five Nordic countries, Luxembourg made a deliberate choice not to involve other Benelux countries in campaigning for its candidature, in order to retain its campaign a national project, to demonstrate its commitment to the UN system, and to prove to other UN member states that its small size would not prove an obstacle.[99] Alongside la Francophonie, another comparative advantage for Luxembourg was its long-held membership in both NATO and the EU,[100] while Finland was not a NATO member but had only close practical cooperation with the organisation.[101]

Both Luxembourg and Finland were also members of the EU, but in some respects, their EU membership proved more of a burden than an asset during their campaigns. The Security Council already has two permanent European members (the United Kingdom and France), while developing countries, particularly those in Africa, are grossly underrepresented in demographic terms. Australia's announcement of its candidature in 2008 marked a game-changer in the competition in the sense that the 'clean slate' (meaning that Finland and Luxembourg would automatically obtain the two available non-permanent seats on the Council allocated to the WEOG) did not apply. The EU membership became a disadvantage for both Finland and Luxembourg in the eyes of many diplomats, particularly those representing the Global South. Conversely, being non-European became an asset for Australia.[102]

---

94   Interviews 7; 11.
95   Interviews 1; 4. The alleged support of France for Luxembourg was neither confirmed nor denied by Luxembourgian interviewees.
96   Interviews 4; 7. In this connection, Interviewee 7 spoke of not only France, but also other nuclear weapon powers, in general.
97   Interviews 1; 2.
98   Interview 1.
99   Interview 6.
100   Interview 7.
101   Interview 8.
102   Interview 1.

In this competition setting, Finland's political actions in the EU regarding Greece's financial crisis before the election inadvertently affected Finland's campaign, since Finland was the only country that required loan guarantees for the EU support to Greece. This undermined Finland's reputation to some degree by revealing selective solidarity on the part of Finland in the EU context, or even a hawkish attitude. Such portrayals also contradicted Finland's self-image as a model student in the EU and on the international stage, at large.[103] One interviewee described the lack of support for Finland from other EU countries as a shock.[104]

To summarise, Finland's campaign message was inconsistent and modest compared to Luxembourg's. When asked, most Finnish interviewees could not specify Finland's main themes or messages, whereas Luxembourg's interviewees had a clear vision of what they had highlighted when campaigning.

4   A Specific Message: Human Rights and Other Key Values

According to an independent study conducted by the International Peace Institute (IPI),[105] Finland's excessive focus on human rights including gender equality may have contributed to its defeat.[106] It was further suggested that Finland had an arrogant and 'besserwisser' attitude towards other countries. However, this section will challenge the notion of the presumed hubris of Finland's human rights policy. We argue that Luxembourg's campaign brought up its active human rights policy more vigorously and decisively than Finland's campaign. Luxembourg's campaign message bore appealing and clear implications to global justice which was the irresistible strength of Luxembourg's message.

Finland's and Luxembourg's strategies significantly differed to the extent that human rights were raised during the campaigns. Unlike their Finnish counterparts, Luxembourg's campaign officials made a deliberate decision not to omit politically sensitive issues, including human rights and international criminal justice, in their discussions with representatives of other UN member states during the campaign. They were aware that such a decision entailed risks for the campaign, but these issues were considered part and parcel of Luxembourg's foreign policy and identity. Therefore, leaving them out would

---

103   Giuli and Hedberg-Paul 2018, 3–17.
104   Interview 8.
105   International Peace Institute 2013.
106   See also YLE News 2012; 2012a;2013.

not have been truthful or honest in relation to other UN member states, in fact it would have proven counterproductive for the campaign in the long run. In campaign meetings Luxembourg reiterated that it would stand by the EU's foreign policy principles during its envisaged Security Council membership, as well.[107]

One interviewee from Luxembourg invoked the French proverb *droit dans ses bottes* – 'standing straight in their boots' – to explain the self-assured, honest, and determined way in which Luxembourg decided to integrate human rights in its campaign, which promoted Luxembourg's brand and contributed to the positive campaign outcome. In particular, the rule of law has been existential for Luxembourg and integral both to its identity and to self-interest.[108] Because of the small size of its territory, natural resources, and army, the sheer existence of Luxembourg itself has throughout its history been dependent on the maintenance of international rule of law, that is, the adherence of states to the principles of sovereignty and territorial integrity, and the non-use of force in international relations. In this regard, the historical experiences of Luxembourg have been similar to those of Finland. Yet Finland decided not to comprehensively integrate human rights into its campaign strategy.[109] This somewhat counterintuitive element of the Finnish campaign will be explored in more detail below.

Interviews with the Finnish representatives revealed that Finland adopted a significantly more modest approach than Luxembourg did about its campaign message on human rights. According to an inside joke within the campaign team, the less democratic a country is, the more likely it was to vote for Finland.[110] One interviewee confirmed that human rights issues were not raised during the campaign.[111] Another interviewee explained the rationale for a cautious approach to human rights by stating that it served to eliminate a hubristic 'besserwisser' image that could potentially be associated with Nordic countries and thus inflict damage on the campaign. The fact that Sweden was campaigning for a seat on the UN Human Rights Commission (now Council) at the same time, was an additional reason for wariness.[112] One interviewee provided a similar rationale, arguing that Finland was, first and foremost, identified as a Nordic candidate, which meant that other Nordic countries might

---

107   Interviews 3; 6.
108   Interview 10.
109   Interviews 1; 2.
110   Interview 1.
111   Interview 7.
112   Interview 2.

be seen as more vocal on human rights issues, and that Finland might consequently be considered complacent or self-righteous by certain UN member states.[113] This proved to be an inaccurate assessment.

Yet, interviewees calculated that the portrayal of Finland being a Nordic country as more advantageous than disadvantageous for the campaign in overall.[114] One interviewee refuted the post-campaign critique that Finland would have been hubristic on human rights issues, since its campaign did not actively bring up such issues in discussions with other UN member states, nor were they raised by counterparts.[115] Another interviewee, however, maintained that Finland did not actually change its approach or message regarding human rights, but in fact upheld the human rights values, gender equality, and the Nordic welfare state model throughout the campaign.[116] Here again, the interviewee emphasised that these values were related to the overall Nordic model, the Nordic brand,[117] as human rights are part of the construction of the Nordic welfare state.

What is showcased above proves that Finland adopted a comparatively modest human rights approach during the campaign, whereas Luxembourg actively and deliberately brought up human rights issues not only as part of its campaign strategy but also, and more crucially, as part of its wider identity-building process: human rights were viewed as corollary to Luxembourg's foreign policy and integral to its identity and self-interest. Luxembourg's campaign managers considered the campaign a unique opportunity for Luxembourg to make itself, its interests and values known among the UN member states – unique in the sense that Luxembourg could not promote its interests and values in the forums and locations where Finland had a more extensive embassy network or greater resources at its disposal. In other words, the campaign per se was regarded as valuable to Luxembourg, regardless of its eventual outcome.

Moreover, the identity-building dimension of Luxembourg's campaign (the active dissemination of Luxembourg's values and interests to other UN member states) contributed to predictability, in that it provided UN members with a clearer sense of what values and interests Luxembourg stood for, and how it was likely to act and vote as an elected member of the Security Council. By side lining human rights in its own campaign, Finland lost that opportunity and could not create a clear or predictable vision of how it would be expected

---

113   Interview 1.
114   Interview 1.
115   Interview 1.
116   Interview 4.
117   Interview 4.

to act on the Security Council, which, in turn, had a negative impact on how UN member states – especially the EU and other Western states – were likely to vote. One possible explanation might be that Finland made an inaccurate calculation when it assumed that others already understood Finland's policy and reputation for human rights and gender equality beforehand. Luxembourg did not want to take anything for granted.

Luxembourg's decision to actively promote human rights during the campaign is clearly reflected in its campaign brochure, which reinstates Luxembourg's commitment to human rights, fundamental freedoms, democracy, good governance, and the rule of law. Notably, the brochure confirms Luxembourg's active support both to the Human Rights Council (HRC) and to the principle of Responsibility to Protect, also known by its acronym RtoP or R2P.[118] The brochure further declares Luxembourg's long-lasting commitment to gender equality by referring to Luxembourg's active and concrete contributions in this field, including its financial support to the UN Women.[119]

The Finnish brochure also points out Finland's commitment to human rights, democracy, the rule of law, and gender equality.[120] However, this affirmation is outlined in generic terms without any referral to concrete contributions, unlike in Luxembourg's brochure. Moreover, the Finnish brochure leaves out politically sensitive topics such as the HRC and RtoP, which are explicitly mentioned in Luxembourg's brochure. Finland's policy on RtoP could, in retrospect, be described as passive and evasive throughout the entire campaign period, although RtoP encompasses human rights, democracy, the rule of law, and gender equality, values which Finland wishes to support. For example, Finland did not present a national statement at the first general debate of the UN General Assembly on RtoP organised in July 2009, as numerous other EU member states and other Nordic countries did, including Iceland, Norway, and Sweden (which spoke on behalf of the European Union), as well as Luxembourg and Australia, all of whom voiced their support for the principle of RtoP.[121] RtoP was elevated to the priorities of the Finnish UN policy only after Finland's defeat in the Security Council election in October 2012, as outlined in the Finnish Foreign Service UN Strategy.[122]

This change in the Finnish policy on RtoP from a passive mode to a more active one would suggest that a modest or passive approach to human rights

---

118   Luxembourg and the United Nations 2013–2014, 8.
119   Luxembourg and the United Nations 2013–2014, 10.
120   Finland to the UN Security Council in 2013–2014, 10.
121   See for example ICRtoP 2009.
122   Ministry for Foreign Affairs of Finland 2013.

had clearly proven counterproductive to the Finnish campaign, and contradictory to the Finnish identity in international community, at large. Finland's refreshed approach to human rights in its UN policy virtually rose from the ashes of its campaign defeat.

5   Showing Competencies by Networking: Activities of Some Key Participants

The common denominator between Finland's and Luxembourg's campaigns was their active efforts to demonstrate their commitment to defend and promote effective multilateralism, and to prove that they possessed sufficient capabilities to fulfil the responsibilities bestowed upon the elected members of the Security Council,[123] despite their perceived images as small states.[124] Luxembourg, on the one side, strove to quell potential scepticism regarding its capacity to effectively act as a nonpermanent member by pointing to its previous track record of prestigious international positions. Luxembourg had numerous times served as the President of the European Union, despite the small size of its foreign administration. Finland, on the other hand, had already served twice as a nonpermanent member of the Security Council. Thus, both candidates were in a position to make a convincing argument that the basic administrative capacities were in place to effectively fulfil the duties of a nonpermanent member.

    Nevertheless, interviews conducted for this research revealed interesting differences between the two candidates in terms of their efforts to portray themselves as competent small states. To explain these differences in more detail, it is useful to draw upon Baldur Thorhallsson's account, which identifies two broad categories of qualitative factors that can determine the ability of small states to influence the work of the Security Council. Firstly, small states should aim to show their internal, or administrative, competence, including the knowledge, initiative, diplomatic, and leadership skills of their representatives, particularly politicians and diplomats, as well as their ability to forge coalitions. Secondly, small states should try to demonstrate their external competence by projecting an image of themselves as neutral actors or norm entrepreneurs in particular policy fields.[125] Both internal and external competencies should relate to the reputation that these states want to construct or uphold.

---

123   Interviews 1; 6.
124   See Ekengren and Möller, Chapter 2 in this book.
125   Thorhallsson 2012, 159.

It could be said that Luxembourg was more effective and successful in demonstrating its internal competence to other UN member states during its campaign, including the proven competence of its UN diplomats to work in leadership positions of UN organs, while Finland focused more on its external competence, particularly its capacity to act as a pioneer, major contributor, and norm-entrepreneur in the policy fields of peacekeeping and mediation. Ultimately Finland's focus on external competence, however, resulted in a confused and somewhat self-contradictory country image.

Regarding internal competence, both Luxembourg and Finland attempted to demonstrate the diplomatic skills of their politicians and officials, but interviewees perceived that Luxembourg ultimately proved more active, effective, and successful in this task. The strong social capabilities and personal commitment of Luxembourg's Foreign Minister Jean Asselborn (as well as Australian Prime Minister Kevin Rudd) were significant assets to Finland's rivals. Some interviewees even believed that Finnish policy makers and diplomats did not possess as fluent social skills as their Luxembourgian colleagues when interacting with foreign representatives.[126]

Luxembourg's candidature was personified by Foreign Minister Asselborn,[127] who travelled far more than his Finnish counterparts[128] and consequently became widely recognised, thanks to his extensive travels.[129] Moreover, Minister Asselborn had been acting as the foreign minister for a long time, nurturing an extensive network of personal and professional relationships, which contributed positively to the campaign.[130] Minister Asselborn also visited New York frequently.[131] Campaigning efforts were often part of a larger agenda.[132] The royal family was involved in the campaign, as well.[133] HRH the Grand Duke of Luxembourg, the Head of State of Luxembourg, addressed the General Assembly in 2012 and participated in the Rio + 20 conference.[134]

Both Luxembourgian and Finnish interviewees felt that Luxembourg's campaign officials demonstrated outstanding diplomatic and leadership skills, which contributed to a successful election outcome. Notably, Sylvie Lucas, who worked as the Permanent Representative of Luxembourg to the UN

---

126   Interviews 1; 2.
127   Interview 7.
128   Interviews 2; 10.
129   Interview 2.
130   Interview 3.
131   Interview 6.
132   Interview 10.
133   Interviews 11; 12.
134   Interviews 6; 10.

during the final years of the campaign, had taken on high-level responsibilities before the Security Council elections, acting as President of the Economic and Social Council from 2009 to 2010, as Chair of the Guinea configuration of the Peacebuilding Commission, and as a mediator and facilitator of international negotiations at the request of the President of the General Assembly, as previously mentioned. The interviewed officials from Luxembourg pointed out that these merits – as well as its other internationally acclaimed and professional diplomats – formed part of Luxembourg's overall attempt to demonstrate its willingness, readiness, and capacity to take on the responsibilities that come with being an elected member of the Security Council.[135] These merits, to use Thorhallsson's terminology here, signalled the 'internal competence' of a small state.

Although opposition parties in Finland did not voice any objections to the campaign, a low level of political interest and a lack of commitment to concrete actions was observed by interviewees.[136] One interviewee noted that Finland's candidature was considered part of its normal UN policy and foreign policy framework, one task among many others relating to foreign policy. In Luxembourg and Australia, by contrast, there was a strong commitment to the candidature by high-level politicians, and it was considered a high national priority.[137]

The general debates at the United Nations General Assembly in September gather all world leaders to the UN headquarters and are thus a valuable opportunity for states to present their candidature and policies. Luxembourg very systematically presented its candidature in the general debate speeches it gave. From 2008 onwards, Luxembourg mentioned its candidature regularly at the end of every speech. In 2010, Luxembourg connected its candidature to European and EU-related values. On other occasions the speeches were made by Foreign Minister Asselborn, but in 2012, the year of election, the speech was made by HRH the Grand Duke of Luxembourg.[138]

Finland, however, discussed its candidature in its general debate speeches only three times during the period from 2008 to 2012. The candidature was left unmentioned during 2008 and 2010. In 2009 and 2011 President Tarja Halonen mentioned the candidature in the middle of her speeches. In 2012, President Sauli Niinistö, mentioned Finland's candidature twice in his speech,

---

135   Interview 6.
136   Interviews 1; 12.
137   Interview 7.
138   See UNGA Speeches Luxembourg 2008–2012.

discussing it in the middle of the speech and returning to it at the end.[139] This can be interpreted as showing the countries' different political approaches to campaigning.

The role of political decisionmakers in any major political campaign undertaken by states, including the Security Council campaign, cannot be underestimated, since they lend domestic political support to the campaign, which is vital to its success. Interviewees regarded the foreign ministers and heads of state as key actors in the Security Council campaign.[140] In this regard, Finnish interviewees also believed that politicians should have taken on more of a leadership role during the campaign.[141] The role of Finnish politicians also remained limited regarding the execution of the campaign, as demonstrated by the lack of travelling on the part of foreign ministers. Strikingly, one of the Finnish foreign ministers was mentioned to have made only one trip solely to campaign,[142] although the foreign ministers did travel and meet their colleagues, for example at the UN, in dozens of bilateral and multilateral meetings, as well as in some multilateral summits. Foreign Minister of Luxembourg Asselborn, by contrast, travelled extensively, visiting every continent except Australia, including countries that were difficult to reach. Finland's ministers never achieved the same level of outreach.[143] The policymakers of Australia were also considered active and positive towards campaign travel, and utilised multilateral meetings skilfully for campaigning, in addition to travelling solely for campaigning purposes.[144]

The fact that the campaign responsibilities were on the level of officials/ diplomats instead of the political level was detrimental to the Finnish campaign since officials were not able to compensate for the political clout that high-level politicians could have brought to the campaign. In his capacity as the Foreign Minister's Special Representative, Ambassador Patokallio met with several presidents bilaterally and at international meetings, but generally speaking, presidents and other high-level policy makers prefer to meet with their direct counterparts, especially in Africa and in hierarchically organised countries.[145]

---

139   See UNGA Speeches Finland 2008–2012.
140   Interviews 2; 10.
141   Interview 7.
142   Interview 4.
143   Interview 10.
144   Interview 2.
145   Interview 2.

The continuity of the governmental policy in Luxembourg was also considered an asset to its campaign, whereas the consistency of Finland's campaign messages and campaign structure was inadvertently affected by numerous changes to the government during the campaign period.[146] Luxembourg, like Finland, applied active outreach measures, although the planning and execution of its campaign was headquartered in New York. In addition to Foreign Minister Asselborn, who campaigned abroad frequently and extensively,[147] Luxembourg assigned four special envoys, thus covering a wider geographical sphere than Finland. In general, the commitment of political decision makers was seen as exceptionally high with regard to Luxembourg's campaign. For Luxembourg, this was a practical way to reach those places where their diplomatic network was weaker.

Both Finland and Luxembourg also engaged other ministers, politicians, and stakeholders in campaigning.[148] The Speaker of the Finnish Parliament, Eero Heinäluoma, actively participated in the campaign.[149] Moreover, the Finnish campaign team provided materials to policymakers representing sectoral ministries when they attended international meetings.[150] Ambassador Kahiluoto also met with relevant officials in sectoral ministries, including the Ministry of Education and Culture and the Ministry of Transport and Communications, to brief them on the campaign.[151] In Luxembourg, the Prime Minister, the Minister for Development Co-operation and Humanitarian Aid, and several other ministers were engaged in the campaign.[152] The campaign was brought up in meetings with foreign representatives whenever possible. Speaking notes and materials were also prepared and given to other ministers by the campaign team.[153]

The Finnish campaign also mobilised some of its preeminent politicians who had proven their diplomatic skills on the international stage, and thus promoted internal competence, to some extent. Particularly, the Former President and Nobel Peace Laureate (2008) Martti Ahtisaari was described as a 'loyal warrior'[154] and an asset to the campaign because of his vast personal networks.[155] In the final stage of the campaign, President Ahtisaari met with

---

146   Interview 7.
147   Interview 10.
148   Interviews 2; 6; 7; 10.
149   Interviews 1; 2; 8.
150   Interview 7.
151   Interview 7.
152   Interview 6.
153   Interview 10.
154   Interview 2.
155   Interview 7.

almost every African PR to the UN, who pledged their support.[156] President Ahtisaari, along with State Secretary Pertti Torstila, participated in the Finnish delegation to the high-level week of the UN General Assembly in autumn 2012 prior to the elections, and the two had many meetings during and after the high-level week.[157]

Some interviewees indicated a potentially serious critique, that Finland, for some reason did not have women in key positions of campaigning efforts,[158] even though Finland claims to be a forerunner in gender equality matters. However, most interviewees did not consider this problematic,[159] although one interviewee did point out that some representatives of UN member states might have taken note of the absence of women in the campaign.[160] The fact that Luxembourg, by contrast, had a highly competent and acclaimed woman as its Permanent Representative to the UN was seen as a positive for Luxembourg's campaign.[161] This may have also increased the perceived contrast between Finland's and Luxembourg's campaigns in the eyes of other UN member states: Luxembourg, unlike Finland, was in the practice of promoting gender parity in its own campaigning. In addition to the fact that gender parity is a question of principle, it is also a question of the country's reputation.

The significance of having special representatives and envoys of policymakers in Security Council campaigns has been debated by some on account of the fact that in many UN member states, the voting decision is ultimately made either by the permanent representative or by the Foreign Ministry.[162] However, it is deemed here that comparison of the special representative/envoy systems between Finland and Luxembourg merits some examination, because they enabled outreach to UN member states, which constituted a crucial factor of a successful campaign, namely networking.

Special representatives and envoys were usually met by their respective counterparts. A special representative of the foreign minister, for example, typically met with the foreign minister. Finland's campaign leader, Ambassador Pasi Patokallio, was named a Special Representative of the Foreign Minister to ease access to political decision makers abroad. Ambassador Patokallio

---

156   Interview 1.
157   Interview 1.
158   Interview 11.
159   Interviews 1; 2; 5; 7.
160   However, this interviewee did not consider the contradiction between Finland's policy of gender equality and the lack of women in its campaign particularly problematic (Interview 1).
161   Interview 11.
162   Interview 9.

travelled frequently as part of the campaign efforts, even establishing diplomatic relations with two countries (Kiribati and South Sudan) which Finland had not previously had any substantial diplomatic communication. By the end of the campaign, Finland had established diplomatic relations with all other UN member states.[163]

The nature of the Finnish political system was such that it ruled out special representatives of the prime minister, as the prime minister is not in charge of foreign or UN policy in Finland.[164] There was, however, discussion in Finland about sending special representatives of the president, but the idea was discarded. One interviewee mentioned that on one special occasion, a Special Representative of the President was used,[165] although another interviewee maintained otherwise and insisted that there was no occasion, despite the efforts of POL-TN, that anyone was designated as a Special Representative of the President. Nevertheless, the lack of Special Representative(s) of the President was, in hindsight, viewed as a downfall, as having this would have enabled access to the highest political level and to the head of state.[166]

Given the importance of the number of votes small Caribbean states possess, POL-TN made good use of the contacts of Ambassador Mikko Pyhälä, who was accredited to those Caribbean countries. He was often accompanied by the Foreign Minister's Special Representative on his visits to the region, too. Ambassador Pyhälä was highly praised by all interviewees who knew him[167] and his work and networking skills were considered unique.[168] CARICOM, the Caribbean Community composed of 15 states, endorsed Finland's candidature as a group.[169] Some stated that this was, to a large extent, due to Ambassador Pyhälä's personal efforts, as he was very well known among the political leaders of the Caribbean.[170] In addition, Ambassador Pyhälä's experience was very much appreciated and admired by African ambassadors, since he had a long career and substantial professional experience of working in many African countries[171] and demonstrated diplomatic skills which would have been useful elsewhere, as well.

---

163   Interview 2.
164   Interview 9.
165   Interview 1.
166   Interview 2.
167   Interviews 1; 2; 4; 7.
168   Interview 4.
169   Interview 7.
170   Interviews 1; 4.
171   Interview 7.

Luxembourg, by contrast, had four special regional envoys: one for the African Union, one for the Caribbean, one for la Francophonie, and one for the Pacific.[172] The special envoys covered those areas that Foreign Minister Asselborn could not.[173] Luxembourg's special envoys were ambassadors that were given additional responsibilities.[174] For example, Luxembourg's ambassador to Beijing was simultaneously the special envoy to the Pacific, and the special envoy to the African Union was a former PR to the UN.[175] Special envoys actively travelled to regions where Luxembourg did not have embassies, delivering the campaign message.[176] There was also a special envoy to the Non-Aligned Movement, but lobbying the NAM proved more difficult than regional organisations.[177] Special envoys also travelled to places that were difficult to reach, sometimes having to wait long periods of time due to demanding circumstances and distances before they could reach their destinations. Special envoys were generally well received by hosting states and governments, and most UN member states were visited at least at the special envoy level.[178] Considering that the diplomatic networks of Finland and Luxembourg were similarly weak in certain regions like Africa, Luxembourg was able to reach a wider geographical area through the special envoys and showcase an interest for less-visited countries.

Finland tried to reach other UN member states by organising two high-level seminars during 2012: one on peacekeeping and another on mediation.[179] Finland also organised an exhibition at the UN headquarters showing its past contributions to UN peacekeeping.[180] Through these events, Finland signalled its competence to work as a pioneer and conceptual architect of peacekeeping and mediation and to further develop these themes during its tenure on the Security Council, like a normative and conceptual *middle power* of UN peace and security – more than a small power, less than a great power.[181] Throughout the campaign, Finland's country image oscillated between a small state and a middle power since, on the one hand, Finland had been portraying itself as 'greater than its size',[182] a major contributor, and norm-entrepreneur in

---

172   Interviews 3; 6.
173   Interview 10.
174   Interview 10.
175   Interviews 6; 10.
176   Interview 10.
177   Interview 3.
178   Interview 10.
179   Interview 1.
180   Interview 7.
181   Robertson 2017.
182   Ministry for Foreign Affairs of Finland 2010.

peacekeeping and mediation, while its actual contributions to these two sectors remained meagre at the time.

The interviewed Finnish campaign actors themselves maintained that the image that Finland was conveying to other states was one of a small state.[183] The interviewed representatives of Luxembourg also pointed out that *both* Luxembourg *and* Finland belong to the Forum of Small States.[184] However, the above analysis reveals that Finland actually portrayed itself as a middle power in many important aspects, including particularly on its focus on external competence in peacekeeping and mediation.[185] Thus, the middle power image broadcast by the Finnish campaign appears to have been an unintended consequence.

Finnish interviewees pointed out that highlighting peacekeeping and mediation as thematic priorities of the campaign was typical for Finland's UN policy over the previous decade, and that nothing new was invented in that regard.[186] So, one can say that the Finnish campaign was consistent but did portray itself as larger than its actual size. Another interviewee stated that Finland lost despite the aforementioned seminars, and would have lost with certainty, had they not been organised at all.[187]

6   Conclusions

Reflecting the theoretical framework from Chapter 2, demonstrating contributions, claiming competencies, and showing ideational commitments, it is possible to draw three main conclusions. First, the analysis has revealed inconsistencies in the Finnish campaign message, which ultimately proved detrimental to the whole campaign. On one hand, Finland projected some elements of an image of itself as a middle power, a global norm-entrepreneur of mediation and peacekeeping. However, these did not match Finland's actual contributions to the UN system, including its peacekeeping contributions, which had hit a historic low at the time, as well as its lower official development assistance (ODA) compared to its smaller European rival. As a result, Finland was oscillating between the images of a small state and middle power, and its campaign message remained unclear. Luxembourg was able to present

---

183   Interviews 2; 5.
184   Interview 6.
185   Ministry for Foreign Affairs of Finland 2010.
186   Interviews 2; 4; 5.
187   Interview 1.

itself as an effective and committed small state candidate due to its focus on its internal competence. Luxembourg created a convincing and coherent image of itself as a competent small state with skilled diplomats and politicians, just as Australia was able to successfully build its campaign upon the identity of a middle power with greater resources.

Secondly, the Finnish defeat can also be attributed to the relative strengths of Luxembourg's campaign, notably the higher commitment of political decision makers and more effective campaign processes, institutions, and networks, which, among other things, enabled it to maintain the consistency of the campaign message, to achieve high visibility in New York among peers due to its high-level positions in main UN organs, and to establish effective outreach to UN member states. One Finnish interviewee admitted that, in Luxembourg, the candidature was seen as a national project, constituting the main undertaking in Luxembourg's foreign policy.[188] Luxembourg's foreign minister, for example, travelled more than his Finnish counterparts.

Thirdly, and perhaps most importantly, this case study has not supported the argument that excessive focus on human rights would have played a major role in the failure of the Finnish campaign. The International Peace Institute (IPI) and the ensuing debate on that report gave rise to the idea that the hubristic moral approach by Finland contributed to its defeat.[189] Head of the IPI, Terje Rød-Larsen, argued at the launching event of the report:

> The core values which the Nordics stand for [...] like human rights, the rule of law, the responsibility to protect, et cetera, is (sic) not necessarily that popular amongst the majority of the membership in the United Nations. And this is paired with a perception that the Nordics consider themselves to be morally superior, that there is a "besserwisser", condescending attitude towards others based on the values and ideological issues.[190]

This idea was also supported when Sweden failed to succeed in their Human Rights Council campaign in 2012, right after Finland's defeat. The results from our case-study rather reveal that Finland downplayed human rights during its campaign, while Luxembourg actively and resolutely brought up human rights issues as part of its campaign strategy.

---

188   Interview 12.
189   IPI 2013.
190   YLE News 2013.

Bibliography

Carr, Bob. *Diary of A Foreign Minister.* (Sydney: New South Publishing, 2014).

Giuli, Marco, Annika Hedberg and Ivan Paul . Finland in the European Union: Frontrunner or Follower? Discussion Paper. Sustainable Prosperity for Europe and Europe in the World Programmes. November 13. *European Policy Centre* (EPC). Retrieved from https://www.epc.eu/en/Publications/Finland-in-the-Europ ean-Union-Frontrunner-or-follower~2045b8, 2018

Global Policy Forum. *Peacekeeping Tables and Charts.* Retrieved from https://www .globalpolicy.org, 2019.

International Coalition for the Responsibility to Protect (ICRtoP). *General Assembly Debate on the Responsibility to Protect and Informal Interactive Dialogue.* Retrieved from https://www.globalr2p.org/resources/, 2009.

International Peace Institute (IPI). *Taking Stock, Moving Forward: Report to the Foreign Ministry of Finland on the 2012 Elections to the United Nations Security Council.* Retrieved from https://www.ipinst.org/wp-content/uploads/2013/04/pdfs_130406 -UNSC_Elections_Report_Final.pdf., 14–15, 2013.

Luxembourg and the United Nations. Candidate for the Security Council 2013 – 2014. Grand-Duché de Luxembourg. *Ministère des Affaires étrangères.*

Ministry for Foreign Affairs of Finland. *Finland vill bli stormakt inom fredsmäkling.* Nyheter, 7.5.2010. Retrieved from https://um.fi/aktuellt/-/asset_publisher/gc654 PySnjTX/content/suomi-tahtaa-rauhanvalityksen-suurvallaksi?curAsset=0&stId =47307, 2010.

Ministry for Foreign Affairs of Finland. *The UN Strategy of the Finnish Foreign Service* 17.7.2013. Publications of MFA 08/2013, 48–50. Retrieved from http://formin.finl and.fi., 2013.

Mäkinen, Juha. *Kadonnutta kunniaa etsimässä.* Ulkopolitiikka 1/2013. Retrieved from http://arkisto.ulkopolitiikka.fi/artikkeli/1102/kadonnutta_kunniaa_etsim_ss/, 2013.

Organisation internationale de la Francophonie, *Welcome to the International Organisation of La Francophonie's Official Website.* Retrieved from https://www .francophonie.org.

Robertson, Jeffrey. 'Middle-power definitions: confusion reign supreme'. *Australian Journal of International Affairs,* 71 (4), (2017), 355–370.

The Luxembourg Government. *The Government.* Retrieved from https://gouvernem ent.lu, 2020.

Thorhallsson, Baldur. 'Small States in the UN Security Council: Means or Influence?'. *The Hague Journal of Diplomacy,* 7(2012), 135–160.

UNGA (United Nations General Assembly) Speeches Finland 2008–2012. 63rd session [2008, 23 September]: A/63/PV.6: President Tarja Halonen.

UNGA (United Nations General Assembly) Speeches Finland 2008–2012. 64th session [2009, 24 September]: A/64/PV.6: President Tarja Halonen.

UNGA (United Nations General Assembly) Speeches Finland 2008–2012. 65th session [2010, 24 September]: A/65/PV.14: President Tarja Halonen.

UNGA (United Nations General Assembly) Speeches Finland 2008–2012. 66th session [2011, 21 September]: A/66/PV.11: President Tarja Halonen.

UNGA (United Nations General Assembly) Speeches Finland 2008–2012. 67th session [2012, 25 September]: A/67/PV.6: President Sauli Niinistö.

UNGA (United Nations General Assembly) Speeches Luxembourg 2008–2012. 63rd session [2008, 26 September]: A/63/PV.12: Deputy Prime Minister Jean Asselborn.

UNGA (United Nations General Assembly) Speeches Luxembourg 2008–2012. 64th session [2009, 25 September]: A/64/PV.8: Deputy Prime Minister Jean Asselborn.

UNGA (United Nations General Assembly) Speeches Luxembourg 2008–2012. 65th session [2010, 24 September]: A/65/PV.14: Deputy Prime Minister Jean Asselborn.

UNGA (United Nations General Assembly) Speeches Luxembourg 2008–2012. 66th session [2011, 24 September]: A/66/PV.24: Deputy Prime Minister Jean Asselborn.

UNGA (United Nations General Assembly) Speeches Luxembourg 2008–2012. 67th session [2012, 26 September]: A/67/PV.9: HRH the Grand Duke of Luxembourg.

United Nations Peacekeeping. *Troop and Police Contributors*. Retrieved from https://peacekeeping.un.org/en/troop-and-police-contributors, 2019.

Ungerer, Carl. 'The "Middle power" Concept in Australian Foreign Policy'. *Australian Journal of Politics and History*, 53(4), (2007), 538–551.

Valtioneuvosto/Statsrådet. *Hallitukset aikajärjestyksessä*. Retrieved from https://valtioneuvosto.fi/tietoa/historiaa/hallitukset-ja-ministerit/raportti/-/r/v2, 2020.

YLE News. Niinistö: Pohjoismaiden on nähty röyhistelevän maailmalla omilla malleillaan. 1.12.2012. Retrieved from https://yle.fi/uutiset/3-6399235, 2012.

YLE News. Niinistö: Suomella ei varaa ylemmyydentunteeseen. 23.12.2012. Retrieved from https://yle.fi/uutiset/3-6427568, 2012a.

YLE News. US Think Tank: Not Everyone Cares for the Nordic 'Know-It-All' Attitude. 9.4.2013. Retrieved from https://yle.fi/uutiset/osasto/news/us_think_tank_not _everyone_cares_for_the_nordic_know-it-all_attitude/6571358 ,2013.

Interviews

Interview 1 2018, 9 March, Interviewer Anni Tervo.
Interview 2 2018, 15 March, Interviewer Anni Tervo.
Interview 3 2018, 6 April, Interviewer Anni Tervo.
Interview 4 2018, 4 April, Interviewer Anni Tervo.
Interview 5 2018, 5 April, Interviewer Anni Tervo.
Interview 6 2018, 6 April, Interviewer Anni Tervo.
Interview 7 2018, 26 March, Interviewer Anni Tervo.

Interview 8 2018, 19 April, Interviewer Anni Tervo.
Interview 9 2018, 3 May, Interviewer Anni Tervo.
Interview 10 2018, 21 May, Interviewer Anni Tervo.
Interview 11 2018, 27 June, Interviewer Anni Tervo.
Interview 12 2018, 29 June, Interviewer Anni Tervo.

CHAPTER 8

Election 2016: Sweden and the Kingdom of the Netherlands

Ann-Marie Ekengren and Ulrika Möller

1 Case Introduction

In the 2016 election for nonpermanent seats on the UNSC, three candidates competed for the two WEOG seats for the term 2017–18: Sweden, the Kingdom of the Netherlands, and Italy. A contested slate between three wealthy and industrialized countries paved the way for an intense round of campaigning. The 2016 election was the first held in June, rather than early autumn, for the purpose of giving incoming members more time to prepare.

This chapter focuses on the campaigns of Sweden and the Kingdom of the Netherlands to gather support for their aspirations to win a seat on the Security Council.[1] It regards the Swedish campaign as the successful case, and the Kingdom of the Netherlands' campaign as the unsuccessful case. The latter was partly successful in the sense that it resulted in one year on the SC (see discussion on design in Chapter 2), but the election outcome from the first round of voting is a clear verdict in favor of Sweden as the candidature with the strongest support. The discussion of the two candidatures is structured into organization, key-participants, activities, message, and domestic debate, which forms the basis of the comparison between them. Results inform conclusions about three different logics of campaigning (as presented in Chapter 2); demonstrating contributions, claiming competence, and proving ideational commitment. As in the other empirical chapters on competing candidatures, the aim is to investigate whether, and how these logics are at play in the campaigning processes. We suggest that the degree to which these logics are present, and the way they are combined, can explain the different outcomes in terms of both success and failure. A decisive difference between

---

1 There are several studies on how Sweden organized its work during the term in the Council and on the objectives obtained, see especially Engelbrekt, 2020; 2023. The Swedish Government's focus on women and children during conflicts is also highlighted in Jormanainen, Kurath & Muvumba Sellström (2022) and Sellström, Wallensteen, Finbakk, Olsson, Chang and Tryggestad (2021).

the campaigns compared in this chapter is the degree to which members of the government were actively involved, which had effects on the competence claims and ideational commitments of each campaign. The Swedish candidature managed to display expertise and commitment relevant to the themes of the campaign and to the position at stake.

In the 2016 election, all three candidates had substantive multilateral merits and considerable previous experience from serving on the SC. With a record of three previous terms on the SC (1957–8, 1975–6,[2] 1997–8), Sweden had been the first to announce its candidature in 2004. Sweden had also been a candidate for the term 1993–4 but was defeated by Spain and New Zeeland in the 1992 election. The Kingdom of the Netherlands followed suit in 2005. The Netherlands had previously served on the SC on five different occasions (1946, 1951–1952, 1965–1966, 1983–1984, 1999–2000) and Italy had previously served on the SC on six occasions (1959–1960, 1971–1972, 1975–1976, 1987–1988, 1995–1996, 2007– 2008).[3] Italy deprived Sweden and the Netherlands of their hopes for a clean slate, by announcing a new candidature just as they completed their most recent term.

Initially, many observers considered Italy to be the stronger candidate, leaving Sweden and the Netherlands to compete over the second seat. The qualified guess among several ambassadors in New York, as late as the spring of 2015, was that Sweden would end up defeated. Instead, Sweden won a first-round victory in the election. For the second seat, the Netherlands and Italy resolved the situation of even support after five rounds of voting through a split-term agreement.[4]

The Swedish government welcomed the victory with relief and happiness. The candidature had not only suffered from a prolonged indecisive period but was completed in the context of a critical domestic debate. The outcome represented an important break from a series of Nordic failures. In terms of candidatures to the Security Council, Iceland was defeated in 2008 and Finland in 2012. Sweden had experienced several related UN-failures; in 2011 Sweden ran for a seat on the International Law Commission (ILC), in 2012 for the Human Rights Council, and in 2014 for the International Criminal Court (ICC). All three attempts failed. These attempts had also directed resources towards other campaigns than the UNSC campaign .[5]

---

2 Mörth 1991.
3 Security Council report, 2016.
4 Interview 18; Security Council Report, 2016.
5 Lidén 2016.

A Social Democratic government announced the Swedish UNSC candidature in 2004, with broad parliamentary support. For most of the candidature, Sweden had a liberal-right coalition government (2006–10, 2010–14). A social democratic-green coalition government (2014–18) took office in October 2014. At this point in a candidature, it is reasonable to expect ongoing active campaigning. However, different approaches between the two coalition governments had a significant impact on the pace and size of the campaign. The two approaches by the two different Swedish governments resulted in a long period of modest activity followed by a concluding high intensity finale.

The Netherlands had several different coalition governments in between the announcement of its UNSC candidature in 2005 and the election in 2016. Prime Minister Jan Peter Balkenende (2002–10) announced the candidature on behalf of his rightwing coalition government. During the first part of the candidature, Christian Democrat Balkenende was Prime Minister of four different coalition governments, ranging ideologically from rightwing to center-left. He was replaced by conservative-liberal Max Rutte (2010-) as Prime Minister, initially for a coalition government with the Christian Democrats, and then from 2012 onward with the Social Democrats.[6] In the Netherlands, the governments had similar approaches to the campaign, and once the phase of intensive campaigning began in 2013, it held a steady pace.

2   Organization of the Campaign: Sweden

The Swedish candidature was a long-spun process (2004–16) and therefore inevitably involved many people, including a mix of politicians, diplomats, and civil servants. Once a decision to run had been made, the candidature becomes the responsibility of the Minister of Foreign Affairs. Over the course of its candidature, Sweden had a shift on this position, which is a common occurrence in context of the prolonged candidature process. The extent to which the shift had an impact on the Swedish campaign is difficult to determine but there was a clear difference in priority between governments. During the initial phase, and for most of its candidature, Carl Bildt was the Swedish Foreign Minister (2006–14) eventually succeeded by Margot Wallström (2014–2019). These two individuals embodied the diverging views of their respective coalition governments on the role of the UN in Swedish foreign policy, as well as how Sweden should go about winning a seat on the Security Council. Foreign Minister Bildt

---

6   Parliaments and Governments Database. See https://www.parlgov.org/.

made a political statement out of the Swedish candidature by launching a 'slim' campaign, mainly restricted to the circulation of international merits in the relevant political and diplomatic circles, summarized as the Swedish 'UN CV'. One person became responsible for coordinating the candidature at the Ministry of Foreign Affairs in August 2012. It took another two years, until September 2014, to have two staff in place at the Swedish representation in New York; a diplomat responsible for coordinating the campaign in New York, and an election officer.[7] When Margot Wallström took office as Foreign Minister, she revised Sweden's campaign strategy in favor of a more ambitious approach, with the full support of the new Prime Minister Stefan Löfven. The government declaration in October 2014 highlighted the UN candidature to set the tone for an increased focus on the campaign.

The secretariat for the Swedish campaign was set up at the Ministry of Foreign Affairs in Stockholm. It was formed in Stockholm during the autumn/winter of 2014 and consisted initially of six people; one manager, four co-workers, and one assistant, but expanded to eight by the time of the campaign's final phase. The initial division of labor meant that each co-worker was responsible for one geographical region. The additional two recruitments were for the purpose of 1) keeping track of the diplomatic interactions and the growing number of voting agreements reached, and 2) handling the documentation of the campaign and other issues raised during the domestic debate around the candidature.[8] An additional center was located at Sweden's Permanent Representation to the United Nations in New York. Intense and friendly contact between Stockholm and New York occurred during the period of active campaigning. The team in New York appreciated that the secretariat in Stockholm trusted the judgements and plans they made as based on efforts and assessments from the New York campaign site.[9] The campaign also engaged Swedish embassies around the world, as well as the delegations in Brussels and Geneva. Yet Sweden had the weakest diplomatic representation by far among the three candidates. By the time of the election, in 2016, Sweden had 107 international missions, compared to 144 for the Netherlands and 205 for Italy.[10] The campaign sought to compensate for this by making the most out of 2015, approaching it as a year with a very busy multilateral schedule. Thus, the reach of the campaign was

---

7   Cronenberg-Mossberg 2017.
8   Interviews 2; 10.
9   Interviews 12; 13.
10   Lowy Diplomacy index. At the beginning of the candidature, in 2005, Sweden had 105 missions (Swedish Government Offices' Yearbook 2005, 35). We have not been able to identify the earlier numbers for the Netherlands or Italy.

increased by engaging in several high-profile multilateral meetings, including
COP21 in Paris and Financing for Development in Addis Ababa, as sites for the
Swedish campaign.[11]

In March 2015, a new ambassador, Olof Skoog, arrived in New York, filling
the position of the Swedish Permanent Representative to the UN. The campaign unit at the Swedish representation also added two additional staff members in 2015: one communications officer and one assistant. As the campaign
intensified, it affected nearly all the work at the mission in New York. The most
important position among the non-diplomatic staff in New York was the election officer. During the final, most intense part of the Swedish campaign, the
team in New York even had two election officers. With only weeks left before
the election, status meetings were held twice a day, where most of the people at the representation attended.[12] The weekly meetings with the PRS of the
Nordic and the Baltic states offered a chance to catch up with information during the campaign in New York. The expectation of the Nordic PRS supporting
each other's candidature through their diplomatic interactions with other UN
colleagues relies on an established practice of collaboration.[13] The Swedish
candidature enjoyed a similar kind of support from the Baltic PRS in New York,
which was a newer occurrence. These weekly updates about the campaign
offered Sweden strategic insights from its close Nordic and Baltic colleagues.[14]
To estimate the amount of support they had received, the Swedish campaign
developed an elaborate tool – internally referred to as 'the SPON list'. This tool
estimated the received responses over time, and at different political levels.
The secretariat in Stockholm and the unit in New York shared the list with each
other. According to people tasked with updating the list during the campaign,
the number of votes Sweden received during in the election in June 2016 corresponded with the number they had predicted when analyzing the list in the
days ahead of the election.[15]

3   Organization of the Campaign: the Kingdom of the Netherlands

The Netherlands had several different coalition governments during its
Security Council candidature (2005–16). Led by two different prime ministers,

---

11   Interviews 2; 11.
12   Cronenberg-Mossberg 2017; Interviews 12; 13.
13   See Chapter 1.
14   Interview 12.
15   Interview 12; 13.

Jan Peter Balkenende and Max Rutte, these governments were consistent in their political views on the relevance of the candidature. The candidature was on behalf of the Kingdom of the Netherlands, and thus included four countries: the Netherlands, Aruba, Curaçao and Sint Maarten. The secretariat for the Kingdom's campaign became located at the Ministry of Foreign Affairs in The Hague. The Permanent Representation to the United Nations in New York was the other important unit. The Hague secretariat began its work in 2013, with two staff members and one intern. It gradually increased in size, and by March 2014, a new campaign manager was in place. By the time the election took place, a staff of eight to ten people were employed. The campaign was coordinated from The Hague, where the campaign was shaped, but in close contact with and through substantial input from New York. The campaign team in New York had seven members, including two interns, for most of the active phase. This number increased to 15 staff members during the final weeks of the campaign.[16] In 2013, the Dutch Foreign Minister, Frans Timmermans, gave a speech at the General Assembly in New York launching the candidature. The Kingdom of the Netherlands was introduced as 'Your partner for peace, justice and development'.[17] This launch coincided with the inauguration of Ambassador Karel J.G. van Oosterom as Permanent Representative of the Kingdom of the Netherlands. This was almost three years before the election. The diplomatic work to reach vote agreements had been underway since the announcement of the Dutch candidature in 2005. From autumn 2013, winning support through bilateral contacts was also a main activity of the new PR. In particular, the target set was that the ambassador should meet bilaterally on three occasions with each of his many diplomatic colleagues.[18]

The campaign also engaged Dutch embassies throughout the world, as well as the diplomatic missions in Brussels and Geneva. Referred to as 'the golden triangle', The Hague, New York, and the embassies were the three main pillars of the campaign. There was a systematic approach in terms of ensuring that additions made to the campaign were distributed to all locations at the same time. It is worth noting that the capitals of the Caribbean countries of the Kingdom were not explicitly factored into this strategic figure, even if coordination between capitals took place. Moreover, since the diplomatic representation for all countries of the Kingdom occurs via a common permanent mission, no additional coordination efforts were made between the countries of the Kingdom regarding a particular campaign site.

---

16   Interview 17.
17   Timmermans, UN, 2013.
18   Interviews 14; 18.

Although the campaign aimed for contacts on the political and diplomatic levels available, conscious efforts were made to focus on the decisionmaker, and the campaign considered that the decisionmaker could vary depending on the country in question. To keep track of the established contacts and to estimate the level of support, the secretariat established a database to which all members of the campaign had access. It included a file on who was identified as the decisionmaker. The estimations of the amount of support relied on a system of confirming and reconfirming on the different political levels. Incionsistency between levels was interpreted as a sign of weakness in the campaign, or a lack of support, which helped to identify relations in need of strengthening. Several campaign members described difficulties with estimating support, and special challenges related to the size of the state. While inconsistencies between levels is a common challenge related to larger states, with smaller states the difficulty is rather to establish dialogue on at least one level to estimate support. Without a bilateral diplomatic relationship, confirmed by embassies located in each capital, the platform for dialogue is between PRS in New York. Getting in touch with the smallest states is especially difficult because of their very limited administrative resources, but it is also particularly important since the PR may very well be the decisionmaker.[19]

4   Comparison of the Campaign Organizations

The Swedish and Dutch candidatures had similar organizational features. They both established secretariats in their capitals, with additional units located at the representation in New York. The interviews offer a glimpse at the close and constructive contacts between these locations. The efforts to reach voting agreements and to spread the previous and current contributions to the UN began even before the establishment of these organizations. The emerging secretariats worked on creating a coherent message, including attempts to display the traits of the candidate, by using slogans and short, prepared speeches, at any given opportunity. Both campaigns relied on their embassies to set up diplomatic and political meetings and to arrange activities. Both were particularly active in New York. Bilateral meetings with other PRS were the single most important task performed by the PRS. Both campaigns set a plan for several such visits by their PR to gather and maintain support. Both campaigns developed a tool to keep track of all contacts and activities over time, on various

---

19   Interview 14; 15; 16.

diplomatic and political levels, and at different sites, and they used these tools for estimating the amount of support. The main difference between the candidatures was that the Dutch organization to prepare and manage active campaigning was set up one year earlier. The Dutch PR began his many visits of diplomatic colleagues in the autumn of 2013, while the gathering of support on behalf of the Swedish campaign in New York was modest until the spring of 2015. The Dutch campaign was swift to introduce the slogan of the Kingdom of the Netherlands as 'Your partner for peace, justice and development'. The Swedish candidature organized to make the most of the many multilateral meetings the year ahead of the election.

The emergence of campaign organizations signifies how the candidatures moved towards the phase of active campaigning. In addition to the attempts to promote the candidature through engagement in the UN, the secretariats in The Hague and Stockholm, in collaboration with their missions in New York, worked on a coherent message based on specific values and priorities that they began to communicate more actively using slogans, in speeches, and in discussions. In both cases, the early candidatures showed the countries' efforts to demonstrate their contributions to the United Nations. In both cases, the shift towards more intense campaigning that followed the establishment of campaign centers, showed the further efforts to demonstrate their many past and present contributions to the UN, combined with initiatives to prove ideational commitment to the UN, as well.

5   Key Participants: Sweden

The political parties that formed the liberal-right coalition government (2006–10, 2010–14) stood behind the 2004 announcement of the candidature in their role as political opposition. As a government, they were more reluctant to move the candidature forward. The Swedish Prime Minister, Fredrik Reinfeldt, showed no special interest in the matter. Two previous Nordic candidatures seemed to have proven that the extensive efforts gave nothing in return. In political circles, there was a critical debate on the increasing competition for a seat in the Security Council. The debate highlighted rising costs and increasing risk of the use of dubious means. More importantly, critical voices claimed that contested slates within the WEOG led to undesired rivalry between members of the EU. The coalition government consisted of parties with their hearts and minds invested in European integration. Carl Bildt contributed to the debate by promoting a rotation schedule for the EU-members. The larger EU states disagreed with a rotation schedule as they aimed for a much more frequent representation on the Council than a rotation would allow.[20] As an additional approach, the Swedish 'slim campaign' would keep it clean and save it from the rampant costs of extensive diplomacy and politicians on the move. Sweden's aim was to be an example of an honest candidate.[21]

In contrast, the 2014 governmental declaration pronounced an active pursuit of the candidature.[22] The new Swedish Prime Minister, Stefan Löfven, had been among the critical voices against the concept of a slim campaign, which the Social Democrats viewed as a profound lack of interest in the candidature.[23] Löfven substantiated his political dedication to the candidature by actively participating in the campaign. The other two most active ministers were Foreign Minister Margot Wallström and Minister for International Development Cooperation Isabella Lövin. Margot Wallström's Cabinet Secretary, Annika Söder, and Isabella Lövin's Cabinet Secretary, Ulrika Modéer, were also very much involved. They all raised the candidature in their external contacts planned for other purposes and traveled to promote the candidature. Not only was the Foreign Ministry more involved in the campaign during the new government, but the Government Offices of Sweden were more integrated in the work, as well.[24] Among Stefan Löfven's political advisors, Efraim Gomez is mentioned as important in facilitating Löfven's interest in the campaign and acting as a link between the Ministry of Foreign Affairs and the Government Offices.

The position as campaign manager was first held by Anna-Karin Eneström and later by Niklas Kvarnström. The responsibility for the campaign in New York was given to Carl Skau, who coordinated the many diplomatic contacts. Olof Skoog was appointed PR in March 2015, with only 15 months left before the election. The obligatory first courtesy visit to meet with colleagues gave an instant opportunity for the new PR to raise the Swedish candidature.[25] By taking on the position as chair of the Peacebuilding Commission, Skoog was also able to bring immediate visibility to the Swedish delegation and candidature.[26]

---

20   See Chapter 1.
21   Interviews 1; 3; 5.
22   Government Declaration, October 3, 2014.
23   DN Debatt October 8, 2013.
24   Interviews 2; 3; 11.
25   Interviews 12; 13.
26   In terms of shaping the Swedish campaign organization and deciding who should be active in its pursuit, it was important to analyze the experiences from previous Swedish and Nordic campaigns, as well as some successful campaigns from other members of the WEOG. A few key individuals, including Cabinet Secretary Annika Söder and diplomat Anders Lidén had experience from previous Swedish candidatures; one failure (1992 election) and one success (1996 election) and these experiences were brought into the

The candidature also engaged Swedish ambassadors throughout the world. To further increase the number of representatives actively promoting the candidature, the secretariat in Stockholm recruited a group of former politicians and senior diplomats. These 'Special Envoys' consisted of former Prime Ministers Göran Persson (1996–2006) and Carl Bildt (1991–1994) (also the most recent former Minister of Foreign Affairs, 2006–2014), former Minister of Foreign Affairs Lena Hjelm Wallén (1994–1998), and former diplomats Marika Fahlén, Pierre Schori, and Henrik Salander. Göran Persson was never actively involved in the campaign but was mentioned as a figurehead. On certain rare occasions, Crown Princess Victoria attended campaign events in Stockholm as an additional highlight to activities related to the campaign.

6   Key Participants: the Kingdom of the Netherlands

The active part of the candidature took place with Max Rutte as Head of a coalition government between his conservative liberal People's Party for Freedom and Democracy and the Social Democrats.[27] Foreign Minister Frans Timmermans promoted the candidature in the General Assembly in September 2013, with a special focus on the legal order supported and promoted by the Netherlands.[28] The proceeding years of active campaigning took place under Bert Koenders as Foreign Minister. Ambassador Bahia Tahzib Lie was campaign manager in The Hague, and the responsibility for the campaign in New York fell on Frans Kemperman.

The strategic concept of 'The Golden Triangle' (The Hague, New York, and diplomatic missions) encapsulated the relevance of ambassadors throughout the world serving as campaign workers. The PR in New York played an

---

planning. The campaign planners considered unsuccessful Nordic candidatures (Iceland 2009–10, Finland 2013–14), and especially the conclusion from the Finnish evaluation that the campaign had 'peaked' too early and lost votes just ahead of the election. New Zealand's candidature was considered as an example of a successful campaign run by a country similar to Sweden in size, which also had an independent foreign policy profile. Insights on the necessity of having support from a country's own political level became part of the Swedish campaign as a direct consequence of the contacts with NZ; therefore, Löfven and other ministers took on important roles in the campaign. Candidatures from the Baltic states and Germany were also mentioned as important during the campaign planning.

27   Dutch Foreign Ministers in office: Christian Democrat Ben Bot (2003–07), Christian Democrat Maxime Verhagen (2007–10), Liberal Uri Rosenthal (2010–12), Social Democrat Frans Timmermans (2012–2014) and Social Democrat Bernt Koenders (2014–17).

28   Timmermans, UN 2013.

important role. The arrival of Karel J.G. van Oosterom in August 2013 marked the start of the campaign in New York. In his previous position as Director-General for Political Affairs in the Ministry of Foreign Affairs Van Oosterom had already been involved in the candidature. Among the members of the government, the Foreign Minister was the most involved in the campaign. The candidature also engaged ministers from the Caribbean part of the Kingdom.

On some occasions, members of the royal family were involved in activities related to the campaign. Most notably, the Dutch speech at the General Assembly in 2015 was held by King Willem-Alexander for the first time. This meant that the Dutch speech was held earlier in the session, since diplomatic protocol puts Heads of States before Prime Ministers. Prime Minister Rutte, Foreign Minister Koenders, and Queen Maxima were also in attendance when King Willem-Alexander delivered his speech. King Willem-Alexander referred to the UN as the 'primary global organisation for peace, justice and development'. A Dutch candidature was seen as a matter of course given the Dutch foreign policy priorities of maintaining a multilateral order and taking an active role in the UN.[29] Members of governments from Aruba, Curaçao, and Sint Maarten were also present. In his speech, King Willem-Alexander referred to Queen Maxima's role, appointed by the General Secretary, as 'Special Advocate for Inclusive Financing for Development', which contributed to highlight the Dutch dedication to the work of the UN.

In addition to members of the royal family, the Dutch campaign showed some involvement from celebrities. In his role as the United Nation's Global Advocate for the Elimination of Mines and Explosive Hazards, actor Daniel Craig ('James Bond') participated in campaign activities supporting the topic. Ambassador van Oosterom tweeted that he was 'Thrilled – perhaps even stirred, not shaken' to raise awareness with Daniel Craig on de-mining issues.

While the campaign organization aimed to have active involvement from members of the government, the task of engaging politicians to pay foreign visits and to participate in campaign-related activities was difficult. To further increase the number of representatives actively promoting the candidature, the secretariat in The Hague recruited a group of former politicians and senior diplomats. These 'Special Envoys' included the senior diplomats Herman Schaper and Laetitia van den Assum. Schaper was the former PR in New York (2009–2013), and van den Assum had previously been posted in Kenya, Mexico, and the UK.[30]

---

29   King Willem-Alexander, UN, 2015.
30   Interviews 13; 14; 15.

7   Comparison of Key Participants

Both campaigns involved a similar mix of politicians, diplomats, and civil servants. In order to increase the reach of the campaign, both secretariats also recruited former politicians and diplomats to launch the candidatures of their countries, through bilateral meetings and in multilateral settings. Both campaigns took the opportunity to involve members of their royal families. The Dutch campaign brought their King to New York. Diplomatic visitors to the capitals, as part of trips arranged due to the candidatures, met with King Wilhelm Alexander and Crown Princess Victoria, respectively. The retired diplomats and former politicians contributed to the campaign with their skills and expertise appreciated in the field of multilateral diplomacy and among the political representatives that they visited. In doing this, they played a useful role to claim competence on behalf of the candidature. The former engagement of these prominent individuals, known to many within the UN, also reiterated and underscored the historical record of contributions to the United Nations on behalf of the candidature. Members of the government also offered their skills and competence to the campaign, confirming an actual and current political dedication to the candidature. When members of the government promoted the message of the campaign it contributed to proving political dedication to the specific values and priorities identified. Furthermore, when members of the government contributed specifically on topics related to their own expertise, this accentuated the claiming of competence made through the campaign. One main difference between the two campaigns was the degree to which members of the government became involved in the actual campaign. The proceeding examination of activities further speaks to this. This has relevance to the capacity of the campaign to prove ideational commitment and to claim competence.

8   Campaign Activities: Sweden

The Swedish candidature was characterized by a low amount of activity with regards to the initial phase, which usually focus on voting agreements. While the diplomatic deliberations that lead to an agreement can take place at different locations, the interaction between PRs in New York is important. The number of agreements reached is something the candidates keep to themselves. However, in March 2015, the close and recurrent dialogue between the Nordic PRs in New York enabled Ambassador Skoog to come to the disappointing conclusion that the Swedish candidature for a seat in 2017–18 had fewer agreements reached than the Norwegian candidature had for a seat 2021–22. Although the number of vote exchange agreements was initially low, support increased once the campaign intensified. In October 2015, Sweden had confirmed support from 101 countries, and 32 of these were considered certain. In May 2016, the support had increased to 129 countries, of which 36 were regarded as certain. Just a few days prior to the election, confirmed support had reached 140 countries, with 39 certain countries.[31]

The member state speeches at the opening of the General Assembly annual sessions represent a much more public push of the candidature in New York. The Head of Government or the Foreign Minister is a common choice of speaker, which was also the case for Sweden in 2012 and 2013. However, neither Foreign Minister Bildt, in 2012, nor Prime Minister Reinfeldt, in 2013, mentioned the Swedish candidature in their speeches. The speech in the 2014 session, given by the Swedish PR at the time, Mårten Grunditz, was the first mentioning of the Swedish candidature. His main points in the speech, with reference to the candidature, were that it has Nordic support, and that the UN needs further reform to meet global challenges.[32] In 2015, Prime Minster Löfven spoke in the GA and brought further attention to the Swedish candidature. He emphasized Sweden as a champion of small and medium-sized states, a country that aims for the equality and fair representation of all states.[33]

At this point, Ambassador Skoog had also begun to approach his fellow PRs to promote Sweden for the SC. The ambition was to meet with the diplomatic representatives of all members states twice. Only very few member states were not approached by the Swedish campaign, and at least 70 follow-up meetings were held.[34] However, the campaign did note that some categories of states were more important than others, and concluded that some states would be difficult, if not impossible, to win over. The Swedish campaign paid special attention to the group of Small Island Developing States (SIDS), a group Prime Minister Löfven met with already in the autumn of 2014. As mentioned, one very practical obstacle was that the small members have limited administrative resources. If the Swedish campaign could not get in touch with the PR of a state due to an understaffed (or lack of) office in New York, then members of the Swedish team made sure to attend gatherings where they expected to find a representative of the state for the purpose of establishing contact and setting up a diplomatic meeting.

---

31   Lidén 2016.
32   Grunditz, UN 2014.
33   Löfven, UN 2015.
34   Interview 2.

The Swedish embassies throughout the world also participated in the campaign, mainly in connection to travels made by the Government or the Ministry of Foreign Affairs. To bring further visibility, the Swedish campaign also seized the opportunity to take an active approach during four major multilateral meetings in 2015. This approach was developed based on the belief that the Swedish campaign was lagging its two competitors, and it involved the opportunity to reach representatives of countries where Sweden did not have an embassy. Hence, multilateral meetings were used for bilateral meetings where the Swedish campaign could be elevated. The activities at these meetings included the presence of a member of the government, such as Foreign Minister Margot Wallström, and – even more importantly – Prime Minister Stefan Löfven. All in all, Prime Minister Löfven made three visits to Addis Abeba and four to New York in order to convince others of the Swedish dedication to its candidature.[35] Margot Wallström visited the Caribbean conference COFCOR twice, developed a special forum for female Foreign Ministers, and invited female PRs in New York to a special meeting.[36]

In addition to the efforts to promote the candidature in multilateral settings, members of the Swedish government traveled extensively to enable bilateral and regional meetings. During the final six months before the election, Wallström visited Kongo-Kinshasa, The Maldives, Sri Lanka, Palau, Micronesia, the United Arab Emirates, Georgia, Armenia, and Azerbaijan.[37] Several other members of the government contributed to the campaign with similar political meetings. For example, two of these included the Minister of International Development Cooperation and Climate, Isabella Lövin, and Minister for Children, the Elderly and Gender Equality, Åsa Regnér. Sweden also welcomed many foreign ministers to Sweden during the final year of the campaign.[38]

The senior politicians and diplomats enlisted as 'Special Envoys' were also sent to selected destinations, both multilateral and bilateral meetings, for the sake of gathering support for Sweden. For example, Marika Fahlén paid visits to African countries where she mainly talked to Prime Ministers and other members of government about peacekeeping and peace promotion. Lena Hjelm Wallén paid visits to other African countries and attended a conference in Turkmenistan where many Asian countries also participated. She attended a seminar in Stockholm with several PRs who had been invited from

---

35   Lidén 2016.
36   Lidén 2016.
37   Lidén 2016.
38   Lidén 2016.

New York (which was heavily criticized, more on that later). Pierre Schori paid visits to Asia, South America, and to the Caribbean. Henrik Salander participated in the 2015 Review Conference of the Parties to the Treaty on the Non-Proliferation of Nuclear Weapons (NPT) in New York, and in additional nuclear non-proliferation meetings.

Rather than giving the Special Envoys detailed instructions regarding the major themes of the campaign, their main contributions consisted of using their established networks and special expertise. Their travels were planned together with the Ministry of Foreign Affairs, and some advice was given regarding the substance of their discussions, but overall, they were given freedom to plan their own conversations. To demonstrate the substantial degree of freedom given to the members of this group, Pierre Schori even took the opportunity to launch his own book during his travels, supposedly to highlight a more progressive past of Swedish foreign policy. In general, these senior politicians and diplomats were encouraged to indulge in dialogue about substantive issues, in which they were considered experts. Henrik Salander participated in the NPT review conference with access to the official pamphlets for the Swedish campaign but chose not to use them. Instead, he focused on discussing topics related to nuclear non-proliferation, and only occasionally touched upon the Swedish campaign. Similarly, Lena Hjelm Wallén chose not to use the campaign slogan but ensured that the content of her discussions stayed on message.

If Stockholm gave few instructions to these Special Envoys, the documentation of their contacts was more careful. Salander held 53 talks with diplomats and politicians during the NPT review conference. He reported these discussions to Stockholm in two written memos, each 12–15 pages long. These memos became part of the aforementioned 'SPON list', so the secretariat could keep track of contacts and their outcomes.

9   Campaign Activities: the Kingdom of the Netherlands

The Dutch began the phase of active campaigning and the launch of their candidature with the slogan 'The Kingdom of the Netherlands: Your partner for peace, justice, and development' in Foreign Minister Frans Timmermans' speech at the 2013 session in the General Assembly. The speech presented the Dutch contributions to the UN and identified some of the main challenges to the global order.[39] At this point, Ambassador van Oosterom had also begun his mission to, in his own words, 'knock on every door'. The ambassador received

---

39   Timmermans, UN 2013.

support from members of the campaign team before every meeting to focus on the correct issues, but the meetings also zoomed in on the main message, as mentioned with the slogan. The Ambassador's reports from each meeting were included in the Dutch database to keep track of contacts and estimate support. Van Oosterom held around eight meetings per week, with a target of meeting each PR two or three times before the election.[40]

In addition to diplomatic bilateral contacts, several activities took place in New York to present the Kingdom of the Netherlands' achievements and priorities within the UN system. The campaign also hosted events to reach politicians and ambassadors outside the New York diplomatic community, such as in The Hague and other capitals, as well as in Brussels. These occasions always included the slogan for the candidature, as well as the main message it summarizes, and the campaign used social media to advertise the activities. These included, for example, expert meetings on special issues, as well as social activities. The chosen issues displayed the Dutch engagement, and a member of the Dutch government was often present. For example, Foreign Minister Koenders attended the above-mentioned seminar on de-mining with actor Daniel Craig. Other topics raised in connection to the campaign included climate change, infrastructure, development issues of the Security Council, and Syria. While the most common format was a 'lunch-meeting with speakers', the campaign also organized a boat-trip on the East River with 40 PRs to highlight the Dutch engagement on water projects. The campaign also arranged events in New York such as a soccer-game involving Dutch players.[41] The campaign arranged meetings in The Hague on three different occasions, hosting around 15 PRs at each. These meetings were held to show The Hague as 'a city of peace and justice' hosting several UN bodies, in order to demonstrate positive Dutch experiences, for example on water management issues, and Dutch UN contributions, for example on peacekeeping. During these meetings, the PRs also met Prime Minister Rutte, as well as with King Willem-Alexander.[42] The campaign also arranged a meeting in Aruba for ambassadors in the SIDS group to address sustainability issues. Foreign Minister Koenders launched the candidature at a reception hosted by the Embassy in Brussels for diplomats from the African, Caribbean, and South Pacific states. In June 2016, with only weeks left before the election, the Dutch Ministry of Foreign Affairs hosted a reception in The Hague for ambassadors working in The Hague, London, and Brussels. Minister for Foreign Trade and Development Cooperation Ploumen attended the

---

40   Interviews 14; 18.
41   Interviews 14; 15.
42   Interviews 14; 17.

event, as did the representatives of Aruba, Curaçao, and Sint Maarten. Foreign Minister Koenders held a speech to launch the main pillars of the candidature; the Netherlands was a champion of all states, including the smaller ones, the UN was in need of reform and, the Netherlands had unique experience managing the effects of water, as well as contributing to development and peace.[43]

10   Comparison of Campaign Activities

To gather support for their candidatures, both Sweden and the Kingdom of the Netherlands focused on bilateral meetings with representatives from other UN member states. They engaged vigorously to establish a meaningful diplomatic dialogue between the PR and colleagues in New York, but there were also substantial efforts made to target members of governments. Both campaigns were aware of the importance of support from the capitals and sought to confirm support on several levels. Both campaigns engaged members of government as well as Special Envoys in initiating bilateral meetings to discuss the candidature. The Swedish campaign had more help from members of their government; The Swedish Prime Minister had an intense travel schedule for the purpose of campaigning, as did the Foreign Minister and other members of the Swedish government. Another difference was that the Swedish campaign took more advantage of major multilateral events as opportunities to initiate bilateral dialogue. Political representations at these multilateral events contributed by displaying dedication to the candidature and to issues of relevance to the candidature. The Swedish campaign also made sure to have political representation at important regional gatherings for groups of member states identified as crucial to attaining the required number of votes, i.e. African states and small island states.

   In addition to the efforts to gather and confirm support through bilateral diplomatic and political contacts, both campaigns engaged in different substantive events and social gatherings. Both the Netherlands and Sweden also invited PRs to seminars and related activities in The Hague and Stockholm, respectively. These events were typically built around relevant issues related to the campaign to demonstrate both engagement and contributions. The Netherlands seems to have been more active with organizing special events focusing on the campaign. These types of activities took place in New York, as well as at other diplomatic sites throughout the world. A higher level of activity

---

43   Diplomatic Magazine, 9 June 2016.

might contribute to further demonstrating UN contributions, as well as to displaying competence and proving a commitment to the candidature. However, the Swedish candidature had a much higher level of activity in terms of bilateral contacts at the political level. The candidature also reached out more actively to countries without a previous relationship to Sweden. In addition to this, the Swedish candidature was more consistent in political representation on the highest political level at multilateral gatherings that were relevant to the message of the campaign, including the environment and the financing of development. The many trips made by members of the Swedish government for the purpose of bilateral dialogue contributed to showing Sweden's ideational commitment, as well as its competence. The presence of government members at multilateral meetings that addressed themes and topics identified as global challenges by the campaign had a similar effect.

11　　　　Campaign Message: Sweden

The initial discussions regarding message at the Ministry of Foreign Affairs during Bildt's time in office resulted in a campaign primarily focusing on merits. Rather than a regular campaign, it was determined that Sweden should seek support mainly through the circulation of its 'UN CV' summarizing contributions made to the United Nations over the years.[44] The CV listed Swedish personnel involved in peacekeeping, their economic support to development, main policy-priorities, and positions and engagements in key areas such as peace building, human rights, sustainable development, and gender equality.[45]

Several people involved in the campaign during this intense period agreed on the relevance of spreading the CV as a foundation, but also insisted that this strategy alone would never have been enough to persuade the necessary number of states to support Sweden's bid.[46] In shaping the active campaign, several members of the team home in on the importance of credibility, which required the message to reflect Sweden's general foreign policy.[47] 'The most important thing was to be honest about who Sweden was, and what we wanted to achieve in the UN'. The campaign was also aware that the choice between the three European countries might appear as one 'between Cola and Pepsi' meaning

---

44　　Ekengren and Möller 2020.
45　　Cronenberg-Mossberg 2017.
46　　Interviews 2; 5; 10; 12.
47　　Interviews 2; 10.

that the smaller details could make all the difference.[48] Sweden would need to appear 'constructive, listening, and transparent'. Pursuing these qualities within several different issue areas would contribute to the trustworthiness of Sweden's candidature. This description of Sweden was considered to reflect the identity of Swedish foreign policy. It was also relevant to appear to be a good representative for the entire General Assembly and, perhaps especially, to the one third of the members of the UN who had not yet been elected to the SC. The campaign also sought to present a diversified portfolio, not limited to security, to earn the opportunity to become the representative of as many members as possible.[49]

It remained important to show Sweden's past of solid contributions to the UN for the sake of international peace and security during the phase of active campaigning, as well. The campaign pamphlet repeated many of the merits circulated by the UN CV, such as the number of Swedish men and women who had served within the UN, Sweden's top ranking on the UN donor list, and the Swedish ODA. In accordance with the CV, the campaign highlighted peace building, respect for international law, human rights, and development as prioritized issues. On peace building, the Swedish campaign emphasized the involvement of women in conflict resolution. On sustainable development, the Swedish campaign focused on climate change action and Sweden's long-time commitment to this issue. Extensive involvement in the campaign by Minister of International Development Cooperation and Climate Isabella Lövin substantiated Sweden's current dedication in this area. On UN reform, the campaign was explicit on improved transparency and efficiency as goals. The campaign was also careful to spell out that Sweden was ready to serve, in the sense that 20 years had passed since the last time, while the other candidates having served more recently.[50]

The campaign made sure to frame Sweden not only as a dedicated UN member but one that had a small state perspective, also. To present and promote Sweden, the campaign began to use the slogan 'Global commitment, independent voice'. The secretariat had presented the slogan and gotten approval for it from the political level, but it became heavily criticized once made public. The political opposition described the slogan as inaccurate – Sweden was not an independent voice but part of the European foreign policy – and it was criticized for playing down Sweden's commitment to the EU. From the campaign members' point of view, the criticism was unfair and expressed a domestic

---

48   Interview 2.
49   Interviews 1; 3; 7.
50   Ekengren and Möller 2020.

conflict dimension of foreign policy. They saw no contradictions between support of the UN and support of the EU, but some believed that the Swedish
candidature could potentially contribute to mutually reinforcing policy processes between the two organizations. The campaign also saw how the slogan
worked well and gained appreciation from other UN member states.[51] Still, the
debate resulted in a political decision to phase out the description of Sweden
as an independent voice and to replace it with Sweden as a voice with integrity.
Rather than phasing out the original slogan, the campaign in New York and in
other UN-arenas toned it down. Yet Sweden as a UN member with integrity
became an important part of the description of a small state that did not hes-
itate to engage in and stand up for its views. The pamphlet described Sweden
as a defender of 'common values and principles'. The campaign also sought
to substantiate the description of Sweden as a globally committed voice with
integrity by referring to Swedish diplomats and politicians who were internationally recognized, including Dag Hammarskjöld, Hans Blix, and Olof Palme.
The campaign also made references to Sweden's military non-alignment for
this purpose, and used recent controversial decisions made by Sweden, such
as its recognition of Palestine.

Whether a campaign deliberately frames its message depending on arena
or type of audience is an important aspect in all campaigning. According to
several members of the Swedish campaign, when this was discussed as part
of the campaign planning, such differentiation of the message was considered
as putting the trustworthiness and honesty of the campaign at risk. So, it was
deemed preferable to stay on message, even if this proved uncomfortable in
some settings.[52]

The interviewees' answers reveal two different descriptions of the messages,
in relation to the receiving member states. Some stress that the message was
similar in all settings and for all receiving member states. Others say that some
parts of the message were used more frequently with specific groups of member states. For example, Sweden would emphasize its dedication to climate
change action when talking with small island states. Sweden promised these
states that it would speak about climate change as often it could, if elected to
the Security Council. When talking to a country in Africa, which had recently
been affected by conflict or war, Sweden would focus more on peacekeeping
and emphasize, for example, the importance of women's role in peace negotiations. However, these were both important components of the broader

---

51   Interviews 1; 2; 10.
52   Interviews 1; 7; 8; 10; 11.

Swedish message, as well as issues where Sweden had an especially strong record of involvement.

The interviewees had a similar view on all messages used in the campaign as related to the general Swedish foreign policy. This can be seen as explicitly ambitious regarding the campaign. Sweden wanted to refrain from sending messages that were not part of the Swedish foreign policy and from negative campaigning.

12   Campaign Message: the Kingdom of the Netherlands

The Dutch campaign for a seat on the Security Council rested on the image of the Netherlands as a country with a genuinely multilateral identity, with a solid reputation in matters related to international law and justice, and on its history of substantively contributing to UN peacekeeping. It also made the most out of the Kingdom of the Netherlands as being comprised of four countries: the Netherlands, Aruba, Curaçao, and Sint Maarten, sharing experiences with European, as well as with Caribbean countries. The three Caribbean countries had a common experience with many other small island developing states. It was important that the campaign expressed a genuine interest in dialogue and partnership with other countries, regardless of their size. The campaign also paid special attention to issues related to sustainable development, climate change, and water management. The need for Security Council reform, explicitly asking for better representation for African countries, and the importance of gender equality for development were other frequently raised topics.[53]

The Dutch campaign message was summarized by the slogan 'The Kingdom of the Netherlands: Your Partner for Peace, Justice and Development'. The slogan, formulated by the campaign office in The Hague during the preparatory phase, became a consistently used message during the campaign's many different activities in the second, and more intense, phase of the candidature. Every annual speech in the General Assembly from 2013 to 2016 referred to the slogan and substantiated its three pillars. In the 2013 Dutch speech to the UN General Assembly, Foreign Minister Frans Timmermans mentioned that partnership was a cornerstone of the Dutch candidature, along with the reassuring words directed immediately to the Secretary General, that 'We will join you on the road to peace, justice and development'.[54]

---

53   Ekengren and Möller 2020.
54   Timmermans, UN, 2013.

In the 2014 Dutch speech to the UNGA, Prime Minister Mark Rutte repeated that 'The Kingdom of the Netherlands, your partner for peace, justice and development, is a candidate for a nonpermanent seat on the Security Council in 2017 and 2018'. Prime Minster Rutte substantiated the message of the slogan by emphasizing the established dedication of the Dutch to the development of an international legal order and to consistent contributions to UN peace-keeping missions. Referring to the SC resolution 1325, he also underscored the relevance of gender equality to peace and development: 'The important role that women play as change agents in politics, economic development and soci-ety cannot be emphasized enough'. Rutte spoke of the importance of Security Council reform for the betterment of efficiency and legitimacy. To enhance 'authority and resolve', he promoted a broader representation of UN members, mentioning that African states, in particular, lacked sufficient representation.[55]

The 2015 Dutch speech to the UNGA was the first held by King Willem-Alexander. It was the third Dutch speech to promote the candidature, but the first to do so with explicit reference to the Kingdom of the Netherlands as composed by four autonomous countries: the Netherlands, Aruba, Curaçao, and Sint Maarten.[56] Like the previous speeches to the UNGA, King Willem-Alexander spoke of peace, justice, and development, characterizing them as 'a trinity – as tied to each other as the blade of a windmill'. He substantiated the Dutch dedication to these three pillars by describing the Dutch contributions to peacekeeping, referring to the Hague as a place where peace and justice are defended, and emphasizing that the Kingdom 'has again increased its contri-bution to humanitarian assistance, making us one of the largest donors in the world'.[57] In contrast to the previous Dutch speeches to the UNGA, this time King Willem-Alexander spoke extensively about sustainable development, climate change, and marine pollution. He referred directly to the Kingdom's countries. Three of the four countries of the Kingdom are small islands, espe-cially vulnerable to the consequences of climate change and marine pollution. The Dutch experience of water management, and the Netherlands as 'one of the best-protected deltas in the world', was also explicitly mentioned.

Similarly, the short texts and pamphlets from the Dutch campaign expressed a genuine interest in dialogue and partnership within the areas of peace, jus-tice, and development. The Dutch engagement, as a founding member of the UN, and its contributions to the UN, especially within peacekeeping, are emphasized. Another angle was the need for broader representation within

---

55   Rutte, UN, 2014.
56   United Nations, 2015.
57   King Willem-Alexander, UN, 2015.

the Security Council, both in terms of future reform and as the Netherlands representing small and middle-power states if elected. The interviews further confirmed that the message sent by the slogan was the core of the campaign. It was carried out on behalf of all the Kingdom's countries, not only the Netherlands. The Netherlands was described as an inherently multilateral country. Especially relevant issues that were frequently mentioned included water management, peacekeeping, and The Hague as the legal capital of the world. This emphasized the Netherlands contributions to the UN system and showed a consistent message.

13   Comparison Regarding Campaign Messages

Both campaigns sought to portray themselves as good members of the UN by referring to their substantial contributions to international peace and security. It was important for both Sweden and the Kingdom of the Netherlands to state that they fulfilled the necessary conditions to run for a seat on the UNSC. This message was even a primary activity done early on by the Swedish campaign, but both candidatures made sure to put their strongest merits in their pamphlets. Both candidates communicated a sincere multilateral dedication and reinforced their small state experiences. The Kingdom of the Netherlands could further substantiate its multilateral identity by referring to The Hague as one of the UN cities of the world. Sweden lacked a similar 'material manifestation' of its dedication to the UN. Both had sustainable development and especially climate as part of their message. The Kingdom of the Netherlands focused more on water management, and Sweden more on the oceans. Their choice of message makes sense based on their strong merits in these fields, but it also displays a strategic awareness of the importance of the large group of Small Island Development States for whom climate change poses a threat to survival. With similar messages in terms of the relevance of climate issues, the Swedish campaign managed to display stronger ideational commitment and competence regarding this issue by actively involving members of the government. The Swedish focus on multilateral meetings to discuss climate and development, along with the presence of political representatives, might have accentuated this even more. Both candidates also sought their mandate based on their identities as countries that welcomed dialogue and engaged in joint efforts for improving areas such as development, sustainable development, marine pollution, and climate change. The main differences regarding these issues seem to primarily have to do with the historic strengths of each candidate. The messages of both campaigns reveal substantial contributions to the UN, as well as strong ideational commitment to the agenda of the UN. However, the degree to which the campaigns managed to underscore the political dedication to these messages of ideational commitment differed. The Swedish campaign benefited from having members of its government speak more frequently about key issues during the campaign. The Swedish campaign could thereby also substantiate the knowledge and competence of several members of its own government, related to the priorities and challenges identified through this message.

14   The Domestic Debate: Sweden[58]

When Prime Minister Göran Persson's Social Democratic government announced Sweden's candidature for a seat on the SC in 2004 it did so with the full support of the political opposition. Just two years later the government changed, and Prime Minister Fredrik Reinfeldt's liberal-right government (2006–14) made plans for a slim campaign. The Social Democrats, in particular, were critical of what they regarded a delayed campaign start and repeatedly asked the government to reveal its plans for a successful Swedish campaign.[59] The Minister for Foreign Affairs, Carl Bildt, explained that Sweden's CV regarding UN matters would speak for itself and that the government did not want to contribute to an irresponsible use of public funds through excessive spending on a large campaign.[60] The opposition, in contrast, was concerned over what they viewed as a lack of interest to promote the Swedish candidature.

With only two and half years left to the election, the government changed once again. In the autumn of 2014, the new Social Democratic and Green government decided to intensify the campaigning. Once the campaigning intensified, the Moderates, the Liberal Party, and the Centre Party repeated their opposition towards excessive spending on the campaign. They were also critical of what they deemed to be too much focus on the UN in Swedish foreign policy. The liberal-right parties feared that the focus on the EU, which they favored, would dissolve.[61] This was quite opposite to the position taken by the

---

58   Documents on the Swedish debate in this section are published on the Swedish Parliament's website www.riksdagen.se/. Documents on the Dutch debate in this section are published on the Dutch Parliament's website www.tweedekamer.nl/kamerstuk ken/plenaire_verslagen. See also Ekengren and Möller 2020.

59   Riksdagen 2012/13: UU15; Riksdagen 2013/14: KU1; Riksdagen 2013/14: 102.

60   Riksdagen 2013/14: 102.

61   Riksdagen 2014/15: UU15.

Swedish Democrats, who instead feared that Sweden would be a megaphone for the EU on the Security Council.[62]

Once the Swedish campaign for a seat on the SC was up and running, the debate between the government and the opposition revolved around both the content of a future seat on the SC as well as the form of the present campaign. In terms of what issues Sweden should focus on, if it received a seat, the Left Party argued during the debate that Sweden should use its seat to highlight the rights of LGBTQ people, especially those in areas of conflict. The government's response was that Sweden would focus on women and women's rights, in particular.[63]

The liberal-right parties hoped that Sweden would work in favor of reforming the UN and the UN system. In their view, the veto right should be limited in its use, as should the use of extensive campaigning for different seats in the UN community.[64] In addition, the liberal-right opposition raised concerns about the fact that Sweden had launched its campaign under the slogan 'Global commitment, independent voice'. This slogan was heavily attacked by the opposition, which ultimately led to a revision. The slogan was taken as a confirmation of the opposition's concern that an increased focus on the UN implied a loss of attention on the EU. The liberal-right parties had concerns that Sweden's membership of the EU, and especially cooperation within the framework of the Common Foreign and Security Policy (CFSP), would be adversely affected by multilateral claims and of an independent Swedish voice.[65] In the revised version of the slogan, independence was replaced by the word 'integrity', intended to signal that Sweden was a country with a distinct set of rules, foundational to a clear and consistent foreign policy.[66] In terms of the form of the campaign, the liberal-right parties were critical of the government for not sufficiently involving and informing the opposition. Given the fact that transparency and openness was part of how the Swedish government wanted to transform the UN, perceived lack of those qualities in the Swedish campaign was used by the opposition to ridicule the government's position. The opposition accused the government of withholding information about the campaign, both regarding content and activities. Especially, the use of vote exchange agreement and the invitation of a group of UN ambassadors to Stockholm attracted media attention. On vote exchange agreements, MPs followed up with questions in the

---

62   Riksdagen 2014/15: UU15.
63   Riksdagen 2016/17: UU15.
64   Riksdagen 2014/15: UU15.
65   Riksdagen 2014/15: 422; Riksdagen 2014/15: 359.
66   Riksdagen 2014/15: 422; Riksdagen 2015/16: 769.

parliament to the government about the type of countries Sweden could reach these agreements with. In her response, Foreign Minister Margot Wallström confirmed the use of vote agreements, referring to them as an established diplomatic practice. She explained that the possibility of entering into any single agreement depended on whether it was compatible with Swedish foreign policy principles and justified the secrecy of the agreements by noting that they affected Sweden's relationships with other states.[67] The opposition was also critical of the government's use of the budget for foreign aid to finance parts of the campaign, including the abovementioned event in Stockholm. According to Foreign Minister Wallström and the Minister of Foreign Aid Isabella Lövin, the use of aid funds to cover the expenses of the event was in line with existing regulations. Through seminars on conflict prevention the event contributed to the goal of knowledge transfer to the world's poorest countries.[68] That this spending was in accordance with existing regulations was later confirmed when the Swedish Parliament analyzed the campaign.[69]

15　　The Domestic Debate: the Netherlands

In 2005, Prime Minister Jan Peter Balkenende officially announced the Netherlands' candidature for a seat on the Security Council. At that time, the Dutch government consisted of three parties: Christian Democratic Appeal, People's Party for Freedom and Democracy, and Democrats 66. In 2014, with the campaign up and running, the first traces of a domestic debate emerged. At that point, Max Rutte was the Prime Minister for a government based on the support of the People's Party for Freedom and Democracy and the Labour Party.[70]

The Dutch campaign had no equivalent to the intense parliamentary debate over the Swedish slogan 'Global commitment, independent voice'. The Netherlands also portrayed itself independent of the EU, and by referring to itself as a kingdom emphasized the political ties outside of Europe. Pressing questions on how the campaign was proceeding were frequently raised, implying a political expectation to succeed, which was also lacking in the Swedish debate.[71]

67　　Riksdagen 2014/15: 422; Riksdagen 2015/16: 769.
68　　Riksdagen 2015/16: 528.
69　　Riksdagen 2015/16: 1072.
70　　Parliaments and Governments Database.
71　　Kamerstukken II 2014/15, 34 200 V, nr. 1; Kamerstukken II 2014/15, 26 150, nr. 146; Kamerstukken II 2015/16, 34 300 V, nr. 9.

The Dutch Parliament also faced questions about the mounting costs of the campaign. However, these questions, regarding the financial costs of the project, were not asked in the same critical tone as they were in Sweden.[72]

The Dutch Parliament frequently discussed matters related to the content of the campaign. According to the Minister of Foreign Affairs, Frans Timmermans, a Dutch term in the Security Council would bring opportuinities to exert more power and promote more of its principles globally.[73] Timmermans, and later his successor Bert Koenders, discussed the Netherlands' responsibility to protect, the enhancement of the ICC, the support of women according to Security Council Resolution 1325, and disarmament.[74] Hence, the Dutch domestic debate addressed substantive themes, as the political opposition demanded the government to set its priorities, if the Netherlands were to win a seat, but the debate played out from a less critical point of view.

16   Conclusions Regarding the Domestic Debate

Both Sweden and the Netherlands had changes in the formation of the coalition government during the candidature, and both campaigns were led by coalition governments. The shift of government had more obvious effects in Sweden than in the Netherlands, in terms of how the campaign was carried out. The Swedish government faced more intense criticism from the opposition than the Dutch did, especially on how Sweden should be displayed, the costs of the campaign, and the type of activities that were financed. The Dutch domestic debate rather revolved around the issues the Netherlands should focus on, if elected. While the Swedish debate revealed rather profound disagreements between the government and the opposition about how Sweden should conduct the campaign, the Dutch debate reflected expectations that the campaign should manage to get the Netherlands elected, thereby focusing on the priorities of the term. We find it especially noteworthy that the perceived tension between political investments in the UN and in the EU that played out in the Swedish domestic debate had no equivalence in the Dutch case. The oppositional discontent after the new government had levelled up the ambitions with the candidature sparked from the emphasis of Sweden's identity as a military non-aligned state rather than as a member of the EU. The

---

72   Kamerstukken II 2014/15, 26 150, nr. 146; Kamerstukken II 2015/16, 34 300 V, nr. 9.
73   Kamerstukken II 2013/14, 33 750 V, nr. 1, 27.
74   Kamerstukken II 2014/15, 34 000 V, nr. 10; Kamerstukken II 2014/15, 26 150, nr. 144.
       Kamerstukken II 2015/16, 26 150, nr. 150.

Dutch campaign contained a similar strategic shift in the center of gravity as regards of state identity; from a middle-sized member of the EU towards the experience of a Caribbean small state(s), without any similar domestic controversy. One possible reason for this variation is that the EU-identity, simply through a longer membership, is more mature and settled in the Netherlands than in Sweden. However, we also suggest that this detected strategic use of the self in these campaigns, and the fact that it sparked controversy in the Swedish case, indicated the relevance of domestic politics for further exploring the status dimension of the Security Council candidature as a foreign policy priority.

17   Conclusions

The description of the Swedish and the Dutch candidatures, based on their organization, key participants, activities, message, and domestic debate enables a comparative analysis regarding the three logics of campaigning: demonstrating contributions, claiming competence, and proving ideational commitment.

As the descriptive parts of the chapter have shown, Sweden and the Kingdom of the Netherlands had many similarities in how they campaigned for a seat on the UNSC, in terms of how they were organized, who their key actors were, what kind of campaign activities they engaged in, and what their campaign messages were. To summarize their main similarities: Both countries used the UN in New York and their respective Foreign Ministries as their primary sites for campaign planning. Both campaigns involved members of the royal family, former diplomats and politicians, and current diplomats and members of their governments. Both campaigns drew upon and extended their current networks to gather support. Both campaigns demonstrated resourcefulness by emphasizing their historic and present commitment to UN operations, treaties, conferences, and overall values when they presented their 'UN CV'.

There are some interesting differences as well. The Dutch candidature had the advantage of an early start, both in terms of the organization and regarding the main message. The early campaign-secretariat in The Hague developed the slogan 'The Kingdom of the Netherlands: Your partner for peace, justice and development' which efficiently summarized the main message of the Dutch campaign. The three pillars of the slogan reflected areas in which the Netherlands were resourceful and displayed past and present contributions to the UN. With three years left to the election, The Hague was ready to send a new PR to New York, prepared to campaign. To kick things off, Foreign Minister Timmerman launched the campaign in his speech to the UN General

Assembly. At that point, in the autumn of 2013, the Netherlands was considered far ahead of Sweden.

The Swedish campaign had no organization, and the dissemination of its message was mainly limited to circulating its UN CV at suitable political and diplomatic opportunities. In contrast to his Dutch colleague, Foreign Minister Carl Bildt did not mention the Swedish candidature in his 2013 speech at the UNGA. After the change of government in autumn 2014, the Swedish campaign increased in scope and ambition, and both campaigns displayed a similar mix of key actors. In addition to ambassadors, most notably the PR in New York, who were tasked with securing votes, both campaigns engaged senior diplomats and former politicians, as well as members of their own governments. Members of the royal families did their part for strategic occasions. Sometimes, although rarely, the Dutch campaign engaged celebrities and athletes in its campaign.

A main difference regarding the involvement of key actors was the number of extensively involved members of the government. Except for the 2015 session at the UNGA, the Dutch campaign depended primarily on the contributions of the Foreign Minister. In contrast, the Swedish campaign engaged the Prime Minister, the Foreign Minister, and additional members of the Swedish government. Not only did these members of government appear at strategically chosen events, but they also travelled extensively for the sake of promoting the Swedish candidature. They attended multilateral meetings, regional events, and engaged in bilateral meetings. The Dutch campaign was mainly forced to rely on the Special Envoys for these kinds of trips. The active participation in the campaign by members of the government, and especially by the Swedish Prime Minister, displayed ideational commitment. More importantly, it also contributed to displaying competence in the sense that the campaigning members of government had political portfolios that corresponded with issues brought up by the message of the campaign.

The Swedish campaign did not reach a similar degree of consistency as the Kingdom of the Netherlands did by coherent use of a slogan throughout the candidature but the most important parts of the Swedish package – development, climate, and equality – were still clear during the active phase of campaigning. Like the Dutch campaign's quest for partnership with states regardless of size, the Swedish campaign attempted to market itself as a country that listened to and engaged in sincere dialogue. As reflected in its slogan, the Dutch campaign was careful to emphasize the Caribbean identity of the Kingdom of the Netherlands, thereby also displaying its small state experience. Being a small state was also part of the Swedish campaign message, along with emphasizing Sweden as being a member of the Nordic countries and being militarily non-aligned.

To conclude, in terms of the logics of campaigning, the main differences between the Dutch and the Swedish candidature consisted of the degree to which each country managed to claim competence and, most importantly, to prove ideational commitment. Both countries convincingly demonstrated their past and current contributions to the UN. The Swedish campaign managed to show their competence through actively involving not only the group of 'special envoys', but also several members of their own government, who had expertise in issues that were important to the campaign. Moreover, the active involvement of members of the government, including the Swedish Prime Minster, benefited the campaign, and offered a confirmation of political dedication to the message, by demonstrating ideational commitment to the themes of the campaign, and to multilateralism through the United Nations.

Bibliography

Cronenberg-Mossberg, Ulrika. 'Uppföljning och utvärdering av kampanjen för Sveriges kandidatur till FN:s säkerhetsråd' (Riksdagens utrikesutskott, 2017). ['Assessment of the Swedish Campaign to the UN Security Council'].

Diplomatic Magazine, 9 June 2016.

DN Debatt, 8 October 2013.

Ekengren, Ann-Marie and Ulrika Möller. 'Campaigning for an Elected Seat in the UN Security Council'. In Shrijver, Nico J. and Niels M. Blokker (Eds.). *Elected Members of the Security Council: Lame Ducks or Key Players?* (Leiden: Brill Nijhoff, 2020).

Engelbrekt, Kjell. *Sveriges medlemskap i FN:s säkerhetsråd 2017–18.* (Stockholm, Försvarshögskolan, 2020).

Engelbrekt, Kjell. 'Sweden's 2017–18 UNSC Formula: Mobilizing the MFA's Competitive Advantages, Highlighting Africa, and Boosting the E10'. *International Peacekeeping*. 2023. DOI: 10.1080/13533312.2023.2196019.

Government Declaration, 3 October 2014.

Grunditz, Mårten. Speech to the United Nations, 29 September 2014.

Jormanainen, Jim, Tina Kurath and Angela Muvumba Sellström. *Women, Peace and Security Strategies at the Horseshoe Table: the Elected ten UN Security Council Members Advancing the WPS Agenda* (NAI Policy Notes 2022: 3, The Nordic Africa Institute).

Kamerstukken II 2013/14, 33 750 V, nr. 1, 27 of November 2013. Begroting Buitenlands Zaken.

Kamerstukken II 2014/15, 34 000 V, nr. 10, 12 of February 2015. Aanhangsel van de Handelingen. Vragen gesteld door de leden der Kamer, met de daarop door de regering gegeven antwoorden.

Kamerstukken II 2014/15, 26 150, nr. 144, 8 March 2016.

Kamerstukken II 2014/15, 26 150, nr. 146.

Kamerstukken II 2015/16, 26 150, nr. 150.

Kamerstukken II 2014/15, 34 200 V, nr. 1.

Kamerstukken II 2015/16, 34 300 V, nr. 9; 11 August 2016. Wijziging van de begrotingsstaten van het Ministerie van Buitenlandse Zaken (wijziging samenhangende met de Voorjaarsnota). Verslag houdende een lijst van vragen en antwoorden.

Lidén, Anders. *Report to the Swedish Foreign Ministry Regarding the Swedish Campaign to the UNSC* (Unpublished Report, 2016).

Lowy diplomacy index, https://globaldiplomacyindex.lowyinstitute.org/ retrieved on the 3 May 2023.

Löfven, Stefan. Speech to the United Nations, 30 September 2015.

Mörth, Ulrika. *Sverige i FN:s säkerhetsråd* (Sundbyberg: Försvarets forskningsanstalt FOA Rapport C 10334–1.2, 1991).

Parliaments and Governments Database, https://www.parlgov.org retrieved on the 3 of May 2023.

Riksdagen 2012/13: UU15. Mänskliga rättigheter i svensk utrikespolitik [Human Rights in Swedish Politics].

Riksdagen 2013/14: KU1. Konstitutionsutskottets betänkande [Committee on the Constitution]; 2013/14: 102. Sveriges kandidatur till FN:s säkerhetsråd, interpellation från Urban Ahlin (s) [The Swedish Candidature for a Seat on the UNSC, major written question posed to a minister by Urban Ahlin (s)].

Riksdagen 2013/14: 102. Sveriges kandidatur till FN:s säkerhetsråd, svar från Carl Bildts på interpellation från Urban Ahlin (s) [The Swedish Candidature for a Seat on the UNSC, answer given by Minister for Foreign Affairs Carl Bildt from a major written question posed to a minister by Urban Ahlin (s)].

Riksdagen 2014/15: UU15. FN och mänskliga rättigheter i svensk utrikespolitik [The UN and Human Rights in Swedish Politics].

Riksdagen 2014/15: 422. Kandidatur till FN:s säkerhetsråd, skriftlig fråga från Kerstin Lundgren (c) [The Swedish Candidature for a Seat on the UNSC, major written question posed to a minister by Kerstin Lundgren (c)].

Riksdagen 2014/15: 422. Kandidatur till FN:s säkerhetsråd, svar från Margot Wallström på skriftlig fråga från Kerstin Lundgren (c) [The Swedish Candidature for a Seat on the UNSC, answer from Margot Wallström to a major written question posed to a minister by Kerstin Lundgren (c)].

Riksdagen 2014/15: 359. Kampanjen för kandidaturen till FN:s säkerhetsråd, skriftlig fråga från Sofia Arkelsten (m) [The Swedish Candidature for a Seat on the UNSC, major written question posed to a minister by Sofia Arkelsten (m)].

Riksdagen 2015/16: 769. Global Commitment, Independent Voice, svar från Margot Wallström på skriftlig fråga från Sofia Arkelsten (m) [Global Commitment, Independent Voice, answer from Margot Wallström to a major written question posed to a minister by Sofia Arkelsten (m)].

Riksdagen 2015/16: 528. FN-ambassadörernas besök, svar från Isabella Lövin på interpellation från Karin Enström (m) [UN Ambassadors' Visit, answer from Isabell Lövin to a major written question posed to a minister by Karin Enström (m)].

Riksdagen 2015/16: 1072. Bistånd och säkerhetsrådskampanjen, skriftlig fråga från Sofia Arkelsten (m) [Foreign Aid and the Candidature for Seat on the UNSC, major written question posed to a minister by Sofia Arkelsten (m)].

Riksdagen 2015/16: 291. Överstatligt beslutsfattande i FN:s säkerhetsråd med parlamentarisk förankring [Supranational Decision-Making on the UNSC Established in the Parliament].

Riksdagen 2016/17: UU15. HBTQ-personers åtnjutande av mänskliga rättigheter [LGBTQ People and Human Rights].

Rutte, Mark. Speech to the United Nations, 25 September 2014.

Security Council Report, 2016.

Sellström, Angela M., Peter Wallensteen, Ingebjorg Finbakk, Louise Olsson, Patty Chang and Torunn Tryggestad. *Sweden as an Elected Member of the UN Security Council* (Oslo: PRIO Paper, 2021).

Timmermans, Frans. Speech to the United Nations, 27 September 2013.

Willem-Alexander, King. Speech to the United Nations, 28 September 2015.

Interviews

Interviews 1–13 with Swedish Diplomats

SWE Interview 1 2017, 28 November, Interviewer Ann-Marie Ekengren.

SWE Interview 2 2017, 5 December, Interviewer Ann-Marie Ekengren.

SWE Interview 3 2017, 5 December, Interviewer Ann-Marie Ekengren.

SWE Interview 4 2017, 15 December, Interviewer Ulrika Möller.

SWE Interview 5 2018, 22 January, Interviewer Ann-Marie Ekengren.

SWE Interview 6 2018, 5 February, Interviewer Ann-Marie Ekengren.

SWE Interview 7 2018, 6 February, Interviewer Ann-Marie Ekengren.

SWE Interview 8 2018, 6 February, Interviewer Ann-Marie Ekengren.

SWE Interview 9 2018, 26 February, Interviewer Ann-Marie Ekengren.

SWE Interview 10 2018, 27 March, Interviewer Ann-Marie Ekengren.

SWE Interview 11 2018, 27 March, Interviewer Ann-Marie Ekengren.

SWE Interview 12 2018, 6 April, Interviewer Ulrika Möller.

SWE Interview 13 2019, 3 June, Interviewer Ulrika Möller.

Interviews 14–18 with Dutch Diplomats

NL Interview 14 2018, 2 May, Interviewer Ulrika Möller.
NL Interview 15 2018, 19 December, Interviewer Ulrika Möller.
NL Interview 16 2019, 19 March, Interviewer Ulrika Möller.
NL Interview 17 2019, 2 April, Interviewer Ulrika Möller.
NL Interview 18 2019, 3 June, Interviewer Ulrika Möller.

CHAPTER 9

Results, Conclusions, and Reflections

Ann-Marie Ekengren and Ulrika Möller

1 Introduction

In this book, we have investigated the candidatures and elections for a nonpermanent seat in the UN Security Council, with a special focus on the campaigns conducted ahead of the annual elections held in the UN General Assembly. Even though all UN member states have equal rights to candidate for an elected seat, this equality of opportunities have not resulted in an equal outcome in terms of access to the Security Council. We have mapped the number of times each state has served as an elected member of the Council, we have also examined the frequency of failed candidatures in the post-Cold War setting. Moreover, we have analyzed the reasoning behind candidatures to and states' expectations of a nonpermanent seat in the Council. Foremost, we have examined how states carry out their campaigns and inferred on successful campaign features. Our empirical inquiry provides novel and elaborated answers to five questions: Who wins a seat? Why do UN member states seek representation in the Security Council? What kind of opportunities do states expect from having a seat? How do they campaign? What accounts for a successful campaign?

Our forthcoming summary of main findings includes suggestions for further inquiry within the expanding study of Security Council elections and elected membership. We also suggest that our inquiry provides inspiration for two additional strands of research. First, the ascribed importance associated with the opportunity to an elected term speaks to the relevance of a comprehensive study of states' international office seeking. Second, we suggest that the domestic debates and controversies detected in some of the cases speaks to the relevance of incorporating candidature decisions into the study of the associations between domestic politics and foreign policy. As our first empirical step, we mapped the distribution of elected terms in the Security Council between states, as well as the candidatures between 1990 and 2022. Nearly one third of the UN member states have never served as nonpermanent members, whereas a handful of states have been elected often and subsequently have a very frequent access to the Council. The overall pattern therefore reflects how a few regional powers have successfully received a higher share of the representative time available for members of the regional groups, who dispose the nonpermanent seat and own the procedure of candidature nomination. The circumstance that several states who have never served in the Council have been candidates speaks against the proposal that the distribution of elected terms reflects the level of interest among the UN members. Instead, the annual elections of nonpermanent members appear as one out of the many expressions of world politics as an unequal struggle for influence between states. The stratified pattern attests to the relevance of our theoretical starting point of the Security Council election as a procedure that reflects and contributes to international hierarchy. However, the pattern over time reveals that there are certainly some interesting deviations from a purely material view of state power in the outcomes of this game; The larger states do not always defeat their smaller contestants, and states with a solid reputation as a prominent voice within UN-politics can suffer electoral defeats. These deviations, we argue, speak to the relevance of our focus on campaigning as a possible means for electoral success, but also to learn more about why states embark on the political and diplomatic journey of a candidature. Thus, as a second empirical step, we examined states representatives' reasoning on three possible power-enhancing benefits, and related purposes, for a candidature and subsequent term in the Security Council. We combined a telephone survey to delegates at the permanent missions in New York and interviews with senior officials and diplomats with candidature experience in six cases. Our telephone survey inquiry revealed the broader pattern regarding expectations to influence, to network, and to gain status as motivational drives for a candidature and subsequent term in the Security Council. We detected similarities and differences in this pattern between members from different regional groups, and between big and small states in the WEOG, as well as the subgroups Nordic states and Nordic-Baltic states. On the rationale for candidatures decisions, our case studies provided additional knowledge about these power enhancing benefits, as well as related purposes ranging from a sense of responsibility to contribute to the multilateral order to instrumental means, such as the candidature and subsequent term as a kind of stress test to educate the foreign services. As a third empirical step, we charted the main features of the campaigns, which helped us to identify some common features from successful campaigns. We conducted three pairwise comparisons and combined interviews with a broad variety of official documentation and public reports. In this chapter, we will summarize our main findings, present our conclusions, and reflect upon the implications they have, to identify venues for further research. We will end this chapter by discussing policy implications for future state campaigning and the limitations of our conclusions.

2   Concluding Summary: Who Wins a Seat

Despite the dominance of the permanent members of the Security Council, we have suggested that it is relevant to consider the selection of nonpermanent members from the lens of a power struggle. If the study of the Security Council only departs from the view of P5 dominance, we fail to account for the intense competition among the remaining UN members to reach representation in this top-level international body. As an analytical departure for this struggle, we looked upon the distribution of elected terms as a stratification of states, which accounts for a hierarchy between them. By taking the selection of nonpermanent members into account, we move from a binary categorization of states on basis of whether they are permanent members or not towards the more fine-grained ranking, which relies on their capacity to maintain recurrent access to global authority over time. This structural frame is useful to make sense to the ascribed relevance of the annual elections of nonpermanent members as a procedure, and the sense of great importance of electoral success and failure felt by diplomats and other state agents.

Our descriptive statistics show an uneven distribution of terms in the Security Council during the period 1946–2022. Four states have been elected eight terms or more, eight states have been elected 6–7 times, 22 states have been elected 4–5 times, 17 states have been elected three times, 29 states have been elected two times, 46 states have been elected on one occasion, and 60 states have not been elected even once. The categorization reveals that regional powers, such as India, Argentina, Brazil, and Japan, are among the states most often present in the Security Council. Among the states with strong performance below this top-team we see an overrepresentation of wealthier states in the WEOG, for example Australia, Denmark, Ireland, Spain, Sweden, and New Zealand. Finally, among states that have never served in the Council we see a clear overrepresentation of small states, and especially small developing states and small island states. A material understanding of state power, along with outspoken ambitions of influence account for a great deal of the distribution of seat takers and non-seat takers. However, we also identified interesting deviations from the overarching pattern that speaks to the relevance of a further inquiry of active campaigning as an opportunity for states to overcome size-related disadvantages in world politics.

The descriptive statistics also reveal uneven chances from regional group membership. This depends to some extent on the varying number of members in each group, and that the number of elected seats vary between groups.

There are also differences between regional groups in their procedures for candidature nomination. Foremost, our results reveal how the within-group dynamics can further reinforce the unequal opportunities between members. The conditions in the Asia-Pacific Group are tough in the first place due to the large number of members. Since the group has four frequent members of the Security Council, including Japan who has been elected six times in the post-Cold War period, this results in the largest shrinking of available time left for other members of a regional group. Consequently, the Asia-Pacific Group has both the one member who have served most terms in the Security Council (Japan, elected 12 times) and the largest share of members who have not served once (50 percent). In contrast, the regional group with the best initial conditions for the average member to reach the Security Council is the WEOG. Not only has the group several permanent representatives, but it has also somewhat more seats in relation to the number of members than other regional groups. While the WEOG has a similar group of successful few as the other regional groups, there is also a large group of states just behind this top-team, including Austria, Ireland, Norway, and Sweden. In future research, we believe that it is worth pursuing further to understand the dynamic in the Asia-Pacific Group to reveal the mechanisms that accounts for reinforcing the uneven distribution of elected terms in the Security Council among its members.

We address the proposal that never elected members of the Security Council are not interested in this representation, and therefore have abstained from making themselves available through a candidature. In our analysis of candidatures during the post-Cold War period, 1990–2022, we see that 45 candidatures have been withdrawn or ended with an electoral loss. Further, 18 out of the 60 states who have never served in the Security Council have launched a candidature but failed. This attests to the intensity of the competition for representation on the highest international level. This also attests to the uneven outcome in the opportunity for states to participate in international organizations more broadly. As an international body at the top-level of global authority, the stratification on basis of access to the Security Council is of special importance as a reflection of international hierarchy. However, since we have illuminated that the bigger and wealthier states also face the risk of losing against a smaller and less wealthy contestant, we see the relevance of studying states' campaigning as a possible means to electoral success.

3   Concluding Summary: Why Do UN Member States Seek
         Representation in the Security Council? What Kind
         of Opportunities Do States Expect from Having a Seat?

The results from our phone interview survey of the permanent missions at the UN in New York reveal that states seek representation on the Security Council foremost with the ambition to influence decision-making. Often, this was expressed in terms of a wish to shape the work of the Council on matters relating to international peace and security, either in general or in relation to specific conflicts.[1] The desire to take international responsibility is another frequently stated reason. For most states, this was expressed in terms of having a sense of responsibility for contributing to a rules-based multilateral order. The opportunities to network and to achieve higher status from the position of an elected seat are also of interest. Networking and raising a country's status are ascribed as more important factors for why other states candidate.

Our inquiry into motivational drives, as part of the comparative and qualitative case studies on candidatures, confirms the presence of considerations, such as taking responsibility and contributing to the multilateral order, but it also gives us a more detailed understanding of what motivates countries to seek representation. There are other, more practical, considerations, as well, such as following a turn-taking order, or running as a candidate within a certain interval as a foreign policy priority. Moreover, these considerations reveal a consistent pattern among the cases regarding the use of the candidature as a means of confirming or trying to ascend to a specific international status. For example, the small states of Iceland and Luxembourg was trying to be sufficiently involved in world politics, Austria and The Netherlands tried to be recognized as European powers with multilateral foundations, and Finland and Sweden tried to pair their identities as Nordic countries with being some of UNs most dedicated friends. Regardless of whether the candidatures lead to a seat, they play an important role as an opportunity to reflect upon and develop the identity of the candidates' foreign policy. If successful, a candidature to the Security Council is an excellent opportunity for states to perform and seek recognition of a foreign policy role that corresponds with the political and diplomatic elite's perceptions of the state identity.

Our study has also shown that the expected benefits from winning a term on the Security Council differ from what motivates countries to run for a seat in the first place. States believe that a term on the Security Council will give them

---

1   Ekengren et al. 2020.

more, in terms of both networking and elevated status, than from an actual impact on decision making, although the motivation to candidate in the first place is dependent on the desire to have influence. While this is the overall pattern, our study has also shown how members of the WEOG are more confident about the benefits that come from a term on the Security Council, when compared to members of other regional groups. One way to understand why members can differ so much in their views is by recognizing that more than 65 percent of the members of the WEOG have served on the Security Council at least twice, while the corresponding number for non-WEOG members is only 40 percent. Members who have never served on the Security Council amounts to 23 percent in WEOG and 35 percent among non-WEOG states. Thus, the greater level of confidence among WEOG members in the benefits following a seat might reflect the resources available to them, and previous positive experiences. Running a campaign and being part of the Security Council requires money and the capacity to maintain qualified diplomatic and administrative competence. The first time a state wins a seat, it might just be relieved by a successful candidature and be happy to get through the term without any severe failures. The actual benefits from holding a seat, in terms of feeling more confident, only come after the initial test. As opposed to non-WEOG states, the WEOG states also consider the Security Council to be a more accessible tool in their endeavors to exercise influence in world politics as well as to obtain a certain social standing.

Still, there are differences even within the WEOG in terms of how size plays a role on the benefits a country can gain from serving a term on the Security Council. Larger states are more confident about their actual impact on decision making, while smaller states hope to improve their network and raise their status. Intriguingly, our focus on the Nordic group within the WEOG has also brought to light that this group seems to have expectations more in line with the group of larger states when it comes to the opportunity to exercise influence. We view this result mainly as informed by the Nordic group's long-term investment in and dedication to the United Nations as the organizational pillar of the multilateral world order. Maybe their positive attitudes and support of the UN and their expectations of what might result from a term on the Security Council are self-reinforcing processes. By investing politically, the Nordic countries might expect to get 'something in return', which has been confirmed as happening when it comes to previous experiences of influence in various parts of UNs work. Certainly, this underscores how catastrophic the Icelandic and Finnish electoral defeats in 2008 and 2012 were to the Nordic group. It is certainly the case that the Nordic states have a high degree of similar expectations on the possible opportunities form an elected seat in the Security Council.

Intriguingly, there is a clustering of views also when we looked at the Nordic-Baltic states as an expanded sub-group with memberships in two different regional groups. Certainly, this might reflect the ongoing process of increased diplomatic coordination among the members of the NB8 that takes place at the UN in New York (and elsewhere). Now, this extended group of states share information relevant to ongoing candidatures as well as during ongoing terms in the Security Council to a similar extent as previously between members of the Nordic group. Effects of this sub-group extension is an increase both in the number of helpful supporters during an ongoing campaign and in terms of maximizing their possible presence in the Security Council. In 2021, both Norway and Estonia served in the Security Council. While they adopted different approaches to exercising their influence, they could also benefit from their established cooperation.[2]

We have summarized the main results on reasons and expectations on a candidature and subsequent term in the Security Council in Table 9.1.

As seen in this table, influence is the main reason for why states want a seat in the Security Council, while expanding networks and gaining status are additional, but secondary reasons. WEOG states have a more positive view of the possible outcomes from having a seat in the Security Council, than other groups of states. They are more confident they will be able to shape UN decisions, that they will get access to a broader network and that their status will increase.

In future research, we suggest that it is worth pursuing further to understand the relevance of the expectations states have when embarking on the candidature journey for how the term is pursued, if elected. These expectations might guide not only the campaign but also affect the planning and prioritizing for the elected membership. A structured comparison with a mixed methods approach, i.e., process tracing and participatory observations is one way to proceed.

4   Concluding Summary: How Do States Campaign? What Leads
        to a Successful Candidature?

To map out campaigns and identify the factors that lead to success, we compared three recent candidates from the Nordic states, a sub-group of the WEOG, to their competitors. Potentially relevant factors, such as financing, diplomatic

---

2   Haugevik et al, 2021.

TABLE 9.1   Summary of identified factors for seeking a seat in the Security Council among UN member states in general, as well as in Finland, Luxembourg, Austria, Iceland, Sweden, and the Netherlands in particular

To shape decisions	To expand network	To raise status
The main reasons for why states want a seat. WEOG states are more confident in the possibility to shape UN decisions, than states outside the WEOG. The Nordic states and large European states are more confident in the possibility to shape UN decisions, than small European states. Finland, influence the UN and the world in a multilateral direction. Luxembourg, influence the UN and the world in a multilateral direction. Austria, influence the UN and the world in a multilateral direction. Sweden, influence the UN and the world in a multilateral direction. The Netherlands, influence the UN and the world in a multilateral direction.	Not the main reason for why states want a seat on the UN Security Council. States believe that a seat on the UN Security Council will give them access to states outside their regular network since they are in close contact with the P5 and have influence. European states and WEOG states have higher expectations of positive network effects, than non-European states or non-WEOG states. The Nordic states and larger European states have higher expectations of positive network side effects, than small, European states. Sweden, extend networks. The Netherlands, extend networks.	Not the main reason for why states want a seat on the UN Security Council. States ascribe status seeking as a main reason for other states' bids to the UN Security Council, but states are less willing to admit this as a reason for their own campaign. A seat is believed to provide states with higher status since they get more attention if they have a seat. European states believe their status will increase more than non-European states. Large European states believe their status will increase more than the Nordic states and small European states. Austria, remain relevant through increased visibility. Iceland, become relevant through increased visibility. Sweden, remain relevant through increased visibility. The Netherlands, remain relevant through increased visibility.

representation, and the number of times a state had been elected before, could not explain the variation in our comparative cases. Some campaigns failed at their goal despite having more funding, access to a more developed diplomatic network, or being a first-time candidate. By focusing on the actual campaigning regarding its organization, key-participants, activities, message, and domestic debate, our aim was to get a better understanding of differences and similarities in the content of and planning of the campaign.

The descriptive case studies on how states run their candidatures have revealed a great deal of similarities between the campaigns. In terms of their organization, the planning and coordination tends to take place in a unit at the Foreign Ministry, in collaboration with the permanent mission in New York. In terms of key participants, these candidatures turn ambassadors and civil servants into campaign workers. The PR in New York becomes particularly busy. Still, the campaign also requires participation by members of government, as well as other public officials. In terms of activities, the bilateral dialogue among diplomats and politicians is a central feature. The campaigns also held a number of events and gatherings to gain attention and attract support. In terms of their message, a strong dedication to the values and mission of the UN are at the core of each campaign. Within this UN frame, however, each campaign attempts to define a few niches where they feel they have a strong record. Still, all three comparisons, between one successful and one unsuccessful candidature, have demonstrated differences in their campaigns.

The table below summarizes the results from the comparisons. As the table shows, all three factors for success – demonstrating resourcefulness, claiming competence, and proving ideational commitment – could be identified in favor of the Austrian campaign. The same pattern could be found in favor of Luxembourg's campaign, but with somewhat less accentuated differences. The Netherlands and Sweden were on equal terms in terms of demonstrating contributions, but the Netherlands came out less favorable when it came to claiming competence, and also in terms of proving ideational commitment.

Some factors are present in both successful and unsuccessful campaigns, which means they are not sufficient for understanding the outcome. For instance, while we have mainly identified organizational weaknesses in the Icelandic campaign, both the Finnish and Swedish campaigns also suffered from a lack of continuity. Both states started their campaigns late and missed opportunities for vote-exchange agreements. This contributed to Finland's defeat, while Sweden still managed to be elected. Domestic criticism was present in both Iceland and Sweden. While domestic criticism is never positive, it did not lead to an electoral loss for Sweden. There were also differences regarding the financing of the campaigns. While Luxembourg and Austria seemed to

TABLE 9.2   Summary of identified factors for success

Factors for success	Iceland and Austria	Finland and Luxembourg	Sweden and the Netherlands
Demonstrating contributions Focus on assets 'in possession' (for example enjoying a prominent historical reputation, a specific cultural/ social capital, access to networks or economic and/or military resources which could be put to the UN's disposal) – Good UN CV – Support from other important states – Support from UN authorities – Resources in terms of money and personnel – Access to networks (for example the Nordic states, La Francophonie, Africa)	Austria had a good UN CV, for example in terms of earlier participation on the Security Council and hosting UN institutions in Vienna. Iceland had support from the Nordic countries. Austria had a strong Foreign Ministry. Austria had a strong diplomatic representation abroad. Austria received support from UN Secretaries General. Austria had good funding for their campaign.	Both Finland and Luxembourg had a good UN CV. Finland had a good UN CV, but its peacekeeping contributions had declined. Luxembourg showed commitment in terms of ODA and peacekeeping contributions per capita. Finland had support from the Nordic countries. Luxembourg had support from La Francophonie. Finland had a strong diplomatic representation abroad.	Both Sweden and KoN had a good UN CV. Sweden had support from the Nordic countries. KoN had a strong diplomatic representation abroad. KoN had good funding for their campaign.

TABLE 9.2   Summary of identified factors for success (*cont.*)

Factors for success	Iceland and Austria	Finland and Luxembourg	Sweden and the Netherlands
Claiming competence Focus on proving current skills in leadership (for example by promoting prominent politicians, diplomats, and experts) – Domestic support (the ability to unite domestic actors) – Political support, active political leadership – Prominent individuals (sports, politics, music, etc.) – Reputation, states want to be perceived in a certain way, holding certain skills – Proving/showing diplomatic skills	Austria had strong domestic support for their campaign. Iceland had limited domestic support for their campaign. Austria's political leadership showed strong commitment to the campaign. Iceland lacked political ownership of the campaign.	Both states had support from domestic actors. Luxembourg's political leadership showed strong commitment to the campaign. Luxembourg had political and diplomatic continuity. Luxembourg showed strong diplomatic skills. Luxembourg had a plan for a campaign during the voting rounds.	KoN had strong domestic support for their candidature. Sweden faced domestic debate regarding the campaigning. Sweden's political leadership showed strong commitment to the campaign. KoN had diplomatic continuity and coherent political support of the candidature. Sweden proved their political skill through ministers talking about certain areas of expertise connected to their political portfolios.

TABLE 9.2   Summary of identified factors for success (*cont.*)

Factors for success	Iceland and Austria	Finland and Luxembourg	Sweden and the Netherlands
Proving ideational commitment Focus on content and consistency of message (for example specific values and principles, or specific issues/ values in certain places) – Credible message – Consistent message – Promotion of certain values – Commitment to certain values/ identities	Austria promoted both soft security, such as climate change, and hard security, such as disarmament and non-proliferation. Iceland promoted sustainability values as well as values of small (formerly poor) states. Iceland's reputation was questioned at the end of the campaign. Iceland aimed for the votes of small states (SIDS).	Both supported multilateralism. Finland promoted peacekeeping and mediation. Some discrepancies between words and deeds were detected. Finland had, in some respects, a vague message. Luxembourg had a credible and consistent message and 'stayed on message' in different settings. Luxembourg highlighted human rights and international law.	Both supported multilateralism. Both sought to have dialogue and 'partnership'. Both claimed small state experience. Both states had a consistent message in different settings. Both states promoted peacekeeping, development, and sustainability. KoN focused on justice and international law. Sweden emphasized climate change.

have the advantage of access to more generous funding, Sweden had a smaller budget than the Netherlands, but still won.

More importantly, the three successful campaigns had several shared features. All three cases displayed political commitment to the candidature. When a prime minister and other members of the government participate in a country's campaign, they contribute at least with their commitment and at

best their expertise. All three successful cases were characterized by clear dedication from the political leadership to pursue the campaign and to declare
their sincere interest in winning the seat. Hence, this contributed to a sense of
political ownership over the campaign. It is not enough to contribute at symbolic meetings and campaign kick-offs at the UN. What matters is having a
prime minister attending meetings and diplomatic gatherings and engaging
in dialogue with other states. If a prime minister attends meetings, he/she has
access to all other decision makers. Utilizing a senior diplomat in the campaign
offers less access to other countries' high-level representatives. The presence of
prime ministers signals a serious campaign with extensive political support. If
you are a dedicated member with the full support of the elites, then you are
more likely to deliver once on the Security Council.

We have also seen that candidates need to work on how to frame their campaign message. In regional groups with contested slates, it is important that
the candidates promote something unique in their activities or messages. Most
candidates promote values and messages related to the UN agenda, or even
the UN foundation, such as peacekeeping, international law, or sustainability.
When two candidates are very similar it seems like small differences, such as
speaking about climate change instead of sustainability, could make a difference in whether they are able to prove their ideational commitment. States are
also seen as more credible when they promote values that they have expertise
in, and government support of, preferably highlighted in their national foreign policy. An example of this is Austria speaking about international law,
or Sweden speaking about climate change. In future research, we believe that
it is worth pursuing further to understand the relevance of variations in how
similar topics are framed differently. Inquiry of respondents of the messages
i.e., through interviews with ambassadors who are exposed to the competing
campaign messages is one way to proceed.

5   Venues for Future Research

The conducted summary of findings includes suggestions for further inquiry
within the expanding study of Security Council elections and non permanent
memberships. We also suggest that our inquiry provides inspiration for two
additional strands of research. First, the ascribed importance associated with
the opportunity to an elected term speaks to the relevance of a comprehensive
study of states' international office seeking. While the study of the Security
Council elections and nonpermanent memberships has now begun to grow,
we have limited knowledge about candidature diplomacy in general and how

states seek to utilize the various international offices. This inquiry is of relevance to the literature on small states in world politics as well as to the literature on states and IOs.[3] Second, the domestic debates and controversies detected in some of the cases speak to the relevance of incorporating candidature decisions into the reinvigorated study of domestic politics and foreign policy.[4] Currently, most empirical studies about the domestic-foreign link address decisions about national contributions to international military missions.[5] Although not associated with the risk of military violence, we suggest that a candidature also qualifies as a priority decision within foreign policy, similarly to the choice on whether to contribute with military capabilities. We also suggest that the choice of a candidature evokes conceptions among the domestic elites about the national role conception and international reputations. Indeed, the Swedish controversy on whether the SC candidature inflicted with Sweden being an EU-member did reflect such competing conceptions. Thus, exploring the SC candidature as a priority decision contributes also to the emerging literature on international reputation, status-seeking, and domestic politics.[6]

6   Some Policy Advice for Decision Makers

Do our results have a more general applicability beyond the cases discussed here? It is our assessment that they do. The design of our study has helped us to identify some common factors in all our successful cases. We suggest that the importance of the identified factors is not limited to the Nordic states, nor do we think that the principles for campaigning diverge all that much from one country to the next. We know that states who are campaigning in a regional group with a clean slate have fewer incentives to invest heavily in their campaigns. In those cases, our results might be less relevant. However, in cases with contested slates, we believe that our factors for success are relevant beyond both the Nordic states and the WEOG. We also propose that our conclusions on factors for success might even be applicable beyond elections for the non-permanent seats to the UN Security Council. Elections between different state candidates are probably guided by a similar logic. It seems to be a reasonable

---

3   Baldacchino and Wivel 2020; Corbett et al. 2018; 2019; Panke 2020.
4   Raunio and Wagner 2020.
5   Wagner et al. 2017, 2018; Haesenbrouck and Mello 2020.
6   Beaumont 2020; Dunton 2020; Yu-Ting and Katada 2022.

assumption that sincere political support for a campaign and the connection between message and competence are important factors for others, as well.

If we are to end with a final piece of advice for decision makers around the globe it would be this: if you decide that your state is going to run for an international position, make sure you have the perseverance and time necessary to campaign on the highest political level. A successful campaign can certainly be a positive boost for your country's reputation, but an unsuccessful campaign can be a burden, and the risk of an unsuccessful campaign increases with a lack of political ownership of the campaign.

Bibliography

Baldacchino, Godfrey and Anders Wivel. 'Small States: Concepts and Theories'. In *Handbook on the Politics of Small States*, Baldacchino. Godfrey and Anders Wivel eds. (Edgar Elgar Publishing, 2020).

Beaumont, Paul. D. *The grammar of Status Competition: International Hierarchies as Domestic Practice* [Dissertation Project]. (Norwegian University of Life Sciences, Faculty of Landscape and Society, Department of the International Environment and Development Studies, 2020).

Corbett, Jack, Xu Yi-Chong and Patrick Weller. 'Small States and the 'Throughput' Legitimacy of International Organizations'. *Cambridge Review of International Affairs*, 31 (2) (2018), 183–202.

Corbett, Jack, Xu Yi-Chong and Patrick Weller. 'Norm Entrepreneurship and Diffusion 'from below' in International Organisations: How the Competent Performance of Vulnerability Generates benefits for Small States'. *Review of International Studies*, 45 (4) (2019), 647–668.

Dunton, Caroline. 'Willing to Serve: Empire, Status, and Canadian Campaigns for the United Nations Security Council (1946–1947)'. *International Journal,* (2020) 75 (4), 529–547.

Ekengren, Ann-Marie, Fredrik D. Hjorthen and Ulrika Möller. 'A Nonpermanent Seat in the United Nations Security Council: Why Bother?'. *Global Governance: a Review of Multilateralism and International Organizations*, (26) (2020), 21–45.

Haesenbrouck, Tim and Patrick A. Mello. 'Patterns of Political Ideology and Security Policy'. *Foreign Policy Analysis,* (2020) 16:4, 565–586.

Haugevik, Kristin, Piret Kuusik, Kristi Raik and Niel Nagelhus Schia. *Small States, Different Approaches Estonia and Norway on the UN Security Council.* (Tallinn: International Centre for Defence and Security Estonian Foreign Policy Institute, 2021).

Panke, Diana. 'Inside International Environmental Organizations. Negotiating the Greening of International Politics'. *Cambridge Review of International Affairs*, Vol. 33, No. 3, 2020, 365–384.

Raunio, Tapio and Wolfgang Wagner. 'The Party Politics of Foreign and Security Policy'. *Foreign Policy Analysis*, (2020) 16, 515–531.

Wagner, Wolfgang, Anna Herranz-Surrallés, Juliet Kaarbo and Falk Ostermann. 'The Party Politics of Legislative–Executive Relations in Security and Defence Policy'. *West European Politics,* 40 (1) (2017) 20–41.

Wagner, Wolfgang, Anna Herranz-Surrallés, Juliet Kaarbo and Falk Ostermann. 'Party Politics at the Water's Edge: Contestation of Military Operations in Europe'. *European Political Science Review,* 10:4 (2018) 537–63.

Yu-Ting Lin, Alex and Saori N. Katada. 'Striving for Greatness: Status Aspirations, Rhetorical Entrapment, and Domestic Reforms'. *Review of International Political Economy*, 29:1 (2022) 175–201.

Index

activities   148, 153, 154, 179, 185, 188, 189, 190,
    192, 194, 195, 199, 203, 205, 206, 220, 224
African Group   10, 50, 53, 54, 55*t*3.2, 57, 63,
    65, 70*t*4.1, 70*t*4.1
Asia Pacific   70*t*4.1, 70*t*4.1, 71*t*4.1
Asia-Pacific   6, 10, 49, 50, 52, 53, 54, 55,
    55*t*3.2, 62, 63, 65, 215
Austria   14, 17, 21, 40, 41, 43, 47, 51*t*3.1, 58*t*3.3,
    65, 70*t*4.1, 96, 98, 100, 101, 102, 103, 112,
    113, 117, 119, 120, 122, 123, 124, 125, 126,
    127, 128, 130, 131, 132, 133, 135, 137, 138,
    139, 140, 141, 142, 215, 216, 219*t*9.1, 219*t*9.1,
    220, 221*t*9.2, 221*t*9.2, 221*t*9.2, 222*t*9.2,
    223*t*9.2, 224

Baltic   40
Bernt Koenders   188*n*27
Bert Koenders   188, 205

campaign   1, 3, 8, 9, 10, 13, 15, 18, 19, 20, 21, 24,
    29, 30, 32, 33, 34, 35, 36, 37, 38, 39, 43,
    53, 63, 65, 67, 98, 99, 100, 101, 102, 104,
    105, 106, 107, 108, 109, 110, 113, 117, 118,
    119, 120, 121, 122, 123, 123*n*16, 125, 126, 127,
    128, 129, 130, 131, 132, 133, 134, 135, 136,
    137, 138, 139, 140, 141, 142, 146, 147, 148,
    149, 150, 151, 152, 152*n*36, 153, 154, 155,
    156, 157, 158, 159, 160, 161, 162, 163, 164,
    165, 166, 167, 168, 169, 170, 171, 171*n*160,
    173, 174, 175, 179, 180, 181, 182, 183, 184,
    185, 186, 187, 187*n*26, 188, 189, 190, 191,
    192, 193, 194, 195, 196, 197, 198, 199,
    200, 201, 202, 203, 204, 205, 206, 207,
    208, 212, 217, 218, 219*t*9.1, 220, 221*t*9.2,
    222*t*9.2, 222*t*9.2, 222*t*9.2, 222*t*9.2, 223,
    223*t*9.2, 224, 226
campaign message   35, 125
campaigns   147, 148, 149, 161, 162, 166, 171
candidature   1, 2, 8, 9, 11, 12, 14, 15, 17, 18, 19,
    21, 24, 27, 29, 30, 30*t*2.1, 32, 33, 35, 36, 37,
    39, 40, 41, 42, 52, 53, 54, 56, 57, 58*t*3.3, 61,
    62, 65, 67, 68, 69, 84, 96, 97, 98, 99, 100,
    102, 103, 104, 105, 106, 108, 109, 110, 111,
    112, 119, 122, 123*n*16, 125, 126, 129, 130, 131,
    133, 135, 136, 138, 139, 140, 150, 160, 161,

167, 168, 175, 179, 180, 181, 182, 182*n*10,
    183, 186, 187, 188, 188*n*26, 189, 190, 191,
    192, 193, 194, 195, 196, 197, 198, 199, 200,
    202, 205, 206, 207, 208, 212, 215, 216, 217,
    218, 220, 222*t*9.2, 223, 224
Carl Bildt   181, 186, 188, 202, 207, 209
commitment   2, 12, 14, 35, 36, 37*t*2.2, 117,
    125, 126, 128, 132, 134, 135, 136, 140, 141,
    147, 148, 149, 159, 161, 165, 166, 167, 168,
    170, 175, 179, 186, 190, 196, 197, 201, 203,
    204, 206, 207, 208, 220, 221*t*9.2, 222*t*9.2,
    222*t*9.2, 223, 224
competence   14, 36, 37*t*2.2, 89, 97, 109, 112,
    117, 118, 122, 125, 127, 128, 132, 133, 135,
    136, 139, 141, 147, 148, 166, 167, 168, 170,
    173, 174, 175, 179, 190, 196, 201, 206, 207,
    208, 217, 220, 222, 226
contested   179, 186
contested elections   21, 54, 120
contested slate   3, 7, 21, 52, 53, 97
contested slates   71
contribution   10, 14, 20, 129, 200
contributions   147, 148, 149, 156, 157, 158, 159,
    160, 165, 173, 174, 220, 221, 221*t*9.2, 225

domestic debate   148, 179, 180, 182, 204, 205,
    206, 220, 222*t*9.2

E10   1, 5, 6, 9, 12
Eastern European Group   10, 40, 52, 71
election   2, 3, 5, 6, 9, 11*n*20, 14, 18, 19, 20, 21,
    22, 33, 34, 35, 40, 41, 42, 49, 52, 57, 61,
    63, 71, 117, 119, 133, 141, 146, 147, 152, 158,
    160, 162, 165, 167, 168, 179, 180, 181, 182,
    183, 184, 187, 187*n*26, 191, 192, 194, 202,
    206, 213
Election Officer   18
elections   212, 214, 224, 225

Finland   8, 14, 21, 40, 41, 42, 51*t*3.1, 59*t*3.3,
    70*t*4.1, 91, 96, 98, 104, 105, 106, 107,
    112, 147, 148, 149, 150, 150*n*12, 151, 152,
    153, 154, 155, 156, 156*n*66, 156*n*67, 157,
    158, 158*n*73, 160, 161, 162, 163, 164, 165,
    165*n*120, 166, 167, 168, 169, 169*n*139, 170,

Finland (*cont.*)
    171, 171*n*160, 172, 173, 174, 175, 176, 177,
    216, 219*t*9.1, 220, 221*t*9.2, 221*t*9.2, 221*t*9.2,
    223*t*9.2
Foreign Minister   98, 99, 101, 102, 106, 107,
    119, 122, 123, 126, 129, 130, 131, 133, 135,
    148, 153, 154, 159, 167, 168, 169, 170, 171,
    172, 173, 176, 181, 184, 187, 188, 189, 191,
    192, 193, 194, 195, 199, 204, 206, 207
foreign ministers   29
Frans Timmermans   184, 188, 188*n*27, 193,
    199, 205
Fredrik Reinfeldt   186, 202

GRULAC   50, 53, 54, 55, 62, 63

Iceland   14, 21, 40, 41, 42, 51*t*3.1, 57, 59*t*3.3,
    70*t*4.1, 96, 98, 99, 100, 103, 104, 105, 112,
    113, 115, 117, 119, 120, 121, 121*n*9, 122, 124,
    125, 126, 126*n*31, 128, 129, 130, 131, 132,
    133, 135, 137, 138, 139, 140, 141, 146, 150,
    165, 216, 219*t*9.1, 220, 221*t*9.2, 222*t*9.2,
    223*t*9.2, 223*t*9.2
influence   3, 4, 5, 6, 9, 12, 13, 16, 18, 24, 26, 29,
    31, 32, 39, 40, 44, 46, 53, 62, 67, 68, 71,
    72, 72*f*4.1, 73, 73*f*4.2, 75, 78, 78*f*4.7, 80, 81,
    81*f*4.10, 82, 84, 85, 90, 92*f*4.13, 93*f*4.16,
    96, 97, 103, 105, 107, 108, 109, 110, 111, 112,
    118, 131, 135, 139, 213, 214, 216, 217, 218,
    219*t*9.1, 219*t*9.1, 219*t*9.1
international hierarchy   5, 19, 22, 49, 65, 67,
    84, 213, 215

Karel J.G. van Oosterom   184, 189
key-participants   148, 179, 220
Kingdom of the Netherlands   179, 184, 199,
    201, 207

Latin American and the Caribbean   10
legitimacy   3, 4, 6, 7, 15, 19*n*2, 43
Luxembourg   3, 7, 14, 21, 41, 51*t*3.1, 60*t*3.3,
    70*t*4.1, 96, 98, 104, 105, 106, 107, 115, 147,
    148, 148*n*4, 149, 151, 152, 154, 155, 156,
    156*n*66, 157, 157*n*71, 157*n*72, 159, 160,
    161, 161*n*95, 162, 163, 164, 165, 165*n*118,
    165*n*119, 166, 167, 168, 168*n*138, 169, 170,
    171, 173, 174, 175, 176, 177, 216, 219*t*9.1,
    220, 221*t*9.2, 221*t*9.2, 222*t*9.2, 222*t*9.2,
    223*t*9.2

Margot Wallström   181, 187, 192, 204, 209, 210
Max Rutte   181, 184, 188, 204
message   147, 148, 156, 157, 162, 163, 164, 173,
    174, 175, 179, 185, 190, 193, 194, 196, 198,
    199, 200, 201, 206, 207, 208, 220, 223*t*9.2,
    223*t*9.2, 223*t*9.2, 224, 226

Netherlands   14, 16, 22, 42, 44, 50, 51*t*3.1,
    60*t*3.3, 66, 70*t*4.1, 97, 98, 108, 110, 112,
    113, 121, 179, 180, 181, 182, 182*n*10, 183,
    186, 188, 193, 194, 195, 199, 200, 201, 204,
    205, 206, 207, 216, 219*t*9.1, 219*t*9.1, 220,
    221*t*9.2, 223
network   13, 25, 26, 30*t*2.1, 34, 67, 73, 75,
    79, 80, 82, 84, 97, 106, 107, 111, 112, 134,
    135, 137, 140, 213, 216, 217, 218, 219*t*9.1,
    219*t*9.1, 220
Network   109, 110
nonpermanent   1, 2, 3, 5, 6, 7, 9, 10, 12, 13, 14,
    18, 19, 20, 22, 24, 26, 30, 33, 34, 35, 36,
    39, 40, 41, 42, 50, 54, 61, 63, 67, 71, 72, 73,
    73*f*4.2, 75, 75*f*4.4, 77*f*4.6, 78, 78*f*4.7, 79,
    80, 81, 81*f*4.10, 82, 84, 92*f*4.13, 93*f*4.16, 96,
    100, 104, 106, 108, 117, 179, 200, 212, 214,
    224, 225
non-WEOG   67, 71, 72, 72*f*4.1, 73, 73*f*4.2,
    74*f*4.3, 75, 75*f*4.4, 76*f*4.5, 77*f*4.6, 84,
    217, 219
Nordic states   8, 14, 31, 38, 39, 41, 67, 69, 77,
    78, 79, 80, 83, 84, 85, 96, 97, 98, 111,
    112, 121, 213, 217, 218, 219*t*9.1, 219*t*9.1,
    221*t*9.2, 225
Nordic-Baltic states   69, 82, 84, 85, 213, 218

Olof Skoog   183, 187
organisation   148, 152, 153, 154, 160, 161
organization   179, 186, 187*n*26, 189, 206,
    207, 220

P5   1, 4, 5, 6, 7, 12, 13, 21, 24, 25, 26, 27, 30*t*2.1,
    64*t*3.4, 65, 75, 90, 214, 219*t*9.1
pairwise comparison   38
pairwise comparisons   14, 213
permanent members   214
permanent membership   1, 4, 5, 22, 62, 63
Permanent Representative   30, 35, 39, 153,
    154, 155, 167, 171, 183, 184
permanent representatives   65
Permanent Representatives   67

power   1, 3, 4, 5, 6, 7, 8, 11, 13, 18, 19, 19n2, 20,
    24, 25, 26, 28, 29, 31, 41, 42, 47, 49, 62,
    68, 84, 85, 85n5, 96, 97, 98, 102, 103, 105,
    108, 111, 113, 138, 213, 214
power enhancing benefits   6, 8, 13, 213
Prime Minister   98, 99, 129, 148, 167, 170, 172,
    177, 181, 182, 186, 187, 189, 191, 192, 195,
    200, 202, 204, 207, 208
prime ministers   29

representation   1, 3, 4, 5, 6, 10, 11, 12, 15, 18, 21,
    26, 49, 50, 53, 54, 55, 63, 64, 65, 67, 85,
    137, 212, 214, 215, 216, 220, 221t9.2, 221t9.2

Security Council   1, 2, 3, 4, 5, 6, 7, 8, 9n14, 10,
    10n19, 11, 12, 13, 14, 15, 16, 17, 18, 19, 19n2,
    20, 22, 23, 24, 25, 26, 28, 29, 30, 30t2.1,
    32, 33, 36, 38, 39, 40, 41, 42, 43, 44, 45,
    46, 47, 48, 49, 50, 51, 51t3.1, 52, 53, 54,
    55, 55t3.2, 56, 57, 61, 62, 63, 64, 65, 66,
    67, 68, 69, 71, 72, 73, 75, 77, 82, 84, 95,
    96, 97, 101, 102, 103, 104, 105, 106, 108,
    110, 111, 118, 120, 123, 145, 146, 147, 148,
    150, 156, 156n66, 156n67, 158n73, 159,
    160, 161, 163, 164, 165, 165n120, 166, 168,
    169, 171, 173, 176, 179, 180, 180n3, 180n4,
    181, 183, 186, 194, 198, 199, 200, 201, 203,
    204, 205, 206, 208, 210, 212, 214, 215,
    216, 217, 218, 219t9.1, 219t9.1, 221t9.2,
    224, 225, 226
small island developing states   199
Small Island Developing States   7, 32, 52, 119,
    121, 126
small states   15, 28, 29, 31, 32, 38, 44, 52, 53,
    64, 68, 69, 76, 78, 79, 80, 81, 82, 84, 85,
    96, 112, 117, 119, 121, 123, 125, 126, 132, 135,
    137, 149, 159, 166, , 174, 176, 213, 214, 216,
    223t9.2, 225, 226
status   2, 9, 13, 23, 27, 28, 29, 30t2.1, 30t2.1, 44,
    47, 48, 49, 67, 68, 71, 73, 74, 75, 76f4.5,

77, 77f4.6, 79, 80, 80f4.9, 82, 83, 83f4.12,
    84, 87, 91, 93f4.15, 94f4.18, 96, 97, 98, 99,
    101, 102, 103, 106, 107, 108, 110, 111, 112,
    118, 126, 129, 138, 139, 213, 216, 217, 218,
    219t9.1, 219t9.1, 225, 226, 227
Stefan Löfven   182, 187, 192
stratification   5, 19, 22, 23, 49, 65, 68
successful   212, 213, 215, 216, 217, 220, 223,
    225, 226
Sweden   14, 16, 21, 40, 41, 42, 44, 50, 51t3.1,
    61t3.3, 66, 70t4.1, 85n5, 95, 96, 98, 104,
    108, 109, 110, 112, 179, 179n1, 180, 181,
    182, 182n10, 183, 186, 187, 188n26, 190,
    191, 192, 195, 196, 197, 198, 199, 201, 202,
    203, 205, 206, 207, 208, 210, 214, 215,
    216, 219t9.1, 219t9.1, 220, 221t9.2, 221t9.2,
    222t9.2, 222t9.2, 223t9.2, 224, 225

turn-taking   3, 7, 20, 34, 69, 71, 77, 81, 108,
    109, 110, 112
turn-taking norm   20, 34

United Nations   1, 2, 5, 12, 14, 15, 16, 17, 20,
    25, 26, 29, 33, 39, 41, 42, 43, 44, 45, 46,
    47, 48, 49, 51, 61, 66, 95, 133, 142, 146,
    148, 156n66, 157, 157n71, 157n72, 165n118,
    165n119, 168, 175, 176, 177

veto   5, 6, 16, 25, 26, 45

WEOG   8, 10, 12, 14, 30, 32, 37, 38, 40, 50, 53,
    54, 55, 62, 63, 65, 67, 68, 69, 70, 71, 72,
    72f4.1, 73, 73f4.2, 74, 74f4.3, 75, 75f4.4,
    76, 76f4.5, 77f4.6, 78, 78f4.7, 79f4.8, 80,
    80f4.9, 81, 81f4.10, 82, 82f4.11, 83f4.12, 84,
    92f4.13, 92f4.14, 93f4.15, 93f4.16, 94f4.17,
    94f4.18, 96, 111, 117, 120, 179, 186, 187n26,
    213, 214, 215, 217, 218, 219, 225
Western European and Other Group   71
Western European and Others Group   8, 12

www.ingramcontent.com/pod-product-compliance
Lightning Source LLC
Chambersburg PA
CBHW060035030426
42334CB00019B/2330